MILITARY MASCULINITIES

MILITARY MASCULINITIES

Identity and the State

PAUL R. HIGATE

Foreword by Jeff Hearn

PRAEGER

Westport, Connecticut
London

Library of Congress Cataloging-in-Publication Data

Military masculinities: identity and the State / edited by Paul R. Higate;
foreword by Jeff Hearn.
   p. cm.
Includes bibliographical references and index.
ISBN 0–275–97558–4 (alk. paper)
   1. Sociology, Military.   2. Men.   3. Masculinity.   I. Higate, Paul.
U21.5.M4975   2003
306.2′7—dc21   2002072545

British Library Cataloguing in Publication Data is available.

Library of Congress Catalog Card Number: 2002072545
ISBN: 0–275–97558–4

First published in 2003

Praeger Publishers, 88 Post Road West, Westport, CT 06881
An imprint of Greenwood Publishing Group, Inc.
www.praeger.com

Printed in the United States of America

The paper used in this book complies with the
Permanent Paper Standard issued by the National
Information Standards Organization (Z39.48–1984).

10 9 8 7 6 5 4 3 2 1

This book is dedicated to Mike Higate

Contents

Acknowledgments

This volume has been in the making for a considerable period and I would like to thank the patience of the contributors and both Elisabetta Linton and Marcia Goldstein, the commissioning editors involved in the project. Many friends and colleagues have helped and guided me through the mechanics of editing, notably Angela Torrington here at the School for Policy Studies, the University of Bristol.

Particular thanks go to Deborah Harrison, Jeff Hearn, John Hockey, Lieutenant Colonel Charles Kirke, Marcia Kovitz, Mandy-Elaine McClenaghan, and Terry Willett. This list is far from exhaustive and I apologize for the omission of other influential colleagues. I accept entire responsibility for the way the volume has been organized. Finally, particular thanks go to friends and family, many of whom have served in the armed forces and have helped to shape my thinking around the nexus linking military service, gender, and identity.

Foreword: On Men, Women, Militarism, and the Military

Jeff Hearn

Military Masculinities clearly and unambiguously brings together two major themes: the military and masculinities. On the one hand, there is the military; this is one of the clearest arenas of social power and of course violence and killing in their many guises. Military matters are urgent and powerful. The way they go and the ways armies and those in them are organized and act are literally questions of life and death for all concerned. This applies whether we are talking of wars of resistance, just wars, unjust wars, peacekeeping, or simply peacetime.

On the other hand, there is the question of men and masculinities. In recent years there has been a concerted attempt, primarily through feminist and pro-feminist scholarship, to examine how men and masculinities are just as gendered as are women and femininities. Though for a long time gender was largely seen as a matter of and for women, men were generally seen as ungendered, natural, or naturalized. Men, masculinity, and men's powers and practices were generally taken for granted; this is now no longer the case. This has both led to and been shown by the recent, rather rapid growth of critical studies on men, and this is a perspective that informs this book.

Strangely, indeed, very strangely enough, these two areas have generally not been put together; that these military persons are largely men has often either been simply accepted or gone unnoticed for other reasons. It is an understatement to say that men, militarism, and the military are historically, profoundly, and blatantly interconnected. Indeed, many armies and other fighting forces of the world have been and still are armies composed exclusively of men, young men, and boys. Yet already there are some complications.

First, it is important not to presume that all armies are made up of men. The historical interrelations of men, militarism, and the military should not obscure the significance of women's military activity in particular times and places. There are indeed many examples of women making up armies. In the mid-ninteenth century it was estimated that out of the king of Dahomey's 12,000-strong army, 5,000 were women. In the 1941 Yugoslav liberation war about 100,000 women carried arms as active fighters, 25,000 were killed in action, and 40,000 were wounded.[1] In the Algerian liberation war, over 10,000 women took part in the struggle, of whom a fifth suffered imprisonment or death. Women's involvement in nation-formation, for example, in revolutionary struggles against colonial and imperialist powers, has also often been formidable. Often such participation has subsequently been undermined with the movement to peacetime.[2]

Second, even armies and other military institutions that are formally made up of men often have women in servicing or administrative positions.

Third, the impact of such military masculinities upon those outside the military—women, men, and children—is, of course, often huge.

And fourth, the exact nature of the connections between men and the military are themselves various and plural—thus there are military *masculinities*, and not just military masculinity. This is itself one of the starting points of *Military Masculinities*. Indeed, this book could have been renamed *Multiple Military Masculinities*.

In short, as has been made clear by feminist scholarship, these are matters of politics and social organization, gender and sexuality, violence and violation, rather than biology. Thus one could summarize the task of this book as twofold: to attend to the *dominant constructions* of military masculinities; and to produce the necessary *deconstructions* and *questioning* of those military masculinities, which have themselves often been naturalized, even left safely to biology.

Military Masculinities takes up these complicating issues and explores them particularly in terms of the complex and variable relation of identities and the state. Let us first consider the relationship between the military and the state. The growth of the modern military state has been very closely associated with the formation, organization, and modernization and management of national armies. The modern state has become a major controller of violence, as well as a major producer of violence, injury, fear, torture, and death. The large scale of human-engineered death, often organized quite specifically by states, parastates, and counterstates, is difficult to appreciate. Men have dominated these individual and collective actions. The extreme case might appear to be the destructive machinery of the state under the Nazi regime of the Third Reich. However, in recent history there abound many other examples of mass persecutions by states, parastates, and counterstates, specifically in the Soviet Union, China, South East Asia, East and Central Africa, and the Balkans as well as elsewhere. Bringing together the analysis of different kinds of violence, such as military violence, rape, and violence to women in the home, is a particular challenge.

The relationship between the military and identities is an equally complex area. The concept of identity is closely connected to the self and the individual; it stands at the intersection of self-perception and the perception of others. Identity can be understood as a relatively fixed sense of self, as a form of subjectivity, as multilayered, as the product of identity-work, as the object of material and discursive regulation. The notion of identity as a fixed and isolated island of the self is flawed. Although the concept has a long history in social psychology, psychoanalytic studies, and interactionist sociologies, it has in recent years been taken up in other traditions. Recent discussion on identity has highlighted the multiplicity, instability, fluidity, fracturing, and threatening of contradictory identities; identity as in a process of becoming; and shifts from personal identity to social identity. Thus, the making of what might be called military gender is a practical, continuous, social accomplishment. Such insights provide for a more variable understanding of the complex forms that military masculinities take at the level of identity. Mundane military processes, such as military training, have major impacts upon individuals and groups. Military organizations provide social and psychological resources for the reproduction and changing of individual psychologies,[3] often around violence, sometimes not. These include the processes of rationalization, distancing, following an organizational role, obeying orders, and trivialization through humor. For example, bomber pilots and crew may adopt trivializing, casual, ironic, and supposedly humorous phrases, such as "There goes the cookie," in continuing their bombing without too much direct thought for the impact of their bombs upon others.[4]

What happens when these two themes of identity and the state are brought together? What are some of the key features to be found here in this book? And what kind of questions are provoked on reading it? Although for me there are a considerable number of contenders, some of them complex, here I will mention just four.

First, there is the rather basic question of historical change: the changing forms of military masculinities, the shifting and sometimes transformed relationship between the state and the military, the military and identity, and so on. Some observers might indeed argue a contemporary weakening of the links between dominant, violent masculinity and militarism, within the current politics of war, peacekeeping, and human rights. Although connections between militarism and masculinism have been remarkably persistent historically, new associations may be developing in what may appear to be post-militarist societies.

Second, more specifically, the construction of men and masculinities in and around the state and the nation has often been very closely allied to the development of complex and sometimes contradictory militaristic identities. For example, David Morgan has examined the interconnections between militarism and dominant, and occasionally counter, forms of masculinities.[5] He has stressed the ways in which both the "boundedness" and the "pervasiveness of the military or militarism seem to be strongly linked to its coding as masculine. These themes of the relationship between institution and practice are taken up in many of the chapters that follow. There are also intense contradictions to be observed—between hypermasculinity and misogyny, on one hand, and softer, more tender masculinities, on the other, not least in the throes of military survival. Furthermore, the recognition of such contradiction and plurality should not obscure and allow us to forget the real persistence and immensity of military violence and violation.

A third key theme is that of space and place, ground and land, domain and terrain—whether it is the personal space of the body or the extended terrain of the nation. The geographies of the military, the "violent cartographies,"[6] are often plain to see, if not always to decipher. To my mind, this broadly spatial perspective raises a mass of questions that deserve much more attention in the future gendered studies of the military, the land and the body.

And fourth, there is the persistent theme of internationalism. Much militarism, especially nation-based militarism, is international by definition and ambition. This book also emphasizes the national and international dimensions of military masculinities. This includes those of the peculiar British case, of Canada, of Israel, of the German-Jewish question, and of the former German Democratic Republic.

In light of all these important questions, it must be considered very surprising that there is not a wealth of books on men, masculinities, and the military. Libraries, archives, and vaults are full of books and documents giving information, often huge amounts of detailed information, on these military worlds, yet few revisit this field in terms of masculinities and men's and women's gendered practices there. This book is part of the project to change that situation. There can be few more urgent tasks than this—academically, politically, and practically. *Military Masculinities* brings together one of the first collections, perhaps the first collection, of detailed and grounded explorations on this subject. It is a fine and timely contribution to these important debates; it deserves to be read widely and, moreover, acted upon.

NOTES

1. Anne Oakley, *Sex, Gender and Society* (London: Temple Smith, 1972), p. 145.

2. P. R. Knauss, *The Persistence of Patriarchy: Class, Gender and Ideology in Twentiuth Century Algeria* (New York: Praeger, 1987).

3. N. Dixon, *On the Psychology of Military Incompetence* (London: Jonathan Cape, 1976).

4. R. Johnson, "Institutions and the Promotion of Violence," in A. Campbell and J. J. Gibbs, eds., *Violent Transactions* (Oxford: Blackwell, 1986), pp. 181–205; and J. Smith, *Misogynies* (London: Faber & Faber, 1993).

5. David Morgan, "Theater of War: Combat, the Military and Masculinities," in H. Brad and M. Kaufman, eds., *Theorizing Masculinities* (Thousand Oaks, CA: Sage, 1994), pp. 165–182.

6. M. J. Shapiro, *Violent Cartographies: Mapping Cultures of War* (Minneapolis: University of Minnesota Press, 1997).

Introduction: Putting Men and the Military on the Agenda

Paul R. Higate

In Britain during the 1990s, there was a fleeting moment in which both media and public became concerned with the disproportionate number of ex-service-men among the single homeless population. Discussion centered on the ways in which the military institutionalized a number of its former members, and most agreed that this explained the presence of rough-sleeping ex-"squaddies" around major British cities.

Thanks to the influence of feminist and pro-feminist thought, simultaneous developments in social theory, focusing on the embodied and emotional groundings of women *and* men grew through the 1990s. These ways of conceptualizing the embodied and gendered actor were used to investigate a wide range of social phenomena, from sociological understandings of love,[1] through men's health,[2] to understanding the role of military experience in disposing some ex-servicemen to homelessness.[3]

The author's research into the links between military experience and homelessness benefited enormously from applying these theoretical insights, not least the importance of *pluralizing* masculinity within the military.[4] However, the relative paucity of both empirical and theoretical material linking the military with masculinity represented an ongoing concern. After all, what could be more enduring to broader images of masculinity than the warrior figure, at one and the same time celebrated and demonized? What light could be shed on masculinity by exploring these potent and paradoxical constructions, many of which crept into the darker corners of everyday (civilian) life, not least through their dysfunctional manifestation after discharge from the military? And, in a sociological sense, how might we begin to make sense of the routine practices of the soldier, sailor, and airman within the context of broader social structures—perhaps even to the level of the state?

The idea of an edited collection exploring these themes received further impetus at the Gender and Militarism conference hosted by Leeds Metropolitan

University in November 1999. It was, quite possibly, the most unusual of gatherings, for it brought together serving military personnel, academics, and radical feminist pacifists. As one can imagine, debate was lively and challenging for audience and presenter alike. Yet, lingering doubts—crystallized by the extent to which individuals representing different interests talked past one another—convinced me further that the themes of the military and masculinity warranted greater synthesis and development. In tandem with these sentiments was the goodwill of a number of the conference presenters who agreed to gentle coercion to contribute to the volume.

The collection has been split into two sections, with the first paying close attention to substantive, empirical, and theoretical issues linked to military masculinity. The second section is pitched at a higher level of abstraction and is focused on nation- or statehood and concomitant military masculine identity construction.

In Chapter 1, "The Roots of Military Masculinity," Marcia Kovitz provides an anthropological analysis of the binding and durable marriage of men and the military. She uses women's marginalization from the most masculine of bastions, combat, as the key point of departure. Drawing on the anthropological record, Kovitz outlines the importance of taking a constructionist rather than essentialist position on sex and gender. Getting "naturally aggressive" men to fight in the face of their alleged bellicosity has never been a straightforward business, though this biological line of reasoning continues to be used to support the "male-female axis of opposition." Kovitz concludes the chapter on a note of optimism; given that "military masculinity is neither universal nor inevitable," she contributes toward arguments, picked up in Chapter 14, about the potentially positive impact of increasing numbers of women on military culture. The theme of combat is further explored in Chapter 2. In "No More Heroes," John Hockey revisits earlier research and, in keeping with the investigative strategy urged by David Morgan,[5] subjects British Army infantry training doctoral fieldnotes to a gendered reading. Hockey explores the following: the socialization of infantrymen, the ubiquitous feminine-masculine dichotomy, homosociability, and post-training experiences of combat, together with the ritualized, alcohol-fueled "blowout." Hockey reminds us that the occupational culture of the soldier is almost entirely driven by the hazardous operational context, a point that can be crowded out at times by more intellectual or epistemological concerns. Three key themes preoccupy Paul Higate in Chapter 3, "'Soft Clerks' and 'Hard Civvies.'" The first is the diversity of military masculinities, of which clerking in the Royal Air Force (RAF) is noted to be among the most feminized or marginal. With this in mind, and through the lens of autobiography, Higate demonstrates how these softer variants of military masculinity might be surpassed in post-discharge life, thereby subverting perceptions of the homogeneous military man, toughened by training and ready to fight. However, although material performance of hegemonic military masculinity (examples of which are those performed by Hockey's infantrymen in Chapter 2), remained elusive for Higate, nevertheless, ideologies supporting hegemonic military masculinity are noted to persist into civilian life, particularly in the company of other ex-servicemen. Evidence is provided here for the gendering of the frequently used term in these contexts, *institutionalization*.[6] The concepts of space and place have impacted across the social sciences in recent years, and in Chapter 4, Rachel Woodward develops these themes to throw light on the gender identity of British Army soldiers. "Locating Military Masculinities" flags aspects of the spatialized elements pivotal to the construction of gendered identity, in particular the centrality of the rural in the making of the soldier. It is on the windswept Ministry of Defence (MoD)-owned hills and plains around Britain that "men are made," as well as—though in less dramatic ways—in army barrack blocks and gymnasiums.

The fragility and contingency of masculine identity has been a recurring theme within the men's studies literature, and in Chapter 5, "The Home Guard in Britain in the Second World War," Penny Summerfield and Corinna Peniston-Bird draw our attention to a particular configuration of wartime military masculinities. The Home Guard, established in 1940 as the last line of defense if invasion by Germany were to occur, was composed of men deemed excessively old, young, or unfit, and others in reserved occupations. Crucially, they were perceived as amateurs, as lesser men, denied the testing ground of combat in the defense of their country. These uncertain masculinities were further compounded by their proximity to women's auxiliary forces toward the end of the war. The British public's continued fascination with the ambiguous status of these hybridized soldiers, highlighted through the endlessly re-run BBC television comedy *Dad's Army*, demonstrates both the affection for and concern with marginal masculinities at such a crucial juncture in the country's history. Violence, mentioned only obliquely so far in this introduction, is the key theme of Chapter 6, "Violence in the Military Community," by Deborah Harrison. This empirical contribution, based on interviews with 112 military and former military wives, and 48 Canadian military members and civilian staff of military facilities clearly demonstrates what might be termed the spillover effects of military masculinity. As Harrison states: "Obsession with control [within the military] supplements the misogynist character of military bonding in helping to account for the relatively high frequency of woman abuse within the military community." In accounting for the unacceptable and relatively disproportionate burden that military wives bear in the form of physical abuse, issues of combat are once again invoked. Combat bonding, combat morale, and the overall psychological environment surrounding the training and maintenance of readiness of fighting men, are, as Harrison notes, deeply inscribed with misogynistic overtones.

The experiences of personnel leaving the Royal Navy is the focus of Chapter 7 by Samantha Regan de Bere, "Masculinity in Work and Family Lives." Using the concept of a naval discourse, she explores occupational and gendered socialization ultimately leading to the "masculine naval man." The interruption of

navy identity discourses, brought about by discharge from the service, presented de Bere's sixty-three male naval interviewees (and families) with a series of challenges that tended to be tackled by recourse to career continuity
when feasible. To these ends, the majority of leavers moved into management,
engineering, and the emergency services, putting their military occupational
capital to good use and in so doing, seeking out masculine and public service
spheres of civilian employment.

The contributions in the later chapters of the book broaden the context of
discussion around military masculinities to include more explicit considera-
tions of the state.

The concept of state militarism is central to Chapter 8, "The State and Military Masculinity," by John Hopton. Here, discussion traces a number of the
myriad connections between militarism and masculinity, from comment on
historical and contemporary military masculine popular-cultural representation, through observations of the masculinized police and the penal systems,
subsumed under gendered political structures. In Chapter 9, "Conscientious
Objectors in the Great War," Lois Bibbings details the "despised and rejected"
status of the conscientious objectors during the First World War. As Bibbings
states: "If the military man was brave, loyal, patriotic, self-sacrificing and true,
the [conscientious objector] had to be cowardly, disloyal, unpatriotic, selfish and
traitorous." To these ends, the hated "CO" was subject to all manner of draconian and sometimes bizarre torture. The core of Bibbings' thesis is that in adher-
ing so firmly to pacific principles, the CO displayed remarkable levels of moral
courage and heroic actions—traits that sit closely with the oppositional figure
of the brave warrior. Eighteenth-century Britain is the setting for Chapter 10
by Robert McGregor, "The Popular Press and the Creation of Military Masculinities in Georgian Britain." The celebrated Royal Navy and the army of the
day featured extensively in the press, with particular focus on the trials and
tribulations of serving officers and judgments about the extent to which their
actions under fire were deemed masculine or effeminate. McGregor argues that
the eighteenth-century press influenced public opinion (not unlike today) and
that they "upheld a hegemonic conception of military masculinity, one that
owed much to a 'victorious' or 'whiggish' interpretation of British history." The
focus is switched to continental Europe in Chapter 11, "The Militarization of
Masculinity in the Former German Democratic Republic," by Andrew Bickford. Drawing on a wide range of sources and methods, including oral history,
archival research, and participant observation in a former unit of the *Nationale
Volksarmee* (NVA), Bickford explores the transitionary period of 1978–1990 in
the former GDR, as it was during these years that military education and conscription were introduced. As Bickford explains: "The vector of militarization
and the family played a key role in shaping male identity in the German Democratic Republic." Gregory A. Caplan continues commentary on Germany in
Chapter 12, "Militarism and Masculinity as Keys to the 'Jewish Question' in
Germany." Opening with a historical overview, Caplan sketches the alternative

paradigm of Jewish masculinity, emphasising humility and restraint rather than, for example, displays of masculinity more usually deemed hegemonic. Mapping the trajectories, tensions, and overlaps between Jewish, Prussian, and German conceptions of masculinity over two centuries, Caplan concludes by arguing that Jews sought a more dominant form of gendered identity through First World War veterans' propagation of dominant military masculinity. The penultimate contribution, Chapter 13, by Uta Klein, "The Military and Masculinities in Israeli Society," illuminates the highly militarized characteristics of the state of Israel. Military socialization commences in kindergarten and culminates in conscription where service in the armed forces represents *the* central *rite de passage*. Women's conscripted role in the Israeli Defense Forces is second to that of men and consequently, Klein asserts, women are marginalized at the symbolic and at the practical level. Gender roles are heavily influenced by the military in Israel, and veteran status brings with it social mobility, with high rank translating into high public office. However, recent trends have begun to problematize aspects of these military masculinities in terms of not only a decline in willingness to serve but also the greater priority given to sexual harassment in the army. Chapter 14, "Concluding Thoughts," by Paul Higate, assesses recent trends in the British armed forces, for example, the greater integration of women into a wider number of posts and the formal toleration of homosexuals. From these developments, brought about principally by a crisis in recruiting and by externally imposed legislation, Higate attempts to predict the ways in which military masculine culture might evolve. Despite these changes, he remains largely pessimistic that these spillover features, including domestic violence in the military home, sexual harassment in the military workplace, and violence in garrison towns, will diminish significantly.

It is hoped that the contributions in *Military Masculinities* might stimulate further research into this exemplary gendered institution, add to the increasing weight of literature that seeks to demonstrate the pervasiveness of the military masculine discourse and, finally, increase the tempo and perspectives from which the naturalized linkage of man and warrior might be unpacked and, ultimately, reformed.

NOTES

1. Stevi Jackson, "Even Sociologists Fall in Love: An Exploration in the Sociology of the Emotions," *Sociology* 27, 2 (1993): 201–220.

2. Jonathan Watson, "Running around like a Lunatic: Coin's Body and the Case of Male Embodiment," in S. Nettleton and J. Watson, eds., *The Body in Everyday Life* (London: Routledge, 1998), pp. 163–179.

3. Paul Higate, "Ex-servicemen on the Road: Travel and Homelessness," in *The Sociological Review* 48, 3 (2000): 331–348; and Paul Higate, "Tough Bodies and Rough Sleeping: Embodying Homelessness amongst Ex-servicemen," in *Housing, Theory and Society* 17, 3 (2000): 97–108.

4. David Morgan's work in this area has benefited my thinking enormously. See David Morgan, "Theater of War: Combat, the Military and Masculinities," in H. Brod and M. Kaufman, eds., *Theorizing Masculinities* (London: Sage, 1994), pp. 165–182.

5. See David Morgan, *Discovering Men* (London: Routledge, 1992).

6. See Paul Higate, "Theorizing Continuity: From Military to Civilian Life," *Armed Forces & Society* 27, 3 (2001): 443–460.

Chapter 1

The Roots of Military Masculinity

Marcia Kovitz

This chapter explores the roots of military masculinity and multiple military masculinities through a number of related questions. Why, despite the long-standing presence of women,[1] is military organization and practice identified and represented as masculine? And why, despite the military's increasing need for and reliance on women,[2] do they remain marginalized within the organization and continue to experience resistance to their service? Straddling the tension points in the ongoing debates regarding women's military service, the chapter uses these debates as prisms for probing the military's construction of masculinity/ies, shifting the reader's focus from problematizing women's service to problematizing that of men. It examines the foundation and some of the parameters of the military's conceptualization, construction and reconstruction of gender, and asks: why is women's service seen as contentious whereas men's is assumed? Given that the activities in which soldiers engage have lethal aims and consequences, why the struggle over who can take part? Furthermore, given the presence of multiple masculinities based on multiple military occupations and unequal ranks, why is military masculinity identified and represented as singular and uniform? To address these questions, the chapter highlights issues frequently raised in the debates around women's military service; it then distills several of the salient points on the social organization of warfare and gender from the extensive anthropological literature on the subject and from accounts of the historical origins of the army as a unique organizational form for waging war. My objectives are to dispel the related myths of a universal gendered division of labor in war and an essential military masculinity; to provide a comparative backdrop for investigating why the military is constructed as masculine, and uniformly so; and to elucidate some of the links between the military's gendered social construction and its authoritarian form of social organization charged with operationalizing its unique mandate.

DEBATING WOMEN'S MILITARY SERVICE

The arguments of supporters and opponents of women's military service center on two ostensibly distinct yet fundamentally related issues: women's *right* to serve and their *capacity* to serve, both are often reduced to what is seen as the last male bastion, combat. Regarding their capacity, the points of contention concern claims of women's innate physiological inferiority to men in everything from strength (especially in the upper body), stature, speed, and metabolism, to the incapacitating effects of menstruation and childbirth. Supporters of women's service cite competent female combatants such as those in twentieth-century guerrilla units or the Soviet Red Army during World War II, or those described in the anthropological literature and discussed later in the chapter. Opponents, in contrast, argue that women's multiple physiological disabilities render them less operationally effective[3] than men, a hindrance compounded by men's need to compensate for women's inferiority and to resist their natural inclination to defend the "weaker sex," especially against the risk of being taken prisoner. Ideas about women's (in)capacities also inform ideas about women's *right* to serve as equal citizens, with equal rights to lay down their lives for their country and thereby reap the benefits that such potential self-sacrifice entails. Here, too, opponents argue that these rights must not be outweighed by the armed forces' primary goal of operational effectiveness. Women's presence interferes with male cohesion and confuses or dilutes men's identity as defenders acting on behalf of the defended, among whom women are categorized.[4] Officers have to make special living and sanitation accommodation for women in the field, and they must cope with the distractions women pose to men. Then there are the inevitable sexual jealousies. Women's domestic responsibilities constitute a further impediment implied by the question, "Who will take care of the children if their mothers—not their fathers—are sent to war?" Justifications either for the need to marginalize or exclude women or to make women feel more welcome are based on other social and cultural issues as well. But at the core, according to some observers, lies the military's (necessarily) deep-seated masculine culture.[5]

A review of these debates reveals internally contradictory features that conspire to paint a picture of essential difference between men and women, and of essential similarity between men themselves. For example, even though the "tooth to tail ratio" has altered over the past century so that combat constitutes only a small portion of modern military practice, combat remains the ultimate measure of women's suitability.[6] And, though changes in military technology have diminished the need for brute strength, it is this difference between men and women that tends to be emphasized. Most curious, however, is that although the express object of the debate on gender integration is women and the problems associated with their service, there is a "deafening silence"[7] concerning men's service. Men's military service is taken for granted. Few, if any, questions are raised regarding men's capacity, willingness, desire, or inclination to serve, or that in war it is the cream of male youth that is sent out to "die for their country." The numbers for the twentieth century alone are staggering: for example, in the World War I Battle of the Somme, over a million men were killed or wounded.[8] A double standard permeates narratives on death in battle, with women's deplored and men's glorified, framed as the ultimate sacrifice.[9] Moreover, men are treated as an internally undifferentiated group rather than as a socially constructed category incorporating disparate individuals exhibiting a spectrum of physical and psychosocial characteristics, interests, and inclinations, including the inclination for or against military service. If there is uniformity among servicemen, little attention is paid to the painstaking efforts expended by militaries to construct it through deliberate social practice, particularly in basic training, part of which includes expelling non-conforming men.[10] In light of the internal contradictions in the arguments used to justify women's marginalization or outright exclusion from the armed forces, we would do well to reflect on some comparative data on gender and the social organization of war.

COMPARATIVE CONSTRUCTIONS OF WAR AND GENDER

The anthropological record is a good starting point for studying the gendered social organization of warfare because it includes an extensive literature on war and gender in pre-state societies, and it directs us to scrutinize features of the military that we might otherwise overlook.[11] An examination of these gendered war practices serves to dispel universalist notions of war as exclusively masculine. As "a total social fact,"[12] warfare in pre-state societies generally extends beyond combat to encompass a host of sacred, political, and other social practices. These include pre-battle rituals to initiate hostilities, as well as mediation or negotiation to prevent or end them; the socialization and training of warriors, as well as a variety of methods, whether spontaneous or institutionalized,[13] to recruit them for particular campaigns; supernatural observances to ensure the safety of combatants and their victory; the supply of food and transportation: the care of the sick and wounded; postwar taboos, ceremonies, and rituals for structuring victory celebrations or mourning the dead and for reintegrating combatants into the community; and disposing of the vanquished, whether dead or taken prisoner.[14] Since war extends beyond combat, there is less likelihood of monopolization by any one group.

This is borne out by the study of a wide array of accounts that turns up no universal gendered division of labor for any of the above-mentioned practices, no generalized exclusions of women or consistent pattern to suggest that any practice, even combat, is everywhere restricted to men. For example, both men and women may be active recruiters, whether in urging warriors to avenge fallen relatives, defend against enemy attack, or launch a preemptive strike against a hostile village.[15] Motivation may also be commercial: Among the nineteenth-century Yoruba, women traditionally controlled the complex marketing system and waged war to open new trade routes, capture slaves, and gain political control of regions that could supply commercially useful goods. For Tonga women, it was their political interests that implicated them in wars of succession.[16]

As with recruitment, there is no consistent or universal gender-restrictive pattern for other war-related practices such as war magic and ritual observances. In some places, these were particular to the home front yet were considered integral to a successful campaign.[17] For example, a Papago woman whose husband had taken a life would join him in observing postwar blood-cleansing taboos, having presumably contributed to the death through the requisite rituals.[18] Recognition of women's non-combative yet critical war contributions was evident where they were invited to play leading roles in victory celebrations and in their receipt of valuable gifts, such as enemy scalps.[19] It is also evident where they were accorded prominent roles in determining and executing the fate of prisoners of war, a fate which usually involved prolonged, ritualized torture.[20]

Women's capacity for violence and cruelty has not only been exhibited against subdued prisoners. It has also been displayed in combat. Contrary to the claim by some that combat has been the exclusive domain of men, there is considerable evidence, additional to that cited above, of female fighters. Among the forced conscripts of the slave-trading regime of eighteenth- and nineteenth-century African Dahomey were female troops known for their effectiveness in taking heads and general brutality.[21] In eighteenth-century South America, a brigade of Andean women soldiers, led by a female member of the Peruvian nobility, successfully fought the Spanish.[22] On the same continent, in the sixteenth century, European explorers named the Amazon River after the Tupinamba women warriors they had encountered in northeastern Brazil.[23] North America also offers numerous examples of women warriors, as do the European Middle Ages, which occasionally saw untitled as well as titled women fight, the latter in fulfillment of the military obligations attached to their fiefs.[24]

But women did not everywhere participate in their society's war practices. Several explanations are offered for women's absence from combat. David Gilmore ties it to men's reproductive expendability, whereas Paola Tabet argues that men's monopoly of tools and weapons is a deliberate means of dominating women. However, Deirdre Meintel disputes this latter position, noting that there is no universal taboo against the bearing of arms by women. Supporting Gilmore, other explanations focus on women's exemption from battle in situations of either natural or artificial demographic imbalance favoring males or where there is a strong cultural aversion to women's presence. In these instances, measures are taken to prevent women from fighting, measures that may include women's physical mutilation as practiced, for example, by the

Dugum Dani. The deliberate exclusion of women from combat may also be explained by the structural contradiction between the institutions of marriage and war: Societies that practice internal warfare are typically patrilocal and exogamous; women marry in to cement alliances.[25] As daughters and sisters of their husbands' enemies, women have conflicting allegiances to their families of origin and procreation.[26] This explanation is supported by evidence from the New Guinea Highlands, where women are excluded for precisely this reason.[27] It is also supported by the Amerindian evidence that when women fought, it was against distant, unrelated enemies. Other reasons may be cultural: Where blood is considered a powerful essence requiring spiritual intervention, bleeding, even by a man, would disrupt activities. Female combatants were generally postmenopausal.

The varied pattern of women's war participation, including ruthless and effective displays of combativeness and brutal treatment of war captives, dispels the notion that the military is masculine because women innately lack the requisite characteristics. But what about an innate disposition in men to wage war and to engage in what is seen as its core practice, combat? Here, again, the most compelling evidence indicates that, on the contrary, inducing and sustaining combativeness in men is difficult. This is especially well documented for the South American Yanomamö, whose internal, lethal warfare reaps a grim harvest in men's lives. Boys are socialized to be fierce. From about the age of eight, they are subjected to practice duels from which they tearfully try to escape, only to be dragged back for more. Adult men also resist going to war, and when they do, it is under considerable duress, bolstered by hallucinogenic drugs and chanting.[28] Older men fire up younger members of a war party to counter their reticence, their tendency to feign illness, and their high rate of desertion. Fearing accusations of cowardice, they are constrained by a system that expects from men violent aggression and revenge. Yet, even in the face of such pressure, many men do abstain: In Chagnon's sample, 38 percent of the men over 41 years of age had never participated in a killing. And those who do kill "appear to feel a deep ambivalence, manifested in what, in our society, might be termed neurotic symptoms of internal decomposition."[29]

That combativeness must be deliberately induced or constructed is equally evident elsewhere. A variety of techniques—including persuasion, sexual and other incentives, taunting and accusations, humiliation, flattery and exaltations, and ideological equations of warriorhood with manhood—may be used to exhort or pressure (mostly) young men to engage in a form of self-sacrifice to which they are not readily disposed.[30] The same holds true for state societies where extreme, traumatizing practices of basic training are employed to transform young (male) civilians into soldiers. Nor is resistance to combat unusual. Throughout history, individual men have attempted various means of evasion that have included flight, prison, self-mutilation, feigning illness, insanity or sexual deviance, hiring surrogates,[31] going AWOL or even committing suicide. Often when they have fought, they have done so under the influence of mood-altering substances[32] or under threat of lethal violence from their superiors. During the Great War Canadian troops were commonly provided extra rations of rum prior to an offensive in order to prepare them for death or killing. Officers also let their men know that they had appointed battle police to shoot laggards or those who hid.[33]

Such evidence dispels essentialist myths of innate male aggressiveness. Rather, it demonstrates that dramatic transformations, along with social boundaries and liminality, are needed to construct and maintain a combative identity and solidarity. In those pre-state societies where warfare is strictly gender segregated and marked as masculine, these practices are often accompanied by discourses of male-female antagonism, ambivalence and fear, the projection of dissension among men onto women, and a displacement of the fear of the dangers of war onto dangers associated with female "pollution." Such gender-divisive devices are actively cultivated in gerontocracies by male elders who themselves display a more relaxed attitude toward women than do the younger men in whom they deliberately induce this exaggerated fear of female contamination.[34] Elsewhere, I describe a similar, though much less exaggerated, dynamic in the Canadian armed forces that fulfills its mandate to wage war against the enemy through an organizational structure and meaning system that together incorporate a number of mutually informing binary oppositions such as war/peace, death/life, strong/weak, military/civilian, defenders/defended, friend/enemy, and uniformity/diversity. It is onto these sets of oppositions that gender is mapped: Men/masculinity is associated with the former (i.e., war, strong, military, uniformity, defenders, friend, etc.) and women/femininity with the latter (i.e., peace, weak, civilian, diversity, defended, enemy, etc.), embodying, in part, impediments to operational effectiveness. What makes women's presence so contentious is not what they *are*—their purported essential physiology—but what they *represent*, their associated social attributes.[35] It is the aspect of femininity that is associated with weakness and other oppositional characteristics cited above that conjures up the enemy. In the same vein, as we will soon see, the military's masculinity has less to do with men's essential characteristics than with what they represent in relation to the military's mandate. The military's need to segregate its members from civilian society and to develop and sustain in them a solidary, combative attitude entails identifying and shunning all that is associated with the debilitating elements of the civilian sphere. And because the value and practices of the civilian sphere are the inverse of those of the military, the conflation of the military with masculinity and violence serves to normalize and legitimate the military's lethal goals and practices.[36]

Thus far we have seen that pre-state and state societies have in common the need to construct and sustain the bellicose identities of their combatants. But there are other commonalities as well. As in pre-states, war in state societies is multifaceted, drawing on a wide range of participants; and it is ritually complex, bound up with sacred meaning and practice.[37] This is as true of Ancient Assyria,

with its cultic functionaries for interpreting omens and providing religious jus-
tification for military campaigns,[38] as it is of early-twentieth-century Canada,
in which propaganda framed World War I as a Christian struggle against the
forces of evil. Clerics of various Christian denominations worked hand in hand
with the military to encourage young men to exhibit a Christian spirit of self-
sacrifice; death in battle was equated with saintliness.[39] In addition to the sacral-
ization of war, the social organization of war in state societies also differentiates
populations into defenders and defended, in varying ways and degrees. And as
is often the case for pre-state societies, as we saw earlier, combatants in state-
sponsored militaries act as proxies for those who cannot or would not fight.[40]

Although pre-state and state societies have this latter point in common, it is
also the point on which they diverge. That is, despite the susceptibility of warriors in pre-state societies to interpersonal pressure or to structural induce-
ments to engage in combat, often as proxies, the absence of an enforceable draft,
of a coercive superior authority, renders the process from recruitment to combat fundamentally democratic: The decision to engage in this form of collective
lethal violence is ultimately voluntary, made by combatants themselves.[41] No
one is shot for refusing to fight. In state societies, in contrast, motivating
soldiers to place themselves in harm's way—with little to gain and much to
lose—is a principal preoccupation. How does the military appropriate the
soldier's autonomy and ensure obedience to orders, especially to those that en-
tail risking one's life?

The organizational answer to the military's motivational dilemma is eluci-
dated by Mumford in his description of the origins of the army as an organizational form at the "dawn of civilization" in the fourth millennium B.C.E. in
Egypt, Mesopotamia, India, China, Yucatan, and Peru. The innovation of the
army as one of several in a constellation of new institutions and cultural inventions lay not in new mechanical inventions but in a new form of social organization that harnessed a human multitude into what comprised the first
gigantic machine, which Mumford terms the "megamachine." It is this human
machine that produced the grand projects, both sacred and profane, many of
which still stand today: temples, pyramids, ziggurats, and giant irrigation
works. The basis of this new culture, with the army as its central paradigm, was
its dedication "to the expansion of collective power...by perfecting new instruments of coercion."[42] The individual initiative of the hero was replaced by
the strict obedience of disciplined troops governed by the technical rationality
that mobilized them into integrated, mechanized groups acting on orders issued by a solitary individual at the top and transmitted through a series of in-
termediaries to the very lowest of units and individuals.[43] For the machine to
function effectively, orders had to be reproduced and followed precisely; rank
was sacrosanct and disobedience intolerable. The army represented a new instrument of coercion, directed not merely at the enemies of a ruling elite but at
its very own subjects. Wittfogel describes a similar dynamic for what he terms
"hydraulic society"; its objective of harnessing water required the harnessing

of the will of populations. He identifies the same shift to authoritarianism in the army, noting that soldiers in the hydraulic state lacked the protection of "democratic check or feudal contracts...they came when they were summoned; they marched where they were told; they fought as long as the ruler wanted them to fight."[44] Feudal armies, by contrast, were notorious for their lack of discipline, with officers as likely to disobey as were the rank and file to be careless and reckless.[45] In sum, this review of the army's ancient origins highlights the internal repression unique to this form of social organization. It is the archaic army's form of authoritarian social organization that has come down to us through the millennia. Whereas warriors in pre-state societies must be induced, persuaded, or humiliated into fighting in the *absence* of overarching coercive structures, in state societies armies *are* coercive structures, and control the principal agents and executors of state violence against their own members.

WHY MILITARY MASCULINITY?

To recapitulate, the above anthropological and historical narratives on war and gender prompt us to question the masculine social organization of warfare in the form of the military and to investigate the military's organizational means for extracting obedience from its members: its authoritarianism. Moreover, these comparative perspectives are mutually informing: examining the military's authoritarianism furthers our understanding of the means by which this organization commits its soldiers to its high-risk, potentially lethal practices, and of how these are gendered. Whereas the problem of getting soldiers to place themselves at risk was difficult under ancient authoritarian rule, motivation for hierarchically controlled lethal violence on the part of those who are structurally excluded from the decision-making processes and benefits of war is far more challenging in democracies, which guarantee the franchise and promise individual rights and freedoms, and where most social practices are ostensibly based on consent. As an anomalous holdover from a distant and largely forgotten past, the military has in many ways remained true to the despotic social conditions in which it originated. Even as Western societies have inched their way toward expanded legal and political rights, the military's segregation from the larger civilian society has allowed it to retain many of the social and legal parameters of its historic roots.[46] In democracies there is a particular tension between the larger society's political and legal institutions and the military's coercive mandate and conditions of service.

This tension exacerbates the military's existing preoccupation with the internal coercion of its members, with maintaining discipline, ensuring obedience, and mitigating resistance to the performance of this hazardous work. Tasks such as peacekeeping or peace enforcement aside, militaries are instruments of lethal force with mandates to deliver collective lethal violence. Managers of violence are carefully distinguished from those responsible for engendering and sustaining the violence of still others who are charged with its execution. Rank marks the internal differentiation, or conflicts of interest, between more and less powerful men.[47] But rather than being transparent, these differences must be camouflaged in order to construct the military's unity of purpose—which is its operational effectiveness. This is the benchmark against which all else is evaluated. How are these differences in interests contained? The most obvious method is through the construction of the ranking system as inviolable, sacrosanct. Challenging rank is in the order of heresy, since it would mean exposing the oppositions of interest inherent in the ranking system's dispersal of power, thereby disrupting the disciplinary system that enforces obedience. The second method of containment consists in the construction of gender along a male-female axis of opposition, evident above in the elaborate discourses of male-female differences in physiological and social characteristics that render women less able to serve. It is this emphasis on male-female difference that serves to deflect attention from the fault lines along which military masculinity fractures internally. Further, it allows for the perpetuation of the military's attachment to a uniform masculinity (uniformity, strength, etc.) and an opposition to femininity (diversity, weakness, etc.) which, as in some pre-state societies, is used to deflect, mask, and contain these tensions between multiple and unequal military masculinities. Masculine unity, an ally of masculine military uniformity, is a third method of containing, as well as actually masking, differences in military masculinities, and it forms the basis for constructing and fostering troop solidarity in order to achieve the military's unity of purpose, which, again, is its operational effectiveness.

CONCLUSION

The objective of this chapter has been to set out some of the parameters for understanding why the military constructs itself as uniformly masculine and why it is disrupted by the entry of women. Comparative cross-cultural and historical perspectives of the gendered social organization of war demonstrate that military masculinity is neither universal nor inevitable. Instead, a uniform military masculinity is carefully constructed through deliberate social practice as a means of operationalizing a unique mandate—waging war—through an authoritarian organization that is preoccupied with ensuring the obedience of potentially resistant practitioners. The military is an organization that values, promotes, and engages in practices that are the inverse of those valued, promoted, and practiced in the civilian sphere. Militaries are mandated to perfect the techniques of lethal violence, of killing; to fulfil this mandate they must construct different kinds of lives and deaths, and they must assign them meaning. Military masculinity has less to do with men's essential characteristics than it does with the characteristics and assigned meanings of the different world—the military world—that soldiers inhabit. It is in describing something of the nature and requisites of this world, and in shifting our sights from the male-female axis of opposition to the oppositions between military men and to the fractures within military masculinity, that we have been able to delineate some of what masculinity and femininity—embodied in real men and women—represent. It remains to be seen what long-term effects the increasing presence of women will have on the military as a gendered organization and on its mandate, values, and practices.

NOTES

1. Women had been involved with European armies as camp followers and private entrepreneurs providing food, mending, laundry, and other services up until the mid-sixteenth to seventeenth centuries, when the system of subcontracting the organization and provisioning of armies was abandoned and these were brought directly under state control. Barton C. Hacker and Sally L. Hacker, "Military Institutions and the Labor Process: Non-economic Sources of Technological Change, Women's Subordination, and the Organization of Work," *Technology and Culture* 28, 4 (1987): 743–775.

2. This has especially become the case with the advent of the all-volunteer force and shrinking pools of draft-age men. See David J. Armor, "Race and Gender in the U.S. Military," *Armed Forces & Society* 23, 1 (1996): 7–27; Mady W. Segal, David R. Segal, Jerald G. Bachman, Peter Freedman-Doan, and Patrick M. O'Malley, "Gender and the Propensity to Enlist in the U.S. Military," *Gender Issues* 16, 3 (1998): 65–87; Regina F. Titunik, "The First Wave: Gender Integration and Military Culture," *Armed Forces & Society* 26, 2 (2000): 229–257; Julie Wheelwright, "'A Brother in Arms, a Sister in Peace': Contemporary Issues of Gender and Military Technology," in *Inventing Women: Science, Technology and Gender,* ed. Gill Kirkup and Lauri Smith Keller (Cambridge: Polity Press, 1992).

3. These are code words for "combat ready."

4. Wheelwright, "'A Brother in Arms, a Sister in Peace.'"

5. Linda Bird Francke, *Ground Zero: The Gender Wars in the Military* (New York: Simon & Schuster, 1997).

6. Titunik, "The First Wave: Gender Integration and Military Culture," is an exception here, sidestepping the question of women in combat and noting in her final footnote that the "question of women serving in combat requires consideration of a number of complex issues that are beyond the scope of this paper" (p. 257). She never indicates what these issues are.

7. Henri Lustiger-Thaler, "Remembering Forgetfully," in *Re-situating Identities: The Politics of Race, Ethnicity and Culture,* ed. Vered Amit-Talai and Caroline Knowles (Peterborough: Broadview Press, 1996: 196).

8. Warren Farrell, *The Myth of Male Power* (New York: Simon & Schuster, 1993).

9. Genevieve Lloyd, "Selfhood, War and Masculinity," in *Feminist Challenges: Social and Political Theory,* ed. Carole Pateman and Elizabeth Gross (Boston: Northeastern University Press, 1987: 63–77), traces the connection between war, citizenship, and gender in the Western philosophical tradition, where sacrificing one's life in battle has long

been conflated with masculinity and has been constructed as a right—even a *privilege*—of male citizenship.

10. Nor is there much discussion of the ongoing processes by which differences between military men and women are socially constructed.

11. Napoleon A. Chagnon, "Yanomamö Social Organization and Warfare," in *War: The Anthropology of Armed Conflict and Aggression*, ed. Morton Fried, Marvin Harris, and Robert Murphy (Garden City, NY: Natural History Press), notes, "Probably no single academic discipline has more facts bearing on the nature and social effects of war than anthropology" (p. 133). However, it is important to keep in mind that academic, as other accounts, are limited, partial, and motivated and must therefore be read critically. The point that Liz James, "Introduction," in *Women, Men and Eunuchs: Gender in Byzantium*, ed. Liz James (London: Routledge, 1997), makes on the representationality of history may apply differently to anthropology, but it applies nonetheless. It certainly is in step with the position of Lawrence H. Keeley, *War before Civilization: The Myth of the Peaceful Savage* (New York: Oxford University Press, 1996), who suggests that conceptions of warfare in pre-state societies have tended to be chauvinistic. The immediate relevance of these qualifications is apparent in the consideration of Chagnon's work *Yanomamö: The Fierce People* (New York: Holt, Rinehart and Winston, 1968), around which there has been recent controversy. Patrick Tierney advances the argument in *Darkness in El Dorado* (New York: W. W. Norton & Co., 2000) that Chagnon is one of many North Americans and Europeans to have exploited indigenous people of South America for research and other purposes; indeed, that Chagnon's interventions triggered warfare between neighboring Yanomamö villages. The impact of this for my own argument is less debilitating, since I emphasize men's reluctance to fight.

12. R. Brian Ferguson, "A Savage Encounter: Western Contact and the Yanomami War Complex," in *War in the Tribal Zone*, ed. R. Brian Ferguson and Neil L. Whitehead (Santa Fe, NM: School of American Research Press, 1992: 201).

13. For example, taking at least one head may be a requirement for marriage.

14. These are elaborated in Marcia Kovitz, "Mining Masculinities in the Canadian Military," Ph.D. dissertation (Montreal: Concordia University, 1998).

15. For vengeance see Karl Heider, *The Dugum Dani: A Papuan Culture in the Highlands of West New Guinea* (Chicago: Aldine Publishing Co., 1970). For defense see Carolyn Niethammer, *Daughters of the Earth: The Lives and Legends of American Indian Women* (New York: Collier Books, 1977), on the Pawnee. On preemptive strikes see Chagnon. *Yanomamö: The Fierce People.*

16. Deirdre Meintel, "Victimes ou protagonistes: les femmes et la guerre," *Anthropologies et Sociétés* 7 (1983): 179–186.

17. Harry H. Turney-High, *Primitive War: Its Practice and Concepts* (Columbia: University of South Carolina Press, 1971).

18. Niethammer, *Daughters of the Earth.*

19. See Ernest Wallace and E. Adamson Hoebel, *The Comanches: Lords of the South Plains* (Norman: University of Oklahoma Press, 1952), on the Comanche; and Turney-High, *Primitive War: Its Practice and Concepts*, on the Omaha and Wind River Shoshone.

20. See Bruce Trigger, *Natives and Newcomers: Canada's "Heroic Age" Reconsidered* (Montreal: McGill-Queen's University Press, 1985:97), on the Huron.

21. Melville J. Herskovits, *Dahomey: An Ancient West African Kingdom,* vol. 1 (Evanston: Northwestern University Press, 1967).

22. Irene Silverblatt, "The Universe has turned inside out.... There is no justice for us here': Andean Women under Spanish Rule," in *Women and Colonization: Anthropological Perspectives,* ed. Mona Etienne and Eleanor Leacock (New York: Praeger, 1980).

23. Walter L. Williams, *The Spirit and the Flesh: Sexual Diversity in American Indian Culture* (Boston: Beacon Press, 1986).

24. For North America see David B. Adams, "Why There Are So Few Women Warriors," *Behaviour Science Research* 18, 3 (1983):196–212; Karen Sacks, *Sisters and Wives* (Westport, CT: Greenwood Press, 1979); and Turney-High, *Primitive War.* For the European Middle Ages see Phillipe Contamine, *War in the Middle Ages* (Oxford: Basil Blackwell, 1984).

25. Nancy Bonvillain, *Women and Men: Cultural Constructs of Gender* (Englewood Cliffs: Prentice-Hall, 1995), explains that internal warfare is practiced between neighboring, ethnically related and linguistically homogeneous communities. For theories on women's absence from combat, see David Gilmore, *Manhood in the Making* (New Haven: Yale University Press, 1990); Paola Tabet, "Hands, Tools, Weapons," *Feminist Issues* 2 (1982): 3–62; Meintel, "Victimes ou protagonistes: les femmes et la guerre." Heider, *The Dugum Dani: A Papuan Culture in the Highlands of West New Guinea,* describes the sacrificial finger-chopping of little girls after the death of a warrior.

26. Adams, "Why There Are So Few Women Warriors."

27. Marilyn G. Gelber, *Gender and Society in the New Guinea Highlands* (Boulder, CO: Westview Press, 1986); and Eric Schwimmer, "La guerre aux femmes (Nouvelle-Guinée). Propos et discussions," *Anthropologie et Sociétés* 7 (1983): 187–192.

28. Chagnon, "Yanomamö Social Organization and Warfare," indicates that upwards of one quarter of all men die as a result of armed combat, a cause of death that is second in importance only to epidemics. He also describes here the socialization of male children to ferocity. On drug taking as a means for bolstering this ferocity, Chagnon, *Yanomamö: The Fierce People,* points out that Yanomamö warfare consists of escalated forms of aggression ranging from the less serious to the more lethal forms, which are raids and treacherous feasts. Competitive fighting is a component of feasts, and the required ferocity is bolstered through drug taking. In "Yanomamö Social Organization and Warfare," Chagnon notes that they "take hallucinogenic drugs to put themselves in a fighting mood" (p. 133). Drug-related practices also build ferocity in other ways. For example, in *Yanomamö: The Fierce People,* Chagnon describes the special ceremony held on the day before a raiding party set out to avenge the death of a warrior. The dead man's relatives "took a snuff tube and blew some of the drug into the gourds containing the ashes [of the slain man] (p. 135). Earlier he describes how eating these ashes "puts them into the appropriate state of rage for the business of killing enemies" (p. 50). Ferocity and resolve are also bolstered by chanting a "war song" as part of the pre-raid departure ritual: One man sings and the remaining warriors repeat in unison, ending with them all "shout[ing] in the direction of the enemy village" (p. 137).

29. R. Brian Ferguson, "A Savage Encounter: Western Contact and the Yanomami War Complex," p. 223. Also see Gilmore, *Manhood in the Making,* who notes, "Numerous studies have shown that the average soldier is extremely timorous in battlefield situations and that he 'regresses' and reacts 'passively' under enemy fire"(p. 121).

30. For Gilmore, *Manhood in the Making,* the ideology of manhood is a means of enlisting men for these and other high-risk activities. Elaine Showalter, "Rivers and Sassoon: The Inscription of Male Gender Anxieties," in *Behind the Lines,* ed. Margaret Randolph Higonnet, Jane Jenson, Sonya Michel, and Margaret Collins Weitz (New Haven: Yale University Press, 1987), details a comparable use of gender ideology in the re-inscription of masculinity anxiety in a World War I shell-shocked soldier.

31. Barbara Ehrenreich, *Blood Rites: Origins and History of the Passions of War* (New York: Metropolitain Books, Henry Holt and Co., 1997).

32. Ibid., and Gilmore, *Manhood in the Making.*

33. Jeffrey A. Keshen, *Propaganda and Censorship during Canada's Great War* (Edmonton: University of Alberta Press, 1996). Also, see Joanna Bourke, *Dismembering the Male: Men's Bodies, Britain, and the Great War* (Chicago: University of Chicago Press, 1996): "Thus, Bert Rudge described having to get drunk before 'zero hour' because he was frightened that he would be one of the men who had to be forced out. As he put it, 'If they didn't go, they was shot'" (p. 78).

34. Gelber, *Gender and Society in the New Guinea Highlands.*

35. See Marcia Kovitz, "The Enemy Within: Female Soldiers in the Canadian Armed Forces," in *Canadian Woman Studies—Women in Conflict Zones,* 19, 4 (2000): 36–41; and Kovitz, "Mining Masculinities in the Canadian Military." Some of the attributes associated with femininity are conflicting: For example, inside the military, feminine weakness is seen as debilitating to operational effectiveness; but outside, it is considered a motivator for soldiers, since it represents the sphere of the defended.

36. David Morgan, "Masculinity and Violence," in *Women, Violence and Social Control,* ed. Jalna Hanmer and Mary Maynard (Atlantic Highlands, NJ: Humanities Press International, 1990), argues that masculinity is also a means of normalizing and legitimating violence, including that of military practice. With the inclusion of women, more of military practice is coming under critical scrutiny.

37. Oracles were consulted, animals or humans sacrificed, or other religious ceremonials and rites performed to solicit divine guidance, support, or intervention or to ensure auspicious conditions. For example, Menelaus, husband of the abducted Helen of Troy, is reported by Herodotus in *The Histories* (Middlesex: Penguin Books, 1954) to have sacrificed two local children while in Egypt in the hopes of accelerating the advent of favorable winds by which to sail.

38. Arthur Ferrill, *The Origins of War* (London: Thames & Hudson, 1985).

39. Keshen, *Propaganda and Censorship during Canada's Great War.*

40. Combatants have certainly fought on their own behalf as well. Trigger, *Natives and Newcomers: Canada's "Heroic Age" Reconsidered,* recounts how warriorhood could also be the sole route to political power or prestige for young Huron men who eagerly sought pretexts for war, sometimes challenging the pacifist policies of their elders who preferred friendly relations with their neighbors.

41. M. I. Finley, *Politics in the Ancient World* (London: Cambridge University Press, 1983), notes the same conditions for Athenian democracy.

42. Lewis Mumford, *The Myth of the Machine: Technics and Human Development* (New York: Harcourt Brace Jovanovich, 1966: 164).

43. For more discussion on this point see Jurgen Habermas, *Theory and Practice* (Boston: Beacon Press, 1973), and Merritt Roe Smith, "Introduction," in *Military Enterprise and Technological Change; Perspectives on the American Experience*, ed. Merritt Roe Smith (Cambridge, Massachusetts: MIT Press, 1985).

44. Karl A. Wittfogel, *Oriental Despotism: A Comparative Study of Total Power* (New Haven: Yale University Press, 1957: 60).

45. Wittfogel, *Oriental Despotism: A Comparative Study of Total Power*. Also see Michael Prestwich, *Armies and Warfare in the Middle Ages: The English Experience* (New Haven: Yale University Press, 1996).

46. For example, in democracies, workers may elect to resign from their jobs at will, although at a cost, whether financial or other if they have failed to give adequate notice. Soldiers, even in all-volunteer forces, have no such freedom: Recruitment may be voluntary, but release is not, except within clearly defined parameters, and then at the military's discretion. Whereas soldiers can be imprisoned for "quitting," civilians cannot.

47. Along with differences in rank can be counted differences in military occupation, differences explored in this anthology. Robert W. Connell, "Masculinity, Violence and War," in *Men's Lives*, ed. Michael S. Kimmel and Michael A. Messner (New York: Macmillan Publishing Co. 1992), differentiates the physically violent masculinity, subordinate to orders; the dominating and organizationally competent; and the professionalized, calculative rationality of the technical specialist (1992). Cynthia Enloe, "Beyond 'Rambo': Women and the Varieties of Militarized Masculinity," in *Women and the Military System*, ed. Eva Isaksson (New York: St. Martin's Press, 1988), distinguishes the low-ranking combat soldier, or "Rambo"; Star Warrior scientists; defense intellectuals; and white-collar middle managers and senior executives.

Chapter 2

No More Heroes: Masculinity in the Infantry

John Hockey

The prime objective of the military organization is to engage in conflict and the resources it deploys are essentially human. Whereas there are increasingly sophisticated technologies utilized by the military,[1] the brutal business of taking and holding ground remains the province of the infantry. Although other combat arms (armor, and artillery) kill the enemy at long distance, it is the infantry alone that normally destroys the enemy at a much closer range. Ensuring that troops accomplish this organizational objective effectively requires an ongoing socialization process; this chapter will focus upon the role 'masculinity' plays within this process. It will depict how masculinity is constructed and perceived by ordinary soldiers. What follows is based upon data acquired during participant observation with a company of infantry in the regular (professional) British Army, on the basis of which an ethnography of the infantryman's subculture was generated.[2] The material presented emanates from fieldnotes gathered in the contexts of barracks, field exercises, and actual combat operations.

Prior to their army service, potential recruits are exposed to a number of information sources that form part of their occupational pre-socialization to the military and the particular kind of masculinity generated within it.[3] There is, within the wider culture, the popular cliché that entry into the British Army '"makes a man of you" and that the army "turns boys into men."'[4] At a more specific level, the UK Ministry of Defence (MoD) publicity available to those aspiring to become infantrymen at the time of the research heavily stressed an image co-relating being a man and being a combat soldier. This action image, the epitome of aggressive masculinity, is still being used by the MoD in its current recruitment literature.[5] Although as part of its definition of the soldierly role the MoD publicity now stresses learning a skill or an occupation, particularly in relation to technical corps (signals, engineers, etc.), the appeal to masculinity remains central to how it portrays the infantryman and his life.

Moreover, it is well worth remembering that the target group for this kind of appeal is young males, mostly aged between 16 and 24 and mostly educated only to secondary school levels,[6] so the potency of this kind of traditional appeal is perhaps not surprising.[7] It is against this background that recruits start their military service, which, for infantrymen at the time of data collection began with a period of eighteen weeks' basic training.

A *RITE DE PASSAGE*

At the start of basic training, recruits are promptly informed by instructional staff that they do not have the *right* to be infantrymen, that in effect they have to earn that status. Basic training is consequently presented to them as a direct challenge, a series of tests that have to be passed. Passing through this initial period of military service constitutes a *rite de passage*.[8] Successful completion of basic training fits Van Gennep's formulation, for it entails a change of status not only from civilian to infantryman but also from boy to man. Role effectiveness is then explicitly linked by instructional staff to masculine potency. Such potency is made up of a series of qualities and behaviors that are seen to be axiomatic to the efficient infantryman, and in the training staff's eyes, there is no possibility of recruits' passing the *rite de passage* without displaying such attributes. As one corporal instructor put it: "Soldiers should be young and fit, rough and nasty, not powderpuffs!" Recruits are propelled through a series of activities that include drill, circuit training, road runs, assault courses, aikido, and forced speed marches carrying heavy loads of equipment. These activities are physically hard on the recruit. The ability to cope with these physical demands constitutes a prime indicator of the individual's masculinity, and this message is repeatedly reinforced by instructional staff. The unfit are then by definition unmasculine, and the only way forward is to try harder, get fitter, and become "real men." Gradually recruits' physical endurance is built by instructional staff as increased distances, loads, and speeds are demanded of them. Accompanying this focus on physical endurance is the development of a particular kind of mental endurance that centers on the toleration of pain and discomfort. This discomfort starts in a minor way on day one of military service, when recruits encounter military clothing, which is usually much rougher on the skin than its civilian counterpart. Legs, unaccustomed to wearing heavy boots all the time, soon begin to tire, and feet have to be "broken in" to accommodate new boots and not vice versa. Any march that involves carrying considerable equipment inevitably produces blistered areas such as feet, shoulders, and hips, from the weight carried, as well as gross fatigue. As Crossley has noted, the mind is inseparable from the body; they remain "reversible aspects of a single fabric."[9] So exposure to physical hardship brings about a bodily toughening; simultaneously the mind comes to cope with this hardship. In effect a certain kind of stoicism is engendered through an acceptance of particular kinds of suffering caused by physical exertion, lack of sleep, and exposure to climatic variation. Infantry soldiers, when in the field live in "shell-scrapes" (small holes dug in the ground) or under a "basha" (primitive shelter). Recruits have to learn to endure, to "soldier on," they are told by instructional staff; and this stoicism is firmly linked, once again, to a particular form of masculinity.

The recruits have been shown how to build a defensive perimeter consisting of trenches which they have dug. They are now squatting in them (as I am!), watching their "arcs" [zones of fire]. It is very cold, windy, and constantly raining. They have no idea how long this situation is going to last. For an hour the novelty intrigues them, after two hours, grumbles begin, and their attention to their arcs begins to wane. They are immediately reprimanded by the NCO [non-commissioned officer] instructors who cite inattention as a cause of death for oneself and one's mates when on real operations. These messages are rammed home to recruits but there is also another one, namely that putting up with this kind of hardship is what real men do. A Corporal squats on top of a trench and looks gravely down at two soaked, shivering recruits, he is also soaked but not shivering: "Little boys with their toys [pointing to the weapons the recruits carry] is it?" The recruits mumble forlornly about the weather conditions. The Corporal replies: "Well, they [the weapons] are not toys and this is not a game. So the sooner you two learn to wear long pants properly the better." (basic training, initial field exercise)

FAILURE, FEMININITY, AND HETEROSEXUALITY

Whereas positive performances result in praise from the training team and are equated with masculinity, failure to perform is often linked with being feminine and thus deemed to be the antithesis of infantry behavior. Physical inadequacy is then portrayed as being weak and womanly and cause for derogatory comment from instructors: Sergeant to a platoon as it is in the middle of a drill movement: "Come on faster, harder! Bang those feet in when you halt. Some of you are like old women coming around that corner." Corporal to recruits indulging in horseplay outside barracks: "Get fell in and stop fucking about! Act like men and not like a bunch of wet tarts!"

Falling behind in any of the numerous physical activities, the recruits are propelled through invariably aroused some kind of NCO derision, equating this lack of physicality with being women, or comments that "girls can do better," or that "you bunch of girls are always at the back!" Displays lacking in stoicism also met this kind of response, for women were caricatured as people who cried, broke down, and refused to go on, whereas supposedly real infantrymen soldiered on in the face of all sorts of hazards and hardships. An additional prized behavior is that of aggression. Instructors repeatedly emphasized to recruits that in the infantry only those who are really aggressive will survive 'contact' with the enemy. Aggression is deemed an extremely valuable commodity, and recruits are taught that they need to display it consistently. Lack of aggression is again correlated with femininity, inadequacy, and, ultimately and quite fundamentally, death. As one corporal indicated to recruits in a bayonet-fighting class: "I want to hear you scream, you sound pathetic, like a bunch of Mary's, no balls at all. Now let's hear some aggression! ... You have to get momentum and drive forward with that bayonet otherwise he [the enemy] will kill you. You will be DEAD, DEAD, DEAD!"

In addition, the infantry role was explicitly portrayed to recruits as one that demanded heterosexual potency. "Real men" chase women, and "real men" should be sexually athletic at every available opportunity:

Corporal to a class of recruits: "Now young soldiers, you are going on leave soon and you WILL have a good time, that's an order! [Class laughs.] So you will need some of these won't you? [He holds up a packet of condoms.] I expect all of you to get shagged out, but remember if you get VD [venereal disease], then that can be a chargeable offence under military law. So give the girls a good time and keep some of these in your wallet!" (He grins and waves condoms.) (weapon training class)

Corporal to an inept recruit, who is having problems loading a magazine with rounds whilst being timed: "Get a grip W____! How do you expect to pass out (of Basic Training) fumbling around like that? Is that how you fumble around with your bird [girlfriend]? I bet she's pissed off with you. [Class laughs.] Look if you pass out, both her and I will be pleased and then you will be a real soldier!"

MEN AND THEIR MATES

While recruits are assailed by their training team with messages correlating masculinity with physical endurance, aggression, stoicism, and sexual athleticism, there is an additional feature that helps form part of this particular type of social construction.[10] The attributes listed are all demanded by instructors from recruits as individuals, but at the same time it is made clear that on operations, survival is dependent upon the close support and cooperation of one's peers:

Corporal (instructing on sentry duty): "If you don't do your job properly and follow the correct procedures, you may be responsible for your whole section being wiped out. Your mates! All it needs is for you to slip up for an instance, and the enemy will tag on as Tail End Charley [last man in a patrol], and get inside the perimeter. Everyone depends on you when you are on sentry, remember that!"

Instilling loyalty to one's peers, or in soldierly argot, "one's mates" or "the lads," is then a crucial component of the infantry socialization process. Patterns of mutual aid, particularly at the patrol, section, or platoon level, are developed very early in basic training. This aid ranges from helping exhausted peers with their loads when on a march, disguising their deviance from military superiors, or eventually (much later in service) covering their movement when on operational patrol. Interestingly, and in contrast to wider cultural norms, this protection and mutual cooperation is presented as thoroughly *masculine* conduct. If one is a real man, one protects one's mates even at the cost of considerable sacrifice (increased fatigue, hunger, a superior's wrath, the hostile intent of the enemy, etc.) to oneself. Failure to do so can bring formal organizational sanctions (fines, jail, court martial, etc.) as well as informal subcultural ones (ostracism, physical attacks, etc.). So, for example, when NCOs interrogate the soldiers to find out whose voice from the back rank of a squad likened the instructor to 'Frankenstein,' no disclosures are forthcoming even though the soldiers well know that extra work, more arduous physical activity, or no weekend leave are the likely repercussions for all. In a similar vein, when on field exercise with the platoon's cigarette ration almost exhausted, recruits are told by their instructors, "Share with your mates." Failure to do so results in derogatory comments because a refusal to share is stigmatized as weak and not the kind of behavior appropriate for real infantrymen:

NCO to a recruit who is reluctant to share his last cigarette with members of his Section: "Don't be such a wanker J____! Pass that fag around your mates rapid! If you keep on acting like that, you can go and join the girls and fairies in the signals or the engineers or some other dipstick [useless] lot, because we don't want you!"

In the above instance, the NCO is deriding the recruit for the selfishness of his conduct, associating it with other parts of the military organization that are viewed as inferior and less masculine than the infantry. All other corps support the infantry; moreover, normally only the infantry confront the enemy close up, in the ultimate test of the combat soldier, the ultimate test of masculinity.[11] The training NCOs depict peer cooperation and support as a necessity for operational survival, but this is not the only message at work, for underpinning this logic is the imperative that real men support their mates in all situations.

Basic training is a lengthy and intense experience for infantry recruits. Whereas all army recruits undergo a similar process, initial infantry socialization is much more intensely focused on physical endurance, aggression, and loyalty to peers—all features NCOs stressed as being masculine. Instructors are role models within the context of a total institution.[12] Because of their operational service, the NCOs seem considerably charismatic to recruits,[13] thus constituting influential significant others. The result is that recruits eventually begin to perceive themselves as rough, tough infantrymen. As Park long ago noted, "The conception which men [and women] form of themselves seems to depend upon their vocation,"[14] and the trade of the infantryman is centrally concerned with proficiency in homicidal techniques, toughness, ruthlessness, and aggression, all of which are underpinned by a virulently traditional masculinity that continues to pervade the life of the infantryman as he passes through his *rite de passage*, moving from basic training to life in an operational unit.

NO MORE HEROES

Once serving in an operational battalion, the newly qualified infantryman experiences an increased demand by his superiors in certain areas of his day-to-day existence. Whereas the imposition of military discipline is relatively relaxed compared to basic training, demands in terms of efficiency in infantry skills, endurance, fitness, aggression, and group loyalty escalate. Exercise-planning staff deliberately simulate operational conditions, and thus infantrymen spend relatively long periods on field exercises, enduring a primitive existence in the countryside, compared to the rather brief forays—termed by NCOs "Boy Scouts outings"—of basic training. It is then normal for the infantry body to be hauling eighty pounds of weapons, ammunition, and equipment for prolonged periods. Day after day and week after week on major exercises, the infantryman's world consists of long marches, together with simulated patrols and ambushes, often on a minimum of sleep, while exposed to the vagaries of climatic variation. This simulated operational environment is not without hazard, for individuals are routinely injured and on occasion die, as they fall under tanks, are crushed by trucks, fail to survive river crossings, and are hit by misdirected shells. These scenarios demand an enhanced investment in and display of the supposedly masculine attributes previously generated in basic training. Suffice it to say that these attributes are deepened and strengthened by the more intensive, repeated exposure to simulated combat evident in routine battalion life, and at this juncture no more effort will be devoted to repeating how these attributes are constructed. Rather, how infantry masculinity is played out in actual operational contexts will now be examined.

Until their exposure to actual operations, the infantrymen have experienced only training. Actual operations constitute a 'real' environment where the enemy is prone to kill or maim the infantrymen using a range of homicidal practices, including sniping, booby traps, mortars, rocket-propelled grenades, and other sundry explosive ordnance. To newcomers to operational service, nothing brings this stark realization home more than the first casualty suffered within their peer group. In the words of one private serving in South Armagh: "Its hard to realize that J____'s dead, you expect him to walk in any minute... It's like a smack in the face and you sort of grow up quickly. You realize this is the fucking sharp-end and unless you switch on [stay alert], you will be going home to Manchester in a body-bag." Simulated combat develops and tests the previously depicted attributes up to a point; beyond that point actual hazard from the enemy impinges upon the conduct and construction of the infantryman's masculinity. The reality of operational service brings about a modification of that masculinity. As Kickbusch has noted, taking risks may be essential to the constructing of particular social identities, and the identity of the infantryman is centrally enmeshed with risking his body in armed conflict.[15] When in training he is taught effectiveness in homicidal techniques and the most effective strategies to liquidate the enemy. On operations the infantryman's prime concern is not to liquidate the enemy but, rather, to survive. Survival does on occasion involve the liquidation of the enemy; however, the need to survive means that various subcultural practices occur at every possible opportunity. These are aimed at lowering the level of risk when dealing with the enemy, as a private in South Armagh indicates: "They [instructors] tell you that when a round is fired, cock weapon and go for cover. That's what they drill into you, before you come to Ireland. Out here, though, it's different, like when PIRA [Provisional IRA] got _____, it was go for cover and then cock your weapon. That's the way it is out here."

In the above extract the private's primary focus is to survive, to find cover, and then to respond to the enemy. The microsecond it requires to cock a weapon[16] before finding cover during a "contact" increases hazard, so the strategy deployed above—to find cover first—minimizes the risk in an already hazardous situation. Warrior-hero myths propagated by popular literature and MoD publicity[17] meet head on the ugly, brutal, sordid business of armed conflict, and a modification of aggressive conduct ensues. Defeating, containing, or suppressing the enemy necessarily involves aggressive patrolling for the infantry soldier. By "switching on" (patrolling effectively), one minimizes the risk to oneself and to one's peers. However, there are other elements at work within the private's operational acceptance frame,[18] elements that reduce the risk as much as is practically possible, but that can also, on occasion, result in the withdrawal of cooperation from peers and superiors, who are considered foolhardy:

Anyway it was a good shoot, long and straight, they [PIRA] could pick you off from up there on the hill. I thought this isn't on. Brian began to move toward the top of the street, so I signaled to him that I wasn't going down, as it was too dodgy. We both took up positions as Brian had sussed it as well.... He [platoon commander] couldn't do anything about it, not on his own, so we just got on with the patrol. (private, South Armagh)

Practices deemed too risky involve, in infantry argot, "sticking your neck out"; thus, although risk is accepted as a normal practice, some patrolling practices and decisions are unacceptable. Individuals who indulged in particularly perilous conduct were viewed with considerable disapproval, as their actions increased the danger for all patrol members, with possibly fatal consequences. The pejorative term "hero" was consistently used in South Armagh to categorize such individuals; the following examples portray the considerable ire directed at such heroes—those who endanger patrol members' lives unduly. Disapproval could, on occasion, manifest itself in informal violence inflicted on such heroes:

In on time and out on time, an hour's what we're supposed to do on urban [patrol]. He keeps us out [of the security base] twenty minutes longer than we're supposed to be. You don't need fucking 'O' levels [educational qualifications] to work out that's a third more risk.

When blokes come over here for the first time [initial operational duty], some of them go over the top.... Well they take too many risks, and then the whole Brick [patrol] is in the shit.... You have to sort them out quickly, and if they don't listen to what you say, if it's really needed you butt-stroke [hit with butt of weapon] them. (privates, South Armagh)

"Heroic" conduct on operations is then construed as stupid and deviant because it places one's peers in unnecessary jeopardy. Prior to operations, the infantryman internalizes and celebrates a particular kind of masculinity that in training contexts remains relatively unchecked and in many aspects approximates the warrior-hero model.[19] However, in contrast, on operations the parameters of this masculinity are amended in order to elevate the chances of survival. Masculinity in the infantry, as in the general culture, is an occasioned context-dependent construct, for the most part played out in the fashion described in this chapter, but subject to revision when the occasion demands. These amendments need not compromise or diminish the infantryman's sense of masculinity, however, for they are collectively established and maintained. They are rationalized on the grounds of survival and good operational strategy. Moreover, from the infantryman's perspective he and his peers, in spite of their caution, remain out there on hostile terrain, confronting a well-armed and skilful foe. This task, if survived, constitutes the ultimate *rite de passage*, the ultimate test of this particular type of masculinity.[20] As one infantryman noted from a helicopter over South Armagh, pointing down to the terrain: "We are the only people who are down there working the cuds [patrolling the rural area]. It's just us and PIRA, so this is where we really earn our trade pay."

ON BLOWOUTS

During extended field exercises and actual operations the ordinary infantryman endures gross physical fatigue, little sleep, climatic exposure, and various kinds of hazards, be these environmental or the direct attention of the enemy. Understandably, the end of these periods of deprivation, discomfort, and hazard has a marked ritual significance and constitutes an occasion for celebration. These occasions, termed "blowouts," involve embarking on a collective spree with all the backpay one can muster. During these blowout periods, pent-up discomfort, frustrations, tensions, and fears are released and the infantryman's role is celebrated. This is accomplished by pursuit of a particular trinity: booze, "birds," and brawling. The swift imbibing of alcohol in large quantities and the energetic seeking of female company are focal concerns of this celebratory process. "Real men" drink, and they drink hard, not merely as a compensation for recent deprivation but also because this is what "real men" *naturally* do. Having survived and endured simulated or actual operations, such occasions are feted, as is the particular form of masculinity underpinning them. The following extract from fieldnotes gives some indication of the scale of conspicuous consumption:

The waitress asks us what we want: glasses or pitchers? The response is pitchers of the local ale. She returns and deposits a very large pitcher full, with enough glasses for the group. There is a silence and all the lads look at each other, as collective smiles emerge. Finally Joe breaks the silence and addresses the waitress: "No, love, we need one each." She turns to him bemused and indicates we have enough glasses. He responds again: "No, one of these each!" He picks up the pitcher, grinning hugely! Collective laughter erupts as she departs to fill the order. (bar, near training area, Canada)

As previously indicated, the role of infantryman places great stress on heterosexual virility; thus, during such celebrations the ardent pursuit of women accompanies the collective drinking. This combination perhaps inevitably provides fertile grounds for brawling and public fracas. Physical confrontations with other troops, civilians, and the military and civilian police constitute what the subculture terms "friendly fighting." These encounters serve to confirm the potency of the infantryman's masculine self-image and reinforce official organizational training and practices that foster aggression and violence.[21] None of this is to say that the ordinary infantryman does not go for a quiet drink, or visit the cinema, or pursue more sophisticated and less dramatic hobbies. Rather, what is asserted is that the trinity of "booze, birds, and brawling" constitutes the practices around which narratives of release from duty are articulated.

AN OCCASIONED AND CONTINUOUS
ACCOMPLISHMENT

Masculinity in the infantry is both an occasioned construct and a "practical and continuous accomplishment."[22] It is continuous because within the subculture there are ongoing formal and informal demands that test the individual's conformity to the behavior and attributes previously described. Sanctions against deviance, which are harsh by civilian standards, are therefore always possible in the form of fines, jail, or abuse, such as being "butt-stroked" after a patrol in South Armagh. Masculinity is occasioned because it is context dependent,[23] and the prime context that generates its modification is operational. It is this context that also allows the display of certain kinds of emotion that are on other occasions viewed as feminine and therefore weak. For in the aftermath of extreme situations that threatened death and mutilation, displays of tears, sadness, and grief for comrades are accepted and handled with much empathy[24] and haptic contact. In the words of one corporal speaking poignantly after the death of a member of his patrol by PIRA action:

He [a private] was crying a lot after B___ got taken out [killed]. So I just told the rest of the lads to clear off for a bit, and I just talked to him quietly, put my arm around him and let him get it out. Then I told him that we had to go back out there [patrol] and he needed to switch on [be alert] and that we were all depending on him. I just kept my eye on him for a bit afterwards, gave him the odd bit of special attention. He's a good lad and he managed it. (security base, South Armagh)

In the aftermath of such horrific instances small subcultural spaces emerge, and the emotions described become expressible and acceptable. These spaces and this conduct have to be rapidly closed off as operational contingencies demand alertness, stoicism, and aggressive patrolling. Such displays, traditionally deemed non-masculine, are then categorized as exceptional and are tolerated because of the exceptional circumstances that generate them. In such instances, returning to patrol effectively once more reaffirms masculine identity and sub-cultural acceptance.

Masculinity in the infantry is a variation of the near hegemonic masculin-ity prevalent in Western industrialized societies.[25] Its construction and routine maintenance require an intensification of a number of attributes (for example, aggression, risk taking, and heterosexuality) dominant in the wider civilian society. Within the military, combat units, in particular the infantry, are as-signed the highest status and face what is considered to be the most difficult test, that of battle. Thus in basic training a valorized masculinity acts as a nexus around which features such as discipline, weapon handling, and tactical skills are learnt by recruits. A particular construction of masculinity is used by the military organization as a device for recruiting young men into combat units at an age when they are in a transitional stage between adolescence and adulthood.[26] Once the men are socialized into the occupational culture of the infantry, this form of masculinity must repeatedly be reaffirmed in the face of arduous and hazardous activities that constitute the normal features of the infantry trade.

ACKNOWLEDGMENT

Thanks are due to Jacquelyn Allen-Collinson for her helpful comments and tolerance of an ex-soldier's stories.

NOTES

1. Chris Hables Gray, *Postmodern War: The New Politics of Conflict* (London: Rout-ledge, 1997).

2. John Hockey, *Squaddies: Portrait of a Subculture* (Exeter: Exeter University Press, 1986).

3. Peter L. Berger. and Thomas Luckman, *The Social Construction of Reality* (Har-mondsworth: Penguin, 1976).

4. See, for example, Nicos P. Mouzelis, "Critical Note on Total Institutions," *Sociol-ogy* 5 (1971): 13–120; William Arkin and Lynn R. Dobrofsky, "Military Socialization and Masculinity," *Journal of Social Issues* 34 (1978): 168; and Amia Lieblich, *Transition to Adulthood during Military Service: The Israeli Case* (Albany: State University of New York Press, 1989).

5. Rachel Woodward, "'It's a Man's Life!': Masculinity and the Countryside," *Gen-der, Place and Culture* 5 (1998): 277–300.

6. Rachel Woodward, "Warrior Heroes and Little Green Men: Soldiers, Military Training and the Construction of Rural Masculinities," *Rural Sociology* 65 (2000): 640–657. Gwyn Harries-Jenkins, "Role Images, Military Attitudes, and the Enlisted

Culture in Great Britain," pp. 254–271, in D. R. Segal and H. W. Sinaiko, eds., *Life in the Rank and File* (Washington, DC: Pergamon-Brassey's, 1986).

7. See, for example, Danny Kaplan and Eyal Ben-Ari, "Brothers and Others in Arms: Managing Gay Identity in Combat Units of the Israeli Army," *Journal of Contemporary Ethnography* 29 (2000): 396–432.

8. Arnold Van Gennep, *The Rites of Passage,* trans. by M. B. Visedom and G. L. Caffe (Chicago: University of Chicago Press, 1960).

9. Nick Crossley, "Merleau-Ponty, the Elusive Body and Carnal Sociology," *Body and Society* 1 (1995): 43–63.

10. R. W. Connell, *Masculinities* (Cambridge: Polity Press, 1995).

11. E. Badinter, *On Masculine Identity* (New York: Columbia University Press, 1995), p. 68.

12. Erving Goffman, *Asylums* (Harmondsworth: Penguin, 1976).

13. Max Weber, *From Max Weber: Essays in Sociology* (London: Routledge & Kegan Paul, 1977).

14. Robert E. Park, "Human Nature, Attitudes and Mores," pp. 17–45, in K. Young, ed., *Social Attitudes* (New York: Holt, 1931): p. 37.

15. Ilona Kickbusch, "New Perspectives for Research in Health Behaviour," pp. 237–243, in R. Anderson, ed., *Health Behaviour Research and Health Promotion* (Oxford: Oxford University Press, 1988).

16. There was an official ban on troops having their weapons cocked (that is, with a round in the chamber and ready to fire) while on patrol in South Armagh. This meant that in the event of a contact with PIRA, weapons had to be cocked and then fired. The difference in time might well be the difference between life and death. The subculture perceived this ban as essentially politically instrumental and viewed it extremely negatively.

17. Woodward, 1998, op. cit.

18. Erving Goffman, *Frame Analysis: An Essay on the Organization of Experience* (New York: Harper & Row, 1974).

19. Woodward, 1998, op. cit.

20. Badinter, 1995, op. cit., p. 68.

21. Joseph A. Blake, "The Organization as Instrument of Violence: The Military Case," *Sociological Quarterly* 11 (1970): 331–350.

22. Douglas Benson and John A. Hughes, *The Perspective of Ethnomethodology* (Harlow: Longman, 1983), p. 18.

23. The only other context in which I observed conduct that could be classified as at variance with the type of virulent masculinity portrayed in this chapter was in the domestic environments of a small minority of married infantrymen who lived out of barracks.

24. David Morgan, "Theater of War: Combat, the Military and Masculinities," pp. 165–182, in H. Brod and M. Kaufman, eds., *Theorizing Masculinities* (London: Sage, 1994), p. 17.

25. Raymond Williams, *Marxism and Literature* (Oxford: Oxford University Press, 1977); R. W. Connell, *Masculinities* (Cambridge: Polity Press, 1995).

26. cf. Kaplan and Ben-Ari, 2000, op. cit.

Chapter 3

"Soft Clerks" and "Hard Civvies": Pluralizing Military Masculinities

Paul R. Higate

INTRODUCTION

Typical portrayals of military masculinity will almost certainly make reference to the defining features of the warrior ethic. Popular cultural representations, from cinema to literature, are constructed around the themes of violence, misogyny, and heterosexuality and in this sense tend to diverge from more routine "everyday" masculinity. These macho extremes reach their apogee in the paramilitary *Rambo* trilogy, where we are presented with a seemingly invulnerable superhu*man*. In addition, although drawn from real-life accounts, a series of recent best-selling books by the former British Special Air Service (SAS) soldiers Andy McNab[1] and Harry McCallion[2] nevertheless echoes narratives turning on physical toughness, aggression, and stoic commitment"—"soldiering on" in the face of overwhelming enemy odds.

Understandings of military men tend to cluster around these extreme variants of masculinity and become attached to common-sense understandings of soldiers, sailors, and airmen; in essence "our boys" who are tough and unrelenting in the face of hardship. When combined with the closed nature of the British Ministry of Defence (MoD)[3] and formulaic tabloid and fly-on-the-wall television documentary portrayal, it is unsurprising that these constructions should stick. Of course, the more destructive variants of the stereotyped squaddie do exist and can have the most devastating impact on the communities in which they live.[4] Witness the horrific murder of a Danish tour guide by four off-duty soldiers in Cyprus, a case in which alcohol, violence, and misogyny played a tragic part. However, these less usual events and the subsequent media constructions, though playing to the primordial fascination with war, death, and the alleged masculine disposition of bellicosity,[5] serve to eclipse the range of masculinities to be found in the military setting.[6] My intentions in this chapter are twofold. First I wish to go beyond these stereotypical constructions of military masculinity by examining civilian-based masculinities noted to be more hypermasculine than those experienced by the author as a Royal Air Force (RAF) personnel administrator. Second, I suggest that gendered performances learned in the military may remain tenacious after discharge from the armed services into civilian life; as such, these ways of performing masculinity can become institutionalized.

The chapter is structured as follows. In the first section I consider recent, and somewhat radical, thinking around gender, together with a more substantive focus on military masculinities. I then discuss the method of intellectual autobiography, together with the ways in which it might be used to illuminate gendered practice within the context of the RAF and beyond into civilian life. Throughout the latter half of the chapter, masculinized institutions of the university and the military are considered by way of context for personal recollections of four masculine performances that straddle both the military and civilian environments. In the conclusion I flag the limitations to reifying military masculinities and suggest that experiences of particular masculinities in the RAF might not be so easily differentiated from those found within the civilian context.

THEORIZING GENDER

Although I am adding to an already extensive literature with regard to the "theorisation of men and masculinity,"[7] it is necessary to outline what is meant when the term "masculinity" is used in this chapter. Crudely put, there have emerged two distinct perspectives concerning formulations of gender more generally—the constructionist and the essentialist. The former has been thrown into sharp focus within the context of Judith Butler's writing, and any discussion of gender would be incomplete without reference to her canon of work.[8] Butler's contribution to the field, though influential and valuable—not least through her optimistic take on the ways in which gender norms can be resignified and reworked[9]—has nonetheless been subject to wide-ranging critique.[10] Commentators have, for example, argued that agency has been neglected through an overemphasis on the discursive production of gender[11] and that, crucially, "gender 'performances' there certainly are, but it is preposterous to reduce gender identity, sexuality and sexual differentiation to the discursive notion...of performativity."[12] With this in mind, it is argued that the social and psychological implications of biological difference are not yet fully understood, and they cannot be ruled out as *preceding* sex and gender.[13] It is Butler's colonization of uncertainties around the nexus that links biology, sexuality, and gender with a radical constructionist position, that "ignores the fact that only a privileged few can play at taking up and putting aside identities."[14] However, despite these critiques, it is important to reclaim the notion of performance. When pitched at a higher level of abstraction, the concept of gender performance represents a valuable shorthand regarding the accomplishment of gendered identity as a process, something that individuals achieve.[15] These performances are interpreted through wider social practices that give them meaning, for example, as marginal or hegemonic.[16] One example of the former might include the status of male clients within the British Probation Service; these men have been referred to as marginally masculine because of their categorization as offenders.[17]

PLURALIZING MILITARY MASCULINITY

The concept "military masculinities" refers to a particular set of gendered attributes typically found within the institution of the armed forces.[18] These traits—both performance and ideology—cluster around violence, aggression, rationality, and a sense of invulnerability, and they share in common certain aspects of civilian-based masculinities such as coolness under pressure. In terms of masculinities and paid employment more generally, "masculinities are not fixed.... [M]ultiplicity of masculinities and diversity are relevant...to the different forms and locations of workplaces...multiple masculinities connect with multiple sites."[19]

Unlike masculinities found in the civilian environment, the central configurations of gendered practices labeled military masculinities are often assumed to have their own exclusive essence, linked ultimately with violence. Although not discussing gender explicitly, Terry Willetts describes this skewed focus:

This view [of the military's sole association with legitimated violence] overemphasises one function and neglects the many others that are...more salient in peacetime...[the military] is not an obedient machine but a human concern that reflects the culture of the host society to which it belongs.[20]

In terms of violence resulting in death, the experience of impoverished communities in the United States, as one of many examples, almost certainly exceeds those of service people in times of peace. Killing is not the exclusive preserve of the military. However, in attempting to isolate the defining attribute of military masculinity, it is important to avoid conflating the range of violence that underlies homicide, on the one hand, with "military killing," which is "state sanctioned" or "legitimate,"[21] on the other. Aside from other armed agents of the state (certain members of the police force, for example, and death row executioners), the authority to kill lies with the military; it is this institutional prerogative that is crucial for the understanding of military masculinities. To these ends service personnel are socialized in different ways with proven and finely tuned mechanisms designed to elicit controlled violence. As Bob Connell states:

The relationship of masculinity to violence is more complex than appears at first sight. Institutionalised violence (e.g., by armies) requires more than one kind of masculinity. The gender practice of the general is different from the practice of the front-line soldier, and armies acknowledge this by training them separately.[22]

One way in which to make sense of the military gender dynamic that Connell identifies regarding this variable relationship to violence is to see it within terms of a hierarchy of masculinities.[23] Here, hegemonic masculinity stands for the idealized warrior ethic as sketched above. Grouped around these dominant gendered identities are peripheral or, to varying degrees, "second best" military masculinities.[24] A continuum marked by highly skilled SAS troops at one extreme through RAF stewards at the other illustrates this point. Members of the first group are *perceived* in terms of their extraordinary physical toughness, stoicism, and reason under pressure. Ironically, commanders may come to overestimate the abilities of their own troops, as demonstrated by the doomed Bravo Two Zero mission during the Gulf conflict.[25] In stark contrast, RAF stewards are usually employed to respond to the domestic needs of the more senior ranks. Working behind bars, serving food, and maintaining the living quarters of commissioned and senior non-commissioned personnel means that they are understood to occupy a feminized rather than soldierly role; crucially, members of both groups could be termed military men. With these points in mind, this chapter aims to respond to the following objectives:

[W]e are seeking to develop analyses that can begin to reflect and comprehend the multiple, shifting but tenacious nature of gendered power regimes as they characterize diverse [workplaces]. We believe that such empirically informed analytical studies have the potential to examine and understand the dynamic, shifting and often contradictory organizational relations through which men's differences and similarities are reproduced and transformed in particular practices and power asymmetries.[26]

How might we begin to explore and to contextualize one variant of military masculinity, and to what extent are these particular performances unique to the armed forces? How does this gendered performance shift across diverse workplace environments? Autobiographical experience provides us with one way of exploring these questions. Consequently, what follows are reflections on my own period of military service. But first, a few words on the method used in this chapter.

METHOD: INTELLECTUAL AUTOBIOGRAPHY

The tools of intellectual autobiography are used here to illuminate masculine performances that straddle civilian and military environments. In my direct experience masculinities in the former civilian context were more extreme than those encountered during my eight years of military service. In using the autobiographical approach, I draw on and develop the work of other commentators who have analyzed their military experiences through the lens of self-reflection.[27] It should be noted, however, that the four accounts included here are constructed for a particular purpose—inclusion in this particular volume—and thus might say as much about the occasion of production as they do about the actual events recounted.[28] Extracts are partial and selective; they would no doubt be open to a range of interpretations when considered through the eyes of others present at those particular moments.[29] Although the value of intellectual autobiography lies in the ways in which it facilitates reflection on the links between self and society,[30] the autobiographical method can, more specifically, serve to deconstruct typically unacknowledged gendered identity.

DEVIANT MILITARY MASCULINITIES? "SOFT CLERKS"

It is significant that the relatively gentler nature of the RAF differentiates it from tougher British Army regimes, where the ideology of violence is more likely to be found.[31] Basic training for the RAF's non-commissioned ranks lasts just six weeks, whereas army programs are at least twice that length and focus on the development of combat skills. Army basic training is more directly concerned with measuring and testing the body. In turn, these programs reproduce and develop military masculine ideologies. However, the requirement for high degrees of physical resilience in the support trades of the RAF (such as clerk, cook, and driver) are less pressing and are supplanted by technical training, for example. Fostering hegemonic masculinities in the RAF's support trades has little urgency because face-to-face violence is less likely amongst clerks than combat troops. This coupled with the "civilianization" of the armed forces—the increased contracting-out of support tasks, such as the provision of food and transportation, to non-military personnel—together with the greater possibility to live off-base, makes the notion of a total institution also less appropriate today, and may further dilute military masculinity. Finally, that I was employed as an administrative clerk and, after further training, as a personnel administrator also shifts the onus from expressions of extreme masculine performance to those more closely aligned with a "feminised task."[32] Military clerks probably occupy the lowest reaches of an informal gender hierarchy[33] and could thus be described as marginally masculine. The ways in which personnel in the armed forces reconcile the tensions between occupational performance and hegemonic military masculine ideology may vary. Whereas I—in league with clerk colleagues—attempted to live up to this ideology by working out in the gym, others parodied the feminized role. One has only to think of the character Klinger in the television series *M*A*S*H* who embraces the perceived femininity of his non-combat role in time of war by dressing in women's clothes and sporting garish cosmetics. Although perceived as less masculine than that of the army, my military social universe was nonetheless significantly influenced by close contact with military men and rather less women, and my views were concomitantly shaped in line with the more extreme ideologies of military masculinity. To gain better insight into the influences that have shaped my reflections on gendered identity, it is important to discuss briefly the context and impact of my post-military experiences of university life.

INSTITUTIONS OF DIFFERENCE? MILITARY VERSUS UNIVERSITY LIFE

It would be tempting to locate the workplace environments of the military and the university—those institutions characterizing my working life—on the polar extremes of a continuum of difference. When subject to analysis through the lens of gender, however, considerable overlap exists. Although there have been increases in the number of women within both environments, both spheres are pervaded by male culture, which remains resistant to change.[34] How might the similarities and differences between the institutions be framed? In terms of the university, there exists considerable overlap; here the culture of competitiveness and macho long working hours could be invoked. Drawing on the observations of W.J.M Mackenzie, Morgan could be referring to male RAF administrative officers in the following quote describing the composition of academic seminars: "They were, indeed, a formidable group of ... powerful mind, strong personality and occasionally sharp tongue, who could stimulate but sometimes intimidate."[35] Within the context of the discipline of sociology, masculinized cross-cutting ideologies of the superiority of rationality and objectivity over emotional response unite this mindset with that of the military. Yet, in the case of both sociology and the military, this is beginning to change, with what counts as science in sociology developing away from these masculinized themes, and in so doing subverting the objective/subjective hierarchy.[36] In the case of the military:

During the Gulf War fighter pilots, interviewed for TV in their planes before taking off, admitted to being afraid. They did this in a matter of fact way. This would have been almost unthinkable in the Second World War, when such behavior would have been equated almost automatically with being fear-ridden.[37]

Although these sentiments were almost certainly echoed by others, including troops on the ground, such attitudes have failed to significantly upset the gendered constellation of the military or to affect universities' imore entrenched masculine notions. Given that I am a male sociologist, then, my experience has been one of surprising continuity between the two employment experiences, with the institutional dynamic—large bureaucracies in office-bound occupations—and local working culture tending to blur the importance of gender.

PERSONAL EXPERIENCE: THE TRANSITION TO CIVILIAN LIFE

Although I frame the process of transition through a linear narrative, my exit from the military had occurred at least two years prior to discharge, the point at which I had disengaged;[38] I was in but not of the institution for a considerable period. In contrast, a number of other ex-members may understand themselves as out of the military, organizing their experiences through linear time in terms of past, present, and future. For these people, however, military masculine dispositions may clash with civilian gendered belief systems, although civilian masculinized settings, including the police force, the prison service, and even, in the extreme, employment as a mercenary, may attract these individuals.[39] In these settings, military masculine ways of being provide ex-servicemen with an ontologically or emotionally secure environment. Biographies that have developed within the intense total-institutional context of the military could remain influential in other ways. This may even be the case for ex-servicemen who appear at first glance *not* to appropriate these ways of being. These individuals might be described as *latently* institutionalized, with the experience of military masculine identity etched deep into flesh and mind, such that it may resurface later in life. This argument partially explains the disproportionate number of servicemen among the single homeless population, some of whom led settled lives for many years after discharge from the military, prior to the onset of more chaotic experiences characterized by relationship breakdown and subsequent desire for homosociability, a key element of the military masculine life.[40]

THE IMPACT OF SOCIOLOGY

My growing ambivalence toward life in the RAF was influenced by an A-level (sub-degree) sociology course I took at the local further education college during my final year of military service. This stimulating experience contributed toward my disenchantment with the impersonal and rigid military hierarchy and for the first time caused me to consider my role in the organization. After discharge from the air force I studied a mix of university social science subjects, with a focus on sociology. Much like the ex-soldier turned sociologist John Hockey, who is characterized by a broadly parallel biography, I discovered in sociology an account of how the world worked. First, it offered explanations connected to my biography (for example, the deeper working of the school system and my performance within it); and second, not so straightforwardly, it directed attention to my largely subconscious gendered identity. Here, I was provided with tools with which to deconstruct masculine belief systems, particularly those directed toward women, with whom I had had little contact during military service. Yet, these transformations should be seen within the context of a troubled institutional identity characterizing my earlier years of military service. I linked these experiences to military postings in which I tended to be the only administrator working among more hegemonic masculinities such as RAF firefighters and jet pilots. In these contexts, clerking was belittled as worthless and unmasculine. One of the catalysts to my questioning my own sense of military masculinity was recognizing that "real men" perceived me as a worthless secretary.

TENSIONS BETWEEN BELIEF SYSTEMS

Although sociology's enlightened anti-discriminatory ethos is a crucial element of the discipline's overall humanist concerns, as a sociologist I occasionally find myself failing to fight in the equal opportunity corner, thereby reproducing hegemonic (military) masculinities to construct particular others. These sentiments are intended, not as alibis or facile excuses[41] but to demonstrate the ways in which military socialization has elaborated and entrenched masculine views resistant to change. Yet immersion in a military environment does not straightforwardly institutionalize individuals, and agency is maintained in the harshest of conditions. Ultimately, I suggest, military experience, including basic and continuation training, produces broad tendencies in values, beliefs, attitudes, and actions that members of the military *may* carry over into civilian life. Individuals who endure (or alternatively, relish) military socialization do not unquestioningly internalize the belief systems shaping the gendered ways of being to which they are intensively subject.[42] Few today join the British Army for the honor of fighting and dying for their country.[43] Rather, a number of individuals may actively resist these masculine ideologies, shaping the largely universal raw materials of basic and continuation training into more idiosyncratic forms. For these individuals, hegemonic military masculinity may be reluctantly learned though carried out to the satisfaction of instructors and peers within the context of basic training. These identities may, however, be quickly subjugated to more benign occupational interests, perhaps involving working on "big boys' toys" such as tanks and fighter aircraft. For these individuals it is likely that face-to-face violence is of secondary importance; destruction can be wreaked on the battlefield from a safe distance, where hypermasculinity is not so obviously invoked.

AUTOBIOGRAPHICAL ACCOUNTS: KEY EVENTS

The following sections sketch key events linked to my experience of the RAF. These highlight the relatively "softer clerking" variant of military masculinity seen from a sociologist's perspective. This first sketch sets the context and offers clues to my lack of explicit concern to embrace the warrior ethic prior to and at the point of enlistment:

I was raised within the sociocultural confines of military establishments (mostly RAF bases) and attended "service schools" for the majority of my years in compulsory education. When I was a little boy, my father would take me to his exciting place of work—the Recruiting Office—or later, while he was serving in RAF Germany, would let me sit in the cockpits of Lightning jet-fighter aircraft. Like my brothers before me, I eventually enlisted into the RAF for a little over eight years, thereby continuing the family tradition. I purchased my discharge from the RAF after feeling let down by "the system" shortly after I missed a promotional opportunity because of an "administrative error."

The stress here is that my enlistment into the military felt *normal*. That any other career was viable had not occurred to me, such was the narrowness of the cultural milieu of military families, of those of us whose fathers' military service set a precedent for offspring service in the armed forces. I did not join to fight—RAF clerks are not known for serving on the front line—and notions of honor, loyalty, and masculinity were at best subconscious and abstract. Rather, I was keen to experience excitement, camaraderie, and a sense of belonging against the backdrop of emotional security.

POST-DISCHARGE REFLECTIONS: TESTING THE BODY AND CIVILIAN SPORT

Real-life accounts of military training tend to emphasize the testing of men's bodies. Extreme physical performance, however, though a key element of military service, is certainly not the unique preserve of the institution. Consider this account drawn, post-discharge, from the civilian context in which I reinforce this point:

I am on a Sunday "club-run" with the local cycle club. These rides can last anywhere between 40 and 100 miles, and on this occasion the larger mileage appears to be the target. It is brutally physical at the front of the "bunch," riding into the wind. After a number of minutes heading the group, both my friend and I swing off and join the sheltered end of the long chain of male riders. The pace is increased, the weather closes in, and we struggle to stay with the other cyclists, eventually ending up on our own, many miles from any source of food or shelter. The riders make no attempt to stop, our level of fitness being deemed unacceptable and limiting to others who are determined to train at a higher level. We struggle home at a slow pace enduring what may well have been mild hypothermia.

This and other similar experiences were considerably more demanding than any physical training required in the RAF, with the main test for recruits linked almost solely to a short, timed run. Further, the example of this particular cycling club is important because it reflects the club's highly masculinized culture. For example, women were constructed as little more than passive sex objects, and on the bike run, chat often involved weaving stories of sexual performance together with masculinized common-sense banter, in ways that mirrored doing gender in the military. In addition, to state that one could not cope with the exigencies of cycle training at these high levels, and thus disclose one's physical and mental suffering,[44] brought one's masculinity into question, though outlets did exist off the bike in which it was legitimate to recount tales of pain and hardship.

DRINKING "LIKE A MAN"

The cultural relevance of frequently excessive alcohol consumption within the military cannot be overestimated.[45] It represents a key element of the public appraisal of masculine performance for many military groupings from commissioned to non-commissioned ranks. An extract from recent fieldwork by the author exploring the links between military service and homelessness illustrates this point. One of the ex-service participants who took part in the study linked high alcohol consumption with high status, even going so far as to suggest, "The Navy taught people to drink heavily." It remains the case that being able to hold one's drink "like a man" is deeply embedded into wider belief systems.[46] For example, the following account concerns the legendary drinking abilities of "Mickey," at the time a first-year fine arts degree student and a friend of the author, here in the Student University Union (SUU) bar:

I am in the bar with "Mickey." He is drinking Tennents Extra, which is one of the strongest lager beers available. For every one pint of normal-strength beer consumed per head of the student group, "Mickey" drinks two 500ml cans of beer. After an unknown, but substantial number of alcohol units, he appears in control and entirely lucid. Others are clearly inebriated and somewhat impressed at his tolerance to alcohol.

The meanings associated with substantial alcohol consumption in contexts as apparently different as the junior ranks club in the military (the Navy, Army and Air Force Institutes, or NAAFI) or the Officers or Sergeants Mess and the SUU bar, converged on the idea of drinking ability as a credible, even revered, sign of masculinity. High consumption, particularly among younger male students—and increasingly among females—with their post-weekend tales of "being totally smashed," was greeted with respect and awe. These stories mirrored others located in the humdrum office environment of the RAF clerk, where the capacity to drink German beer (while living abroad) played out in parallel ways.

MASCULINITIES AND MISOGYNY

David Morgan argues, "There is no doubt that masculinities form a major element in the construction of military identities and that much of this will appear as aggressive, threatening and deeply misogynist."[47] Whereas notions of misogyny are generally understood to refer to the hatred of women, it is likely that manifestations of this hate can take a variety of forms, from the serial murder and horrific mutilation of women, as in the case of the serial killer Peter Sutcliffe, the so-called Yorkshire Ripper, to protracted objectification such that women may be ideologically constructed and related to in terms purely of their disembodied sexual characteristics.[48] Here, things are done *to* women, as men "rightfully" assume their power over woman as the passive sex-object;

indeed, women, it is argued, secretly desire sexual violation.[49] The difficulties in separating rape from its broader culturally heterosexual context is not so straightforward,[50] however, so shades of misogyny might be noted to dwell within masculinized talk. Their deeply embedded normalization, reinforced by the relatively disempowered position of women serves to sustain and reinforce the patriarchal status quo. An example of objectification, drawn from the civilian context of a research exercise designed to explore the discursive subordination of the other (i.e., women and gay men), is the following extract:

G: Spoke t' Daisy the other night n all.

D: Yeah?

. . .

G: She's got paps, big time.

D: Paps wi' the baps.

D: Got huge breasts ... they're just fuckin' huge, they are really big.[51]

The ubiquity of these sentiments across a range of masculinized contexts renders this extract largely unremarkable. Building sites, rugby clubs, and other, uniformed settings such as the police force[52] or the prison service exist on a staple diet of verbal, if not actual, denigration of women; or, at the very least, masculinities are offset against femininities.[53] Thus, the nexus that links "military" with "misogyny" is far from unique, although the actual violence done to women by military constellations of one sort or another returns us to a more centrally defining feature of military masculinity. Here, the extent to which aggression might be informally accepted as legitimate within the context of domestic violence in military communities (see Harrison, Chapter 6, this volume) represents a disturbing manifestation of hegemonic military masculinity.

The final example, framed in terms of authorial biography, is intended to tease out contradictions in masculinized identity performance, not least those contradictions linked to the blurring of military-civilian boundaries:

I meet a work colleague in the Probation Service hostel where we work, some years after discharge; he is the ex-soldier "Robbo." In conversation, we quickly move on to the subject of women in terms that I find uncomfortable but familiar. Nevertheless, I experience myself following and contributing to this particular pejorative framing of the other. After the event I reflect on the ease with which I collude in this somewhat formulaic banter and consider the alternative course I could have taken.

Although several complex things are happening here, I want to focus only on those factors that serve to maintain and reproduce this particular masculinized talk. First, there is the interpersonal dynamic, identifiable as a power relationship in which I do not wish to lose face; this dynamic ultimately leads to my collusion with the sentiments expressed. Like most talk-action, this sequence of events is characterized by apparent spontaneity, against the backdrop of the "absent presence" of the military. Military masculine belief system, giving way to speech performance, emerged intersubjectively within the context of a dialogue between two ex-servicemen. Although "Robbo" may have experienced a moment of reflection similar to the one just outlined—asking oneself whether saying these things is okay—his motive for the conversation probably lay in his attempt to subvert the equal opportunity culture of the workplace that suppressed such talk. This gives rise to a number of questions, the most important of which concerns what he *felt* about airing such views. Was it a case of using derogatory language to elicit response from me and thus empower himself (he was undoubtedly conscious of the controversial framing), or did he really believe that women were inferior and "good for one thing only"?

A second crucial concern linked to this particular description of women can be explored through the dramaturgical metaphor.[54] Here, role limitations—defined through my sometimes contradictory status as ex-serviceman and sociologist—allowed me, like "Robbo," who also worked in an equal opportunity setting, to hold two things in mind simultaneously. The first was characterized by hegemonic (military) masculinity; the second, informed by my encounter of the feminist enterprise, through sociology, which has raised my awareness of women's issues. Although this episode could be said to have involved me in "deep-acting,"[55] this interaction was shaped by and congruent with my colleague's predicted response and left me surprised by how tenacious military masculine belief systems had remained and by how effortlessly they resurfaced.

MILITARY MASCULINE HOMOSOCIABILITY

Women constitute less than 10 percent of military forces.[56] Given the relatively small number of women within the ranks, it is entirely possible that servicemen mix rarely with members of the opposite sex. Posting to an isolated military base—the Malvinas/Falkland Islands or the Shetland Isles, for example—may compound this unfamiliarity, in the minds of servicemen reinforcing women's status as the mercurial other. Resonance of this metaphorical and actual distance may pervade the relationships of married servicemen, with women forced to compete with the camaraderie of soldier colleagues. Discharge into the civilian environment may make a series of demands on ex-servicemen, including those demands linked to the forming and sustaining of relationships with women. It is this homosociability, this "being with the boys," through which the problematic nature of relationships with women spills over into civilian life. Although failing to achieve the intense levels of camaraderie characteristic of army life, men's company was nevertheless considerably safer and easier than that of women.

CONCLUSIONS

This chapter has considered issues of military masculinity, performance, ideology, and gender theory through a mix of data sources, from fieldwork exploring the relationship between military service and homelessness to authorial accounts drawn from the civilian environment where gender institutionalization and overlap were highlighted. From these discussions it is evident that multiple sites of masculinities are ranged across apparently diverse contexts, of which the military is one. Certainly, more extreme masculinities could be identified by drawing on narrative accounts from individuals who appropriate the more brutal manifestations of these gendered ideologies, as Woodward demonstrates in Chapter 4 of this volume. And yet, it is argued here that in peacetime, within the support or "tail," rather than "tooth," end of military occupations, my experiences are broadly representative, particularly within the context of the RAF.

Clearly, however, serious questions remain around the linkage of military masculine culture in the broadest sense with "mass rape, military sexual slavery and forced prostitution."[57] To these ends there has been an attempt in this chapter to move the debate forward by carving out a degree of conceptual space in which servicemen's encounter with military masculinity is cautiously and tentatively unpicked, and it has been argued to be a more complex process than might be popularly thought. It has been suggested that the military-civilian interface cannot be straightforwardly differentiated along lines of masculinities (commonly understood as hyper" in the former and "softer" in the latter). Multiple sites of masculinities—some extreme in the civilian environment, and others emotionally expressive—serve to blur this dichotomy in which the military has been prone to reification when considered in terms of masculinity.

NOTES

1. Andy McNab, *Immediate Action* (London: Bantam, 1995).

2. Harry McCallion, *Killing Zone* (London: Bloomsbury, 1996).

3. Antony Beevor, *Inside the British Army* (London: Corgi Books, 1991); Chris Jessup, *Breaking Ranks: Social Change in Military Communities* (London: Brassey's, 1996): and David Morgan, "Theater of War; Combat, the Military and Masculinities," in H. Brod and M. Kaufman, eds., *Theorizing Masculinities* (London: Sage, 1994), pp. 165–182.

4. C. J. Stone, *Fierce Dancing* (London: Faber & Faber, 1996).

5. Ruth Jolly, *Changing Step: From Military to Civilian Life: People in Transition* (London: Brassey's, 1996).

6. Morgan, *Theater of War*, pp. 165–182.

7. Jeff Hearn, "A Critique of the Concept of Masculinity/Masculinities," in M. Mac an Ghaill, ed., *Understanding Masculinities* (Buckingham: Open University Press, 1996).

8. John Hood-Williams and Wendy Cealey Harrison, "Trouble with Gender," in *The Sociological Review* 46, 1 (1998): 73–94.

9. Moya Lloyd, "Performativity, Parody, Politics," in *Theory, Culture and Society* 16, 2 (1999): 195–213.

10. Hood-Williams and Harrison, "Trouble with Gender," pp 73–94; Lois McNay, "Subject, Psyche and Agency: The Work of Judith Butler," in *Theory, Culture and Society* 16, 2 (1999): 175–193; Greg Philo and David Miller, *Market Killing* (London: Longman, 2001), pp. 60–61.

11. Lloyd, "Performativity," p. 209.

12. Philo and Miller, *Market Killing,* p. 61.

13. Ted Benton, "Biology and Social Science: Why the Return of the Repressed Should Be Given a (Cautious) Welcome," in *Sociology* 25, 1 (1991):. 1–29; Barbara Epstein, "Postmodernism and the Left," *New Politics* 6, 2 (1997).

14. Epstein, "Postmodernism," quoted in Philo and Miller, *Market Killing,* pp. 60–61.

15. David Morgan, *Discovering Men* (London: Routledge, 1992).

16. Bob Connell, *Masculinities* (Cambridge: Polity Press, 1995).

17. S. Holland and J. B. Scourfield, "Managing Masculinities: Men and Probation," in *Journal of Gender Studies* 9, 2 (2000): 199–211.

18. Connell, *Masculinities;* Morgan, *Discovering Men.*

19. Jeff Hearn and David Collinson, *Men as Managers, Managers as Men: Critical Perspectives on Men, Masculinities and Managements* (London: Sage, 1996), p. 66.

20. Terry Willetts, *Canada's Militia: A Heritage at Risk* (Canada: Conference of Defense Associations Institute, 1990), p. 13.

21. Samuel Huntington, *The Soldier and the State: The Theory and Politics of Civil-Military Relations* (Cambridge: Harvard University Press, 1957); Morris Janowitz, *The Professional Soldier: A Social and Political Portrait* (New York: Free Press, 1971). The debate around what exactly constitutes combat is complex. For example, one police chief stated: 'There's been a lot of talk about women in combat these days.... The Los Angeles Police Department's women are in combat all the time. There's a war right here and it's been fierce.... If you think the war is just in the Persian Gulf, you are wrong. Our casualties are greater in proportion to the casualties in the Persian Gulf" [quoted in Chris Hables Gray, *Postmodern War* (London: Routledge, 1997), p. 43].

22. Connell, *Masculinities,* p. 7.

23. Frank J. Barrett, "The Organizational Construction of Hegemonic Masculinity: The Case of the US Navy," in *Genderwork and Organization* 3, 3 (1996): 129–142.

24. Paul Higate, "The Body Resists: Everyday Clerking and Unmilitary Practice," in S. Nettleton and J. Watson, eds., *The Body in Everyday Life* (London: Routledge, 1998), pp. 180–198.

25. Andy McNab, *Bravo Two Zero* (London: Bantam, 1994).

26. Hearn and Collinson, *Men as Managers,* p. 73.

27. John Hockey, "Putting down Smoke: Emotion and Engagement in Participant Observation," in K. Carter and S. Delamont, eds., *Qualitative Research: The Emotional Dimension* (Aldershot: Avebury, 1996), p. 86.

28. David Morgan, "It Will Make a Man of You: Notes on National Service, Masculinity and Autobiography," in *Studies in Sexual Politics* 17 (Manchester: University of Manchester Department of Sociology), pp. 1–90.

29. Ibid., p. 5.

30. C. Wright Mills, *The Sociological Imagination* (New York: Oxford University Press, 1959).

31. Morgan, "It Will Make a Man of You," p. 11; Trevor Royle, *The Best Years of Their Lives: The National Service Experience, 1945–1963*, 2nd ed. (London: John Murray).

32. Rosemary Pringle, *Secretaries Talk: Sexuality, Power and Work* (London: Verso, 1989).

33. Higate, "The Body Resists," p. 180.

34. David Morgan, "Men, Masculinity and the Process of Sociological Enquiry," in H. Roberts, ed., *Doing Feminist Research* (London: Routledge & Kegan Paul), pp. 95–112.

35. Ibid., p. 102.

36. Liz Stanley and Sue Wise, *Breaking out Again* (London: Routledge), p. 173.

37. Cas Wouters, "On Status Competition and Emotion Management," in M. Featherstone, ed., *Cultural Theory and Cultural Change* (London: Sage, 1992), p. 229.

38. Helen E. Fuchs, *Becoming an Ex: The Process of Role Exit* (Chicago: University of Chicago Press, 1986).

39. Paul R. Higate, "Theorizing Continuity: From Military to Civilian Life," in *Armed Forces and Society* 27, 3 (2001): 443–460; Jolly, *Changing Step*, p. 103.

40. Paul Higate, "Theorising Homelessness amongst Ex-servicemen," in R. Burrows, D. Quilgars, and N. Pleace, eds., *Homelessness and Social Policy* (London: Routledge), pp. 109–122.

41. Morgan, *Discovering Men*, p. 86.

42. Beevor, *Inside the British Army*, pp. 28–46; Martin Edmonds, *Armed Forces and Society* (Leicester: Leicester University Press, 1988).

43. Stephen O'Brien, "Morale and the Inner Life in the Armed Forces," in *Therapeutic Communities* 14, 4 (1993): 285–295.

44. Jean Duncombe and David Marsden, "Love and Intimacy: The Gender Division of Emotion and 'Emotion Work,'" in *Sociology* 27, 2 (1998): 221–241.

45. Morgan, *Theater of War*, p. 178.

46. B. Gough and G. Edwards, "The Beer Talking: Four Lads, a Carry Out and the Reproduction of Masculinities," in *The Sociological Review* 46, 3 (1998): 409–435.

47. Morgan, *Theater of War*, p. 177.

48. John Stoltenberg, *What Makes Pornography Sexy?* (Minneapolis: Milkweed Editions, 1994).

49. S. Scott, "Fragmented Selves in Late Modernity: Making Sociological Sense of Multiple Personalities," in *The Sociological Review* 47, 3 (1998): 432–460.

50. Lynne Segal, *Slow Motion: Changing Masculinities, Changing Men* (London: Virago, 1990), p. 234.

51. Gough and Edwards, *The Beer Talking*, p. 422.

52. Roger Graef, *Talking Blues: The Police in Their Own Words* (London: Fontana, 1990).

53. Hearn and Collinson, *Men as Managers*, p. 36; John Hockey, *Squaddies: Portrait of a Subculture*, p. 35.

54. Erving Goffman, *The Presentation of Self in Everyday Life* (Penguin: London, 1959).

55. Arnie Hochschild, *The Managed Heart: Commercialization of Human Feelings* (Berkeley: University of California Press, 1983).

56. Christopher Dandeker, "New Times for the Military: Some Sociological Remarks on the Changing Role and Structure of the Armed Forces of the Advanced Societies," in *British Journal of Sociology* 45, 4 (1994): 637–654.

57. World Health Organization, *Violence against Women in Situations of Armed Conflict and Displacement* (WHO information sheet, undated).

Chapter 4

Locating Military Masculinities: Space, Place, and the Formation of Gender Identity in the British Army

Rachel Woodward

INTRODUCTION

Gender identities are central to the construction of the soldier. For Ken Lukowiak, writing about his life in the British Army as a paratrooper, the identification of a specific construction of masculinity with the soldier was a prime motivator to his joining up. "To put it plainly and simply, my reason for joining up was that I wanted to become a 'real man.'"[1] Lukowiak may be unusual in drawing this connection so explicitly, but as numerous accounts of the soldiering experience show, the identity of the soldier is intimately bound up with that soldier's own sense of gender identity.

The very process of becoming a soldier involves the construction, negotiation, and reproduction of gendered identities, and this process is critical to armed forces. Armed forces set themselves apart from other institutional or social groups (and the logic for this and mechanisms by which this specificity is negotiated with wider civilian society has provided military sociology with a rich field for critical inquiry). One way in which that specificity is defined is through the mobilization of specific gender identities. Gender identities, of course, are critical in constituting the identities of us all; what we believe ourselves to be and how we act in daily life are informed by our beliefs about what it is to be male and female.[2] Within the armed forces, that general process has highly specific outcomes. A key role of the military—the formation and mobilization of a body of individuals capable of engaging in military activities, be they peacekeeping or engagement in battle—requires the inculcation within that group of a set of values of sufficient potency and tenacity as to enable that group to do those tasks. Those values rely extensively on specific ideas about the necessary attributes of those individuals. Needless to say, those attributes are gendered in that they are constructed with reference to the sexed subjectivity of the individual. This chapter is a contribution toward an ongoing intellectual project exploring the gendering of soldierly identities.

This chapter explores this practice, of the formation of gender identities, and does so with reference to space, place, and location. The key idea informing this chapter is that military identities, and gender identities within the military, are constituted and expressed not only socially but also spatially. The purpose of the chapter is to examine how gendered military identities—in this case, masculinities—are made and given expression with reference to the locations in which they are constructed.[3] The chapter argues that gender identities are spatialized, and that the spaces and places in which those identities are developed in turn feed into that process of construction.

MILITARY MASCULINITIES IN THE BRITISH ARMY

The concept "military masculinity," which informs the contributions of this volume, has emerged over the past decade or so as a means of identifying and explaining the operation of gendered identities within the armed forces. The origins of wider social constructions of masculinity within military cultures have also been of interest. Definitions vary, but there is consensus within the gender studies, cultural studies, and sociological literatures that there exists an array of gendered cultural attributes informing the practice of military life, identifiable as features of masculine military identity. These attributes include pride in physical prowess, particularly the ability to withstand physical hardships; aggressive heterosexuality and homophobia, combined with a celebration of homosociability within the team; the ability to deploy controlled physical aggression; and a commitment to the completion of assigned tasks with minimal complaint.[4]

As a number of scholars of the military and of masculinities have argued, it makes more sense conceptually to talk of military masculinities, a range of models of gendered military behavior, operating in relation to one another, rather than as a single monolithic gendered military identity. For example, Connell argues that the basis of much military organization is the relationship between different forms of masculinity.[5] Barrett's study of masculinities within the U.S. Navy illustrates this point well through his analysis of the relationships between different navy communities, with aviators drawing upon ideas of autonomy and risk taking, surface warfare officers drawing upon themes of perseverance and endurance, and supply officers drawing upon themes of technical rationality.[6] Hockey's study of British Army infantrymen similarly traces the construction and reproduction of gendered models of military behavior and their interrelationships.[7]

The concept of military masculinity is intuitively appealing for many, not least because it strikes a chord with many popular British cultural ideas about soldiers, armies, and military life. The cultural stereotype of the squaddie, a particular model of military masculinity, is celebrated as a risk-taking jack-the-lad, for example, in the popular British television drama *Soldier Soldier*. Publications such as *Combat and Survival* magazine feed the aspirational dreams of a largely young, male readership with handy tips on the aggressive conduct of war and paramilitary activities. Novels such as Andy McNab's *Immediate Action* feed a seemingly insatiable public appetite for accounts of soldierly heroism, bravery, and cunning, appetites whetted by real-life accounts of military engagements that celebrate the mental, physical, and emotional strength of men in battle, transcending physical danger and mental fears in order to complete the mission; see, for example, McNab's *Bravo Two Zero* and Chris Ryan's *The One That Got Away*.[8] The veracity and legitimacy of these stories aside, models of military masculinity provide characters to flesh out stories of daring and tales of adventure.

The British armed forces and the Ministry of Defence (MoD) in turn deploy ideas of military masculinity to great effect. Masculinities, as Connell and others remind us, are historically and culturally contingent.[9] In the British case, we can track the development of models of military masculinities and their deployment for recruitment and publicity purposes over the past century to illustrate this. First World War recruitment posters celebrate "a man's life in the army" with reference to contemporary ideas about the natural role of men as honorable fighting sportsmen, an idea with its roots in notions of muscular Christianity. During the Second World War, one approach was to celebrate the bravery, physical prowess, and courage demonstrated by fighting men in the face of adversity; "Back them up!" says one contemporary poster showing how "British guns blast a way through Axis defenses in North Africa," the caption superimposed on a colored chalk drawing of scantily clad men heaving weighty shells into the chamber of a heavy field gun.[10] In the mid-1980s, at a time when the British armed forces' current recruitment crisis first appeared, cinema audiences were enticed toward a career in the army by being asked to aspire to an all-male, highly physical, adventurous, sports-dominated life, rewarded by the certainty of sexual conquest (by men, of women, of course). As the recruitment crisis persisted into the 1990s, and as the realization dawned on the armed forces about the need to make a forces career attractive to a wider audience, potential recruits were encouraged to consider the personal skills, such as rationality, diplomacy, and negotiation, that an army career might require; the tone of army advertisements moves away from ideas about physical prowess and toward an emphasis on a different set of gendered personal attributes.

GENDER IDENTITIES AND SPACE

The purpose of this chapter is not just to explore the process by which military masculinities are constructed but also to locate that process. The construction, operation, and reproduction of military masculinities are processes operating across space (in the abstract) and in place (as physical location). In this chapter, I argue that an understanding of the relationships between space, place, and the construction of military masculinities enhances our understanding of the ways in which military masculinities are constituted and expressed.

Feminist geography has long identified the geographical constitution and expression of gender relations as a means of exploring the wider politics of gender.[11] The engagement of feminist geographers with post-structuralist social theory has expanded this body of work to include an exploration of the ways in which gender identities—masculinities and femininities—operate as social constructions that are geographically constituted and expressed.[12] Gender identities, it is argued, are not neutral to space, but shape the ways in which different social spaces are perceived and the ways in which they are discursively constructed and politically controlled. Furthermore, gender identities are themselves shaped by the geographies in which they operate. It is this conceptualization of the geographical constitution and expression of gender identities that guides this exploration of the "locatedness" of military masculinities.[13]

THE GEOGRAPHICAL CONSTITUTION AND EXPRESSION OF MILITARY MASCULINITIES

In this section, I explore how military masculinities can be seen as geographically constituted and expressed, doing so with reference to two locations where this process operates—the army's training areas and within the domestic confines of military barracks. I do this by drawing on three main sources. The first is documentation produced by the British Army itself and aimed primarily at a young audience of potential recruits. The purpose of this documentation—primarily publicity brochures and recruitment packs for individual units within the army—is to paint an attractive picture of army life while emphasizing some of the (necessary) hardships and challenges that such a life entails. The second source for this chapter is autobiographical accounts of soldiering activity. A number of these are currently in print and available to choose from for an exploration such as this.[14] Such accounts have a primary purpose in narrating both career progression (successful or otherwise) and tales of active service. A defining feature of these accounts, though, is their use in an introductory section of descriptions of the army training process. They are invaluable, then, in providing a set of narratives about the practices through which soldiers' identities are constructed and about the role of space in that process. They are also valuable for the reflection many of them contain on the relationships between the formation of the soldier and the construction of gendered identities. The third source is a television documentary series shown on BBC television in 1999 and 2000, *Soldiers to Be,* which over twelve half-hour episodes showed the training process of a group of men and women recruits to the British Army.

Location consolidates the construction of forms of masculinity specifically associated with soldiering. I have argued elsewhere, and will continue to do so here, that rural areas—the countryside—provides an important backdrop and context to the constitution of military masculinities within the British Army.[15] This is not to argue that the rural offers the sole arena for that process; the domestic spaces of the army, such as military towns, garrisons, and barrack blocks are significant too, and I go on to explore these below. The huge army field training centers, places such as Sennybridge on the borders of the Brecon Beacons, Salisbury Plain in the center of Wiltshire, and the 22,000 hectares of the Otterburn training area in the Cheviot foothills of Northumberland are significant, though, for their role as the crucible in which gendered military identities are forged. This is where soldiers are made.

Rural areas provide the location and backdrop to most army training, and the vast majority of army recruitment literature introduces army life to the potential recruit with reference to this location. For example, a University Officer Training Corps brochure urges suitable candidates to join through the deployment of pictures of healthy, young, fit individuals out and about engaging in outdoor pursuits.[16] *Army* magazine, a publication aimed at teenagers with a potential interest in the forces, places great emphasis on the active life of a soldier in an incredible variety of outdoor locations ranging from forest, woodland, and moorlands of the British Isles to the snow-covered slopes of Norway, the grasslands of Kenya, and the jungles of Belize. The reference points to brochures for all branches of the army, be they engineering, intelligence, artillery, or infantry, all deploy this imagery of an active outdoor life. The ruralities depicted are sometimes the tame bucolic rurality bound up in classic images of the idyllic English countryside, but more usually they are the wild, open, windswept moorlands of upland Britain. These portrayals of cold, wet wilderness are used frequently as a backdrop, a challenging location against which the soldier-recruit is pitted, and in response to which the skills and identities of the solder-to-be are constructed.

The Army operates in all sorts of climates and terrains around the world and its men and women have to be ready to take up that challenge at a moment's notice. From steamy jungles to snowy mountains, you will be trained to carry out your specialist and military roles quickly and effectively. You will become fitter and stronger than you have ever been and you will learn to think on your feet and respond to rapidly changing circumstances.[17]

Into this environment, the recruit is launched. The physical attributes of the solider, such as high levels of physical fitness necessary for the infantry soldier to carry out designated tasks, are developed over this terrain. A BBC television documentary series about the army training process, *Soldiers to Be*, showed this in action, with recruits undergoing a series of marches over tough terrain, in which oblivion to the discomfort engendered by one's surroundings was trained into the soldiers. This type of marching—known as tabbing (after its acronym, Tactical Advance to Battle)—was defined as "your bread and butter," the staple of infantry soldiering.[18] This is hard work, outdoors; the trainee recruit has to learn to transcend the seemingly overwhelming desire to go back to a warm barrack. The autobiographical accounts of soldiering mentioned earlier all contain vivid accounts of this process. Adam Ballinger, training for the Special Forces reservists, reflects frequently on these activities:

[W]e walked, climbed and ran in our squadrons for nine hours without a break. We rarely used paths and never roads. We went from A to B, usually on a compass bearing. At the end, high up in the hills of North Wales, Scott [an officer] stopped us and each man sat on his bergen, grateful for the rest. We sat in a curve, two or three rows deep, around him. The wind whistled over the ridge, and our smocks, soaked with sweat, flapped against our skin.[19]

The inhospitable outdoors is used not just as the location and device for developing physical fitness but also as the location for the inculcation of particular mental attitudes and attributes deemed central to some aspects of soldiering. In the *Soldiers to Be* series, a non-commissioned officer (NCO) explained how this process worked:

Well, with Guardsmen, you have to train them for an aggressive eventuality. At the end of the day they're the ones that's going actually to go in and kill the enemy, so they've got to have a little bit of physical robustness as well as a bit of aggression as well—once they hit the pain barrier then they start to get annoyed, you hear all the grunts and groans and aggression coming out, and that's what they're basically looking for, in an Infantryman anyway.[20]

The inculcation of controlled aggression in troops is a skill. Again, the environment is central. Ken Lukowiak provides an illustration of this process in his account of training for entry into the Parachute Regiment.

If I had one major problem during basic training—that is, besides the physical exercise and the weather conditions and the food you could never get enough of and the lack of sleep and the mornings before dawn and the late nights, oh, and the drill and the discipline and the constant cleaning and scrubbing, not to mention the persistent shouting— then I guess it was my aggression. Or should I say my lack of it? If I was to become one of our nation's elite killers, then this was obviously something they were going to have to change in me, and change it they did. [21]

Lukowiak describes a ten-mile march one freezing morning at Aldershot, the platoon clad in T-shirts and carrying thirty pounds of sand in their webbing. Before the march begins, a corporal finds that Lukowiak's water bottle isn't completely full, so he pours the contents over Lukowiak's head:

I broke ranks and ran off to the platoon washrooms, and by the time I got there I was in tears. And make no mistake, they *were* sorry-for-myself tears. By this time a few weeks of basic training had passed and I just didn't think I could take any more. I didn't feel I "belonged." [22]

The platoon completes the march, returning by quick-march along the banks of the Basingstoke canal.

The corporal who had poured the water over my head earlier appeared at my side as we marched and asked, "How's my little mummy's boy, then?" And then he pushed me into the canal. As I hit the water I broke ice, screaming with the shock. [23]

Lukowiak climbs out of the canal, "shivering uncontrollably with the cold," and the corporal laughs at him. Lukowiak shouts at him that he's a "fucking bastard." The corporal laughs harder, smiles, and whispers, "Why don't you come and fucking kill me then." Then he kicks Lukowiak back into the canal (p.18). Enraged, Lukowiak jumps out of the canals and runs after the corporal back to barracks. As they wait for the others to catch up, the platoon sergeant makes clear the division between those who have completed the run and those still to come in, and the consequences in battle of being let down by men unable to complete an exercise.

While the sergeant continued his morning reading from the sacred book of Para, the corporal who had pushed me into the canal came over to me. I braced myself for at least a punch in the face for my earlier outburst, but it never came. Instead, he put an arm round my shoulder, playfully pushed his fist into my stomach, and said, "That was better. Good man." Then he gave me an all-boys-together punch on the shoulder and walked off. I felt ten feet tall. I "belonged" after all.[24]

The development of physical fitness and the ability to transcend one's environment to complete the task are quite clearly correlated in soldiers' tales with the identification of masculinity—or more correctly, they are a specific model of military masculinity. Ballinger reports an NCO's comments on this with reference to a particular exercise called Long Drag, a 65 km forced march across open countryside:

I always say, lads, Long Drag is a landmark in a man's life. You're still only a third of the way through the course, but it's Long Drag that makes a man. Even TQ [tactical questioning] is different. When a man gets through Long Drag, I respect him. I always listen to what he has to say, even if he goes on to fail the course.[25]

As with other tests during the training process, these exercises are both physical tests and rites of passage. Failure is equated with effeminacy; to succeed is to attain one's identity as a soldier and as a man: "Each time someone dropped out, a cross was inked over their face on the photo, and we were told by our corporal instructors that the ones with the crosses hadn't been man enough to become paratroopers."[26]

As I noted above, although the wet, wild, windy rural area constitutes a primary space for the constitution of military masculinities, it is not the sole space in which this process is developed. The domestic spaces of the barrack block provide the setting for the inculcation of more soldierly values, and their examination reveals different facets to this mysterious entity, military masculinity. In these spaces, order, cleanliness, and hygiene are promoted unremittingly. The care of domestic space is a task associated, culturally and socially, with the role of women. One could even argue that domestic reproduction is a feminized process.[27] Military masculinities are not usually defined as encompassing values such as care of the domestic sphere and pride in the dirt-free, the cleaned, the sparkling. Yet training soldiers in the care of their domestic environment is an essential part of basic training, and as with the great outdoors, gendered identities are formed through interaction with and response to that environment. Documentaries such as *Soldiers to Be* and autobiographical accounts of soldiering provide an insight into how this process operates.

The living space of recruits in shared barrack rooms is regulated and controlled space. New recruits are instructed on the maintenance of that space to predetermined standards. For example, instruction is given on the correct way in which the clothing within lockers should be arranged, for example, with all the hangers containing uniforms facing the same way and all hung three fingers' width apart on their rails. "Uniformity—make sure your locker looks just like that, OK?"[28] "It's something they instil in you. Its like on *Star Trek*, the Borg [laughs] ... resistance is futile, you will be assimilated.' You just become one of t'drones, there's nowt else you can do about it."[29]

In order to achieve and maintain the standards required, recruits are subjected to regular room inspections. "We'll motivate them!" laughs one NCO to another prior to an inspection where recruits are reprimanded, loudly, for failures in cleanliness and personal hygiene such as food remnants between the tines of a fork, specks of dirt on the soles of PT shoes, and the shadow of old soap suds around the rim of a soap dish.[30] As one officer noted to camera prior to an inspection, "The guys have probably been up most of the night, tidying up."[31] The idea of young men spending their evenings tidying up their domestic space runs counter to strong cultural ideas about both the appropriate activities of young men of an evening and the levels of order, cleanliness, and hygiene often thought to be exhibited by this group. On another inspection, two officers and two NCOs round on nervous recruits standing to attention with comments such as "Did you make your bed this morning?" "Is that how you normally sleep?" "Look at the color on those sheets, they're not clean.' The recruits fail the inspection, are called together, and are shouted at by a sergeant:

Well, congratulations, you fucking failed, you failed the company commander. Lockers, bags, fucking civvy lockers with no fucking clothes in, fucking beds with one sheet on, beds with no fucking mattress covers, fucking quilts without no fucking quilt covers. Who the fucking hell do we think we are?[32]

The point to emphasize here is that models of military masculinity draw reference not only from traditionally male activities conducted in the public sphere, such as physical training in the army's ranges. They also draw reference from activities in the private, domestic sphere, a space culturally associated with femininities, but used in this context for the inculcation of soldierly values (cleanliness, hygiene) not often associated with military masculinities.

THE BODY AND TRANSFORMATION

The body is critical to this conceptualization of the ways in which gender identities are formed and performed; the politics of social space are embodied within the individual. The body, the surface on which gender identities are inscribed, performed, and often resisted, operates in and reflects social space. As McDowell and Sharp put it, "[T]he differences in physicality that construct and reflect gender norms create ways of being in space."[33] It is through the body that the transformation from civilian to soldier is experienced and expressed. This is a spatialized process in that the body's physical location and its occupancy of space contribute to that experience and expression of transformation. The relationship between space and the body is reflexive. Bodies and environments reproduce each other. The training areas and barrack rooms produce the soldier's body, and this in turn is reinscribed and projected back onto those places.

The body is an object labored over in order to conform to some idealized view of an appropriate masculinity or femininity.[34] Transformation narratives appear in many accounts of the military training process. As an army recruitment brochure puts it, "The ten-week initial training is designed to turn you from a civilian into a person who not only looks like a soldier but acts and thinks like one."[35] This transformation entails quite fundamental change. "Just getting dressed in uniform is not going to make you into a soldier."[36] But this change of clothing is important, as Ballinger notes:

Dressed, I looked at the others and was struck by the transformation. Until a few minutes ago we had been wearing different civilian clothes. But now, all outward signs of individuality had gone. We stood in camouflage, concealed by each other. [...] Dozens of [men] stood around three small mirrors checking their appearances. When I did the same I received a sharp shock, for this was more than a transformation of dress, and I felt uncomfortable. It was not that the uniform did not fit, or that I was one of many, for such things did not bother me. It was that I felt different. Nothing looked quite the same. "Good," said Commando [another recruit], adjusting my cap-comforter until it met his exacting standards. "Now you look like a soldier."[37]

The uniformed body is then trained to become a soldier. This is a physical process involving bodily transformation. Through this process, gender identities are fashioned, as Judith Butler notes, through the endless repetition of stylized movements in performance.[38]

Such acts, gestures, enactments, generally construed, are performative in the sense that the essence of identity that they otherwise purport to express becomes a *fabrication* manufactured and sustained through corporeal signs and other discursive means.[39]

The two spaces considered in this chapter—the training ranges and the barrack blocks—are the location for these transformations and performances. Outside on the ranges, bodies are changed through the enactment of physical tasks building up the body of the soldier, equipping it with the skills and capabilities required for its military role. Inside domestic space, the body is preened and labored over to conform to the exacting standards of physical appearance expected by commanding officers. The *Soldiers to Be* documentary, for example, shows examples such as instructing in basic washing and hygiene, inspections of shaving methods and outcomes, control over hair, and scrupulous attention to the smartness of the uniformed body. In turn, the recruits can be observed finding new ways of using their bodies, new ways of occupying their bodies, new ways of presenting their bodies. It is an unremitting process, designed explicitly for the production of the soldier. This process is never un-gendered.

CONCLUSION: THE INSTABILITIES OF MILITARY MASCULINITIES

In this chapter I have examined how gendered identities within the army are constructed with reference to place and space. My key argument is that the study of military masculinities needs to recognize not only the processes by which these identities are constructed but also the ways in which those identities are constructed and reproduced with reference to the locations in which those processes occur.

In conclusion, there are two wider observations I wish to make. The first is to underline the importance of recognizing the inherent fluidity and instability within constructions of military masculinities. The hegemonic models of military masculinity—the warrior-hero, the squaddie, and so on—are highly contingent. Within the armed forces, there is growing recognition of the fragility and implausibility of these models. A recruitment crisis across the armed forces (with the army currently around 5,000 personnel under strength) has forced those responsible for recruitment to become aware of the unacceptability of such models for many potential recruits from non-traditional sources; in its attempts to include more women and members of ethnic minorities within the armed forces, the MoD is aware that different gendered models for soldiers are required. How this shapes the training process is open to question. What is clearly apparent, however, is the need for new models of military masculinity to reflect changing social expectations of what a soldier is and should be. Furthermore, with the gradual increase in the proportion of women in the army (currently around 7.5 percent), there is less sense in examining military masculinities, and more in examining gendered identities among both men and women, including relationships between the two.

The second observation follows from this, which is to raise a question about the very utility of the concept of military masculinities. The concept has been valuable in providing a framework for thinking through the politics of male gendered identities within the armed forces, particularly some of its more extreme attributes. We should recognize, however, the conceptual difficulties associated with the concept of masculinity. As Collier notes, the concept is slippery, politically ambiguous, and conceptually imprecise.[40] The time appears ripe for a critical discussion of the very utility of the concept of military masculinity for understanding the array of gender relations within the armed forces, and for conceptualizing the politics of these relations in an institution facing fundamental (gendered) change.

ACKNOWLEDGMENT

I would like to thank Trish Winter, who contributed to the development of many of the ideas contained in this chapter.

NOTES

1. Ken Lukowiak, *Marijuana Time: Join the Army, See the World, Meet Interesting People and Smoke All Their Dope* (London: Orion, 2000), p. 9.

2. Gender is by no means the sole factor delimiting the specificity of armed forces; it is highlighted here because of the focus of the chapter on gendered identities.

3. This chapter deals exclusively with military masculinities, leaving aside the question of female gender identities within the armed forces. The latter constitutes a rich field of inquiry in its own right. Although the dynamics surrounding the inclusion of women in the British armed forces has received some attention, the question of gender identities has not been fully considered to date. See Christine Cnossen, *Token or Full Member of the Team? An Examination of the Utilization and Status of Women in Combat Arms Positions in the Armed Forces of Canada, the United Kingdom and the United States of America* (Ph.D. thesis, University of Hull, 1994), and Christopher Dandeker and Maddy Wechsler Segal, "Gender Integration in the Armed Forces: Recent Policy Developments in the United Kingdom," *Armed Forces & Society* 23, 1 (1994): 29–47.

4. The social construction of masculinity within military forces has been studied in a variety of national contexts; see Uta Klein, "'Our Best Boys': The Gendered Nature of Civil-Military Relations in Israel," *Men and Masculinities* 2, 1 (1999): 47–65; Lesley Gill, "Creating Citizens, Making Men: The Military and Masculinity in Bolivia," *Cultural Anthropology* 12, 4 (1997): 527–550; Saraswati Sunindyo, "When the Earth Is Female and the Nation Is Mother: Gender, the Armed Forces and Nationalism in Indonesia," *Feminist Review* 58, 1 (1998): 1–21; Anna Simon, *The Company They Keep* (New York: Avon Books, 1999).

5. Bob Connell, "Masculinity, Violence and War," in Michael Kimmel and Michael Messner, eds., *Men's Lives*, 3rd ed., (Boston: Allyn & Bacon, 1995).

6. Frank Barrett, "The Organisational Construction of Hegemonic Masculinity: The Case of the US Navy," *Gender, Work and Organization* 3 (1996): 129–142.

7. John Hockey, *Squaddies: Portrait of a Subculture* (Exeter: Exeter University Press, 1986).

8. Andy McNab, *Bravo Two Zero* (London: Corgi, 1993); Chris Ryan, *The One That Got Away* (London: Ted Smart, 1995); Cameron Spence, *Sabre Squadron* (Harmondsworth: Penguin, 1997).

9. See Bob Connell, *Masculinities* (Cambridge: Polity Press, 1995).

10. Imperial War Museum poster, H16 (London: HMSO, 1990).

11. See Women and Geography Study Group, *Geography and Gender: An Introduction to Feminist Geography* (London: Hutchinson, 1984).

12. Women and Geography Study Group, *Feminist Geographies: Explorations in Diversity and Difference* (London: Longman, 1997), and Nina Laurie et al., *Geographies of New Femininities* (Harlow: Longman, 1999).

13. For a more detailed exposition of this theoretical approach, see Rachel Woodward, "'It's a Man's Life!': Soldiers, Masculinity and the Countryside," *Gender, Place and Culture* 5, 3 (1998): 277–300.

14. Examples include Adam Ballinger, *The Quiet Soldier: On Selection with 21 SAS* (London: Orion, 1992); Ken Lukowiak, *A Soldier's Song: True Stories from the Falklands* (London: Phoenix, 1993); Andy McNab, *Bravo Two Zero* (London: Corgi, 1993); Peter de la Billière, *Looking for Trouble: SAS to Gulf Command: The Autobiography* (London: HarperCollins, 1994); Chris Ryan, *The One That Got Away* (London: Ted Smart, 1995); Cameron Spence, *Sabre Squadron* (Harmondsworth: Penguin, 1997); Sarah Ford, *One Up: A Woman in Action with the SAS* (London: Harper Collins, 1997); Cameron Spence, *All Necessary Measures* (Harmondsworth: Penguin, 1998); Jackie George with Susan Ottaway, *She Who Dared: Covert Operations in Northern Ireland with the SAS* (London: Leo Cooper, 1999); Ken Lukowiak, *Marijuana Time: Join the Army, See the World, Meet Interesting People and Smoke All Their Dope* (London, Orion, 2000).

15. See Rachel Woodward, "'It's a Man's Life!': Soldiers, Masculinity and the Countryside," *Gender, Place and Culture* 5, 3 (1998): 277–300, and "Warrior Heroes and Little Green Men: Soldiers, Military Training and the Construction of Rural Masculinities," *Rural Sociology* 65, 4 (2000): 640–657, for discussions of how rurality and masculinity as social constructions reproduce each other in the context of the British Army.

16. Ministry of Defence, *University Officer Training Corps: Adventure, Challenge, Fun.* CP (A) 93–4 (London: Army Recruiting Group, 1999).

17. Army Recruiting Group, *Experience Life as a Soldier* CP (A) 96 (London: Army recruitment brochure, undated).

18. BBC Television, *Soldiers to Be* (London: BBC Television, 1999 and 2000); Ken Lukowiak, *Marijuana Time: Join the Army, See the World, Meet Interesting People and Smoke All Their Dope* (London, Orion, 2000).

19. Adam Ballinger, *The Quiet Soldier: On Selection with 21 SAS* (London: Orion, 1992), p. 57.

20. Staff Sergeant, ATR Pirbright, *Soldiers to Be*, Series 1, Episode 1, "A New Life," Broadcast 3 August 1999.

21. Ken Lukowiak, *Marijuana Time: Join the Army, See the World, Meet Interesting People and Smoke All Their Dope* (London, Orion, 2000), p. 17.

22. Ibid., p. 18.

23. Ibid.

24. Ibid., p. 19.

25. Adam Ballinger, *The Quiet Soldier: On Selection with 21 SAS* (London: Orion, 1992), p. 113.

26. Ken Lukowiak, *Marijuana Time: Join the Army, See the World, Meet Interesting People and Smoke All Their Dope* (London, Orion, 2000), p. 15.

27. See, for example, Ann Oakley, *The Sociology of Housework* (London: Robertson, 1974).

28. Corporal, ATR Winchester, *Soldiers to Be*, Series 1, Episode 1, "A New Life," Broadcast 3 August 1999.

29. Recruit, ATR Winchester, *Soldiers to Be*, Series 1, Episode 1, "A New Life," Broadcast 3 August 1999.

30. Ibid.

31. Ibid.

32. *Soldiers to Be*, Series 1, Episode 2, Broadcast 10 August 1999.

33. Linda McDowell and Joanne Sharp, "Body Maps: Editors' Introduction to Section 4," in *Space, Gender, Knowledge: Feminist Readings* (London: Arnold, 1997), pp. 201–207.

34. Ibid., p. 203.

35. Ministry of Defence, *Infantry Soldier...for Real Soldiering* (London: HMSO, 1995), p. 10.

36. Ibid.

37. Adam Ballinger, *The Quiet Soldier: On Selection with 21 SAS* (London: Orion, 1992), p. 27.

38. Judith Butler, "Gender Trouble: Feminist Theory and Psychoanalytic Discourses," in Linda Nicholson, ed., *Feminism/Postmodernism* (London: Routledge, 1990), pp. 324–340.

39. Ibid., p. 336.

40. Richard Collier, *Masculinities, Crime and Criminology: Men, Heterosexuality and the Criminal(ised) Other* (London: Sage, 1998).

Chapter 5

The Home Guard in Britain in the Second World War: Uncertain Masculinities?

Penny Summerfield and Corinna Peniston-Bird

INTRODUCTION

The Second World War in Britain was a period in which an association between masculinity and military participation was strongly constructed in political discourse and in popular memory. National Service Acts, the first of which was passed on 1 October 1939, made men aged 18 to 41, extended to 51 in December 1941, liable for military service.[1] Selection processes exempted those regarded as unfit, as well as those on a shifting list of "reserved occupations," identified by government as essential for industrial production and the continuity of civilian life. By 1944 mobilization was extensive. There were 4.5 million servicemen in the British Army, Royal Air Force, and Royal Navy and 10.3 million men in civil employment.[2]

Even though many men were prevented from joining the military because of their age, fitness or position within the occupational structure, representations of men in wartime emphasized the serviceman. The RAF pilots of the Battle of Britain were "the few" to whom so many owed so much; the men of the Royal Navy engaged fearlessly with U-boats in the treacherous waters of the Atlantic; the cheerful British Tommy achieved a significant victory at El Alamein (November 1942) and swept victoriously into Europe after D-Day. Of them all, the flight crew of the RAF retained the most heroic status.[3] This wartime configuration of masculinity was built upon traditional notions that it was a man's patriotic duty to defend the nation and the women and children within it, iterated in modernist ways. This was a just war for peace and freedom against the forces of fascist tyranny. It was fought by men in harness with modern technology, the fighter and bomber plane, the tank, the submarine.[4] The dynamism of its warfare marked the Second World War off from the squalor and stagnation, stoicism and sacrifice of the trenches of the First World War (for all that there were occasions when it was far from dynamic). Political rhetoric of the Second World War recast and rehabilitated the heroism of soldiering.

As in earlier wars, to be a soldier was to be manly, and to be manly in wartime was to be a soldier. But in the Second World War the possession of the military territory by men alone was contested. A new and pervasive military femininity was present. Women's military participation as auxiliaries to the male armed forces had been tried in 1917–1918. It was extensively developed in the period 1939–1945. Women were recruited to three women's forces: the Auxiliary Territorial Service (ATS, the women's branch of the army), the Women's Auxiliary Air Force (WAAF), and the Women's Royal Naval Service (WRNS). At first they had to volunteer, but as labor requirements mounted, an element of compulsion was introduced. Under the National Service Number Two Act of December 1941 single women were conscripted by age group, starting with 20-year-olds. They were supposed to be allowed some choice, in particular between military and industrial war service, but in practice officials of the Ministry of Labour and National Service directed young women conscripts to areas of greatest labor shortage.[5] By 1944 there were 468,800 servicewomen.[6]

Women in military service were defined as auxiliaries. They were there to help and support the male military rather than to engage in active service themselves. At the heart of this gender differentiation was the requirement that women (but not men) must sign a letter of consent before using lethal weapons. But this functional boundary could not be firmly drawn for reasons of technical change as well as labor shortage. For example, ATS women who worked on anti-aircraft batteries were supposed to aim but not fire the guns, but by the end of the war technical changes had made the distinction academic. Women in the WAAF armed fighter and bomber planes with the armaments made by other women in ordnance factories. Women in branches of all three services maintained and repaired fighting machinery.[7] In short, women's auxiliary functions not only extended to sustaining the bodies of the men who used such machinery at the battlefront but also were deeply implicated in military activity.

There were gender differences in the armed forces in terms of the position of women under military law and the authority of servicewomen over men.[8] Nonetheless, the visible presence and functional role of servicewomen breached the all-male boundary that had hitherto contained the male military. Second World War military masculinity was offset by this new military femininity. Military masculinity's legitimacy was as a result particularly strongly linked to *fighting*, since active service was the major differentiator of the roles of the two sexes.

This configuration of military masculinity in the Second World War made the gender identity of a special force, formed for the first time in 1940, problematic. This was the Home Guard, first known as the Local Defence Volunteers, or LDV, a force of volunteers formed rapidly and enthusiastically in May 1940 to help defend Britain against invasion.[9] In the first month of its existence 1,456,000 men joined.[10] They were part-time soldiers, putting on and taking off their military identity with their uniforms at least twice a week unless the advent of an invasion necessitated their full-time service. Over time they acquired the trappings of the military male: uniform, weapons, ranks, and military training in duty, discipline, and combat. They were a visible public presence; but as a group of civilian men debarred from the armed forces yet recruited and trained for military tasks, they occupied an extraordinary position in the relationship between civilian and military male roles.

The ambiguities of the Home Guard as an armed force spanned an extensive register, encompassing its composition, its signifiers, and its functions. In each of these areas, as we shall see, the military status of the Home Guard was constructed in political discourse and popular memory as being, at least partly, in deficit. Discursively and in practice, attempts were made to compensate and restore certainty to its military and therefore masculine identity. But the involvement in Home Guard activities demanded by some civilian *women* in turn destabilized these attempts.

COMPOSITION OF THE HOME GUARD

When the position of the Home Guard was regularized as a section of the army, rules about membership were established. Home Guards were civilians who could not join the armed forces because they were too old, too young, too unfit, or in reserved occupations. These excluded categories are both large and suggestive of a negative definition. In representations of the Home Guard during the war and after it, there were question marks over who its members were and about their competency for the job they might have had to do.

Even issues that would appear to be relatively simple matters of evidence, like the age profile of the Home Guard, were contested. According to the official regulations men aged 17 to 65 could join, so the age profile spanned pre-conscription-age youths (under 18), men of military service age who were in reserved occupations or deemed medically unfit, and men over this age (above 45 in the years 1939–1941, then from 1942 to the end of the war above 50 years of age).[11] The earliest historian of the Home Guard, Charles Graves, states, however, that the average age of members was that which would "normally betoken a pensioner," and this is repeated in other accounts.[12] A pensioner in 1940 was 65 or over. A recent historian, S. P. Mackenzie, challenges the notion that the Home Guard was a collection of pensioners with a calculation that the average age was in fact 35.[13] Although such an average flattens the likely peaks at the younger and older points of the age spectrum, it is a salutary reminder of the approximately 10 million civilian men between the ages of 18 and 65 from whom members could have been drawn.

As well as debating evidence about the age composition of the Home Guard, one can ask questions about the *meaning* of the emphasis on men of pensionable age. This representation is coupled with reiteration of the idea that the Home Guard was a force of veterans of the First World War, who had fought in "the last winning British Army" and could therefore be trusted to defend Britain again.[14] In his speeches Churchill laid claim not only to the sagacity but also to the virility of Home Guards, "many of whom served in the last war, who are full of vigour and experience."[15] It is a representation that connects with the cultural construction that, in the words of a song popular in the army in the First World War, "old soldiers never die."[16] Their patriotic instincts and military knowledge would revive the moment the nation was again menaced by an enemy. This version of the age composition of the Home Guard contradicted evidence of its greater youthfulness (and, by implication, lack of military experience), and was also in contradiction with various salient aspects of the experience of the "winning British Army" of 1914–1918, not least how nearly it lost. Representing the Home Guard as a collection of tough old veterans helped to erase the emasculating effects of the First World War, the pitiable condition of some ex-servicemen in the interwar years, and the defeat of the young army at Dunkirk. It connected the Home Guard with a heroic history of soldiering within a British voluntarist tradition.

As far as gender was concerned, the Home Guard was enduringly represented as masculine. Yet from summer 1940 women formally asked to join on the grounds that civilian women should be trained and equipped to defend themselves and their country so they could take their place alongside men in the event of an invasion.[17] In addition, some joined informally, and others formed their own Women's Home Defence organization.[18] Nonetheless, they were officially excluded until 1943, the stated grounds being shortages of equipment, uniforms, and instructors and simply that there was no place for them in the Home Guard whether as combatants or non-combatants.[19] Women were eventually permitted to join the Home Guard as a result of a combination of feminist pressure and the response of local Home Guard commanders to labor shortages, but they were allowed only limited functions as Women Home Guard Auxiliaries and were denied almost all the signifiers of the male Home Guard. And during and since the Second World War, their presence has been routinely denied, belittled, or overlooked in historical and popular representations.

The ambiguities of the status of the Home Guard in relation to the construction of masculinity in wartime help to make sense of this dogged exclusion of women. The Home Guard was not only about providing a last line of defense in the event of a succession of defeats of the regular forces, leading to invasion. It was also about men's morale. Participation could give civilian men who otherwise felt powerless a sense of involvement in the military war effort. Sir Edward Grigg, Under Secretary of State for War, for example, said in Parliament in November 1940 that the Home Guard had been formed by "men of all ages in all parts of the country" who "were eating their hearts out because for one reason or another they had no opportunity for offering military service.... The morale of this country was never low, but action raises morale. The Home Guard has thus enabled all sorts and conditions of patriotic men to express themselves in service, with tonic effect."[20] Had women been admitted to its ranks in the desperate first three years of the war, these morale-raising effects could have been lost. The need to bestow on civilian men some of the energizing effects of military status in wartime outweighed in the policymakers' minds the advantages, which MPs like Edith Summerskill urged, of allowing women to join, such as an increased supply of fit and efficient recruits. The Home Guard could not be presented as a force of militarily effective men defending the nation's women and children if women were included in that defense.

SIGNIFIERS

Government propaganda emphasized the forging of an efficient military force from the heterogeneous collection of men who volunteered for the LDV in May 1940. In official photographs and film the keen but disorganized volunteers of 1940, dressed in civilian garb and bearing sticks and pitchforks, rapidly become disciplined companies of men clad in khaki and armed with rifles.[21] In practice, though, the signifiers of the transformation from amateurs playing at soldiers to a professional force of military men were slow to arrive. The delays in equipping the Home Guard with uniforms and weapons were caused, on the one hand, by the higher priority given to the army's needs after the loss of equipment on the beaches of northern France in June 1940 and, on the other, by the rapid growth of Home Guard membership, which outpaced the increase in military supplies.

Accounts of the Home Guard stress the story of inadequate uniforms and arms. Thus cartoonists celebrated the fact that the first uniform issued to the LDV was no more than a brassard and that although by June denim overalls and service caps were being issued, there were problems with both dissemination and sizing.[22] Throughout its four-and-a-half-year existence, the Home Guard was associated by humorists with outdated and makeshift weapons, such as pikes (bayonets welded to piping) and Molotov cocktails.[23] Such commentaries contributed to the construction of arms and uniforms as important signifiers of authentic military status by emphasizing the implications of the lack of them for the Home Guard's military identity. The humor lay in the exploitation of the Home Guard's spare-time soldier image and the lack of seriousness, not only of individuals but also of the force as a whole, that it implied. Historical accounts followed suit, typically deploring the fact that at the end of June 1940 there was only one rifle for every six men and that it was "not until" the winter of 1940–1941 that most of the Home Guard were wearing battledress.[24]

There is, however, an alternative reading of the history of the equipping of the Home Guard. The provision of military uniform for 1.5 million men within seven months of the formation of this new force, and of a firearm for every man by 1943, could indicate the relatively high priority the government gave the force in spite of the declining likelihood of invasion after the entry of the Soviet Union and the United States to the war during 1941. Concern expressed in Parliament that in the event of an invasion men without uniforms could be shot as *franc-tireurs* underlined that a uniform served as a signifier of the legitimacy of the bearer's claim to a military identity, protected under international law. The government appears to have recognized the importance of retaining the Home Guard as a properly dressed and equipped military force not only for such functional reasons but also for symbolic ones having to do with maintaining male morale. A commitment to the public status of the Home Guard was expressed in the support given to the wartime anniversaries of the Home Guard by the King (Colonel in Chief to the Home Guard) and the prime minister. In film and photographs of 1941–1944 the Home Guard appears to be indistinguishable from the British Regular Army. Only the practiced eye can spot the differences in badges and belts, although the difference in the latter is telling. The army was issued with khaki webbing belts, whereas the Home Guard, less likely to engage in active service and therefore less in need of the camouflage effects of webbing, was given shiny leather belts.[25]

A comparison with the equipping of the women admitted to the Home Guard in 1943 throws into sharp relief the meaning of provision for male Home Guards. Whereas women in the auxiliary forces and in official civilian organizations (such as the Women's Land Army, the Women's Voluntary Services, the National Fire Service) were issued official uniforms, Women Home Guard Auxiliaries were steadfastly refused any form of uniform beyond a plastic badge. Women Home Guards took matters into their own hands, adapting male uniforms with their feminine skills and acquiring weapons training.[26] Officially, however, the woman Home Guard was to be as invisible as possible, whereas the male Home Guard was dressed and equipped to pass in public as an authentic military presence.

FUNCTION

Probably the most important issue affecting understandings of the Home Guard during and after the war was that it was established to defend Britain against an invasion that never came. Yet, despite the reduction of the threat, the Home Guard was not disbanded until December 1944. The lack of clarity about its function in the absence of an invasion contributed to the uncertainty of its military and therefore masculine identity.

The original intention in summer 1940, when an invasion was anticipated, was that the Home Guard should be characterized by "simplicity, elasticity and decentralized control, and a minimum of regulations and formalities."[27] However, decentralization rapidly became problematic to the government. Were Home Guards, as one MP put it, "to use their own initiative and military knowledge in improvising defence and offence measures in their areas to defend their localities…and use *every* means of sabotaging and defeating the enemy?" Or, as Eden replied, would these actions "unless in conformity with a general plan…do more harm than good"?[28]

Increasingly concerned that it would not be able to control the development and role of the Home Guard, the War Office took steps from June to October 1940 to bring Home Guard procedures into line with those of the army and place it under army supervision. In October, for example, the Home Guard came under the King's Regulations, which involved the introduction of army ranks and enabled the War Office to eliminate those members it deemed unsuitable for service, whether for reasons of incompetence or political affiliation. A voluntary training school at Osterley Park, staffed in part by left-wing veterans of the Spanish Civil War, was brought under War Office control. A permanent staff instructor and an administrative officer were supplied from the British Regular Army to each Home Guard battalion. Later, under the National Service (Number 2) Act of December 1941, men aged 18 to 51 who were not in the armed forces could henceforth be compelled to serve in the Home Guard, introducing an element of state compulsion that significantly eroded the voluntary principle. The function of the Home Guard was not to be that of roving bands of volunteer guerrillas.

On the contrary, as the war continued, the Home Guard was increasingly used to perform military duties in support of the army. The humor in the uncertainty of its function, mobile or static, and independent of or subordinate to army command, was captured in a satirical verse in *Punch* in 1942:

No doubt some high strategic plan

Beyond the ken of common man

Dictates these changes in our job

From mob. to stat. and stat. to mob.

Still it would help us all to know

More positively where to go

In case, when Boches do appear,

We cannot find a brigadier.[29]

In general the War Office favored the static option, that is, that the Home Guard should replace army personnel in guard duties and on gun emplacements. By "taking the burden of home defence on to themselves," as Churchill put it in 1943, the Home Guard not only permitted the regular forces to be more mobile but freed up troops for service overseas.[30] However, no doubt

inadvertently, he contributed to the image of the Home Guard having an uncertain function and an insecure collective identity.

He implied that until 1943–1944, the Home Guard's function had been unclear, writing that the Home Guard at last found "a worth-while job" in the run
up to the D-Day landings: "[N]ot only were they manning sections of anti-
aircraft and coast defences, but they also took over many routine and security
duties, thus releasing other soldiers for battle." Churchill regarded the Home
Guard as making a serious contribution to British home defense. In the statements quoted above he associated the Home Guard with "other soldiers." However, there was a problem of gender alignment in this characterization of the
function of the Home Guard.

This problem arose because of the similarity of the Home Guard's functions
of 1943–1944 to those of the women's military forces. For example, members of
the ATS, the WAAF, and the WRNS worked on anti-aircraft gunsites, sometimes on opposite shifts to the Home Guard, as well as doing routine and security duties. Both the Home Guard and the women's services were releasing
men, by implication "real men," for frontline duties. Furthermore, there was
the possibility that what the Home Guard did was done more effectively by
servicewomen, who had the advantages of being young adults and having full-
time fully trained status. This similarity of function points to the importance of
the combat taboo as a gender differentiator. The cultural construction that it
was inappropriate for women to kill ensured that regular British servicewomen
in the Second World War were not allowed to fire weapons on a gunsite, as a
guard, or in any other role. The combat taboo, then, salvaged the Home Guard's
manhood from the effects upon it of their alignment with servicewomen. But
the position of the taboo was precarious. As we have seen, it was barely upheld
in the women's forces, and it was menaced in the Home Guard by women's demands for weapons training. The repeated insistence of officials that women in
the Home Guard must not be issued with weapons or given arms training can
be seen as a desperate attempt to preserve this classically masculine function
for men. The need to reiterate the combat taboo also serves as an indication that
both men and women in some Home Guard units were ignoring it.

One function the Home Guard fulfilled that marked it as quite different from
the women's auxiliaries was its contribution to training the army. Military exercises were organized in which British Regular Army and Home Guard battalions engaged as if in action, to give army personnel experience of the
military maneuvers they might experience on active service. However, at the
same time as bringing the Home Guard into the ambit of "authentic militarism," such exercises provided opportunities for humiliating representations
of the Home Guard. The most well-known account of a Regular Army–Home
Guard exercise is probably in the Powell and Pressberger film *The Life and
Death of Colonel Blimp* (1943). The Blimp character commanding the Home
Guard, General Wynne Candy, is caught by the army in the steam room of his
London club's Turkish bath. He is unprepared for their arrival because the rules

of the exercise state that "war begins at midnight" and it is still early evening. The young, mobile, vigorous army units involved have decided not to obey the rules, however, and begin the exercise at six P.M. instead, winning outright and securing Candy's dismissal from the Home Guard and the war effort. The message of the film is complex. There is considerable nostalgia for the rules of war, represented by the Home Guard and embodied by its commander, Candy, the Blimp character, a British soldier who has fought in every war since the Boer War. At the same time the film presents a critique of the inadequacies of following these rules when confronting such an enemy as Nazi Germany. The film gives a special twist to the insecure military masculinity of the Home Guard—it can be both military and masculine, but this counts for nothing if it is not modern.

Exercises had their farcical side even when the Home Guard was not walked over in such ways, and perhaps especially when the exercises were between Home Guard divisions rather than between the British Regular Army, genuinely preparing for combat, and the Home Guard. Because live ammunition was obviously not used, umpires decided whether participants were alive, dead, or injured or should be taken prisoner. The exercises were sent up in films, in sketches, and in numerous cartoons.[31] By infantilizing the Home Guards as boys playing war games, these constructions added to the insecurity of the masculinity of Home Guards, who would never get closer to genuine combat than this. Such representations were in precarious balance with the usefulness of such exercises for army training and for keeping the Home Guard in a state of military preparedness.

CONCLUSION

The Home Guard is a site in which masculinity was ambiguous. There were numerous ways in which joining it might compensate for being a civilian and might raise men's morale as the government intended. Nevertheless, the men in the Home Guard were not, and could not be, proper soldiers. The images that clung to them because of their exclusion from the wartime military forces, namely, that of being primarily civilians of extreme youth and seniority, worked against the transformation orchestrated by the War Office, turning them from ramshackle crowds of volunteers desperate to snipe at parachutists to regulated units of disciplined soldiers under the control of the army. Even though the British Army of the Second World War was composed primarily of conscripted civilians, it was a professional, full-time force whose military prowess was repeatedly tried and tested. The Home Guard, in contrast, was part-time, amateur, and unpaid, and it bore no Second World War battle scars, however smartly it might march and trimly turned out it might appear. As a result the tensions between the British Regular Army and the Home Guard were both considerable and complex.[32]

Furthermore, the presence of women in the auxiliary forces, who were arguably closer to active service than the men of the Home Guard, contributed to the distancing of members of that force from a military identity. The presence of women within the Home Guard itself was as a result especially unwelcome, at least in political discourse: It could rob the force of its last vestige of military masculinity and hence undermine the positive effects on male morale that it was meant to have. At the level of political culture (if not in the memos exchanged within the War Office, which were persistently opaque on the reasons for refusing membership of the Home Guard), the logic of polarized gender identities informed the lengthy resistance of women's demands for membership.

The importance of gender differentiation, as well as differentiation from civilian status, to the Home Guard is thus clarified and explained by our argument about the salience of the particular configuration of Second World War military masculinity. It was, of course, incompletely successful. The ambiguities in the masculinity of the Home Guard in Britain in the Second World War are enduring.

ACKNOWLEDGMENTS

The research on which this chapter is based was undertaken with the aid of a Leverhulme Research Grant, F/185/AK 1999–2000, awarded to P. Summerfield, Lancaster University, for the project "The Gendering of British National Defence, 1939–1945: The Case of the Home Guard." The grant enabled the employment of C. M. Peniston-Bird as a research fellow. We are grateful for this assistance and would also like to acknowledge the constructive criticism of forerunners of this chapter that we received at Leeds Metropolitan and at Lancaster Universities in November 1999.

NOTES

1. H.M.D. Parker, *Manpower: A Study of War-Time Policy and Administration* (London: HMSO, 1957), pp. 150–163.

2. Central Statistical Office: *Fighting with Figures: A Statistical Digest of the Second World War* (London: HMSO, 1995), Tables 3.3 and 3.4.

3. See, for example, Robert Rhodes James, *Winston S. Churchill: His Complete Speeches*, vols. VI and VII (New York and London: Chelsea House Publishers, 1974); J. B. Priestley, *Postscripts* (London: William Heinemann, 1940), pp. 69, 41; J. Derracott and B. Loftus, *Second World War Posters* (London: Imperial War Museum, 1972), p. 54, discussion of Jonathan Foss's recruitment posters "Volunteer for Flying Duties" and "Serve in the WAAF with the Men Who Fly."

4. B. H. Liddell Hart, *Dynamic Defence* (London, 1940); T. Wintringham, *New Ways of War* (London, 1940).

5. H.M.D. Parker, *Manpower: A Study of War-Time Policy and Administration* (London: HMSO, 1957), p. 113, pp. 286–287.

6. Central Statistical Office, *Fighting with Figures* (London: HMSO, 1995), Table 3.4. The majority, 206,200, were in the ATS, followed by 175,500 in the WAAF and 68,600 in the WRNS.

7. Gerard DeGroot, "Whose Finger on the Trigger? Mixed Anti-aircraft Batteries and the Female Combat Taboo," *War in History* 4, 4 (1997): 434–453; Peggy Scott, *They Made Invasion Possible* (London: Hutchinson, 1944).

8. See Jane Rosenzweig, "The Construction of Policy for Women in the British Armed Forces, 1938–1945" (unpublished M. Litt. thesis, University of Oxford, 1993), chap. 6; Tessa Stone "Creating a (Gendered?) Military Identity: The Women's Auxiliary Air Force in Great Britain in the Second World War," *Women's History Review* 8, 4 (1999): 605–624.

9. S.P. Mackenzie, *The Home Guard: The Real Story of "Dad's Army"* (Oxford: OUP, 1995).

10. Central Statistical Office, *Fighting with Figures* (London; HMSO, 1995), Table 3.9.

11. Ibid., p. 36. "[T]he wartime national service acts of 1939–42…made males aged 18–50 liable for military service."

12. Charles Graves, *The Home Guard of Britain* (London: Hutchinson & Co, 1943), p. 13. Ernest Raymond in his autobiography says that some members were younger men in reserved occupations, "but the majority of us were well over military age." Ernest Raymond, *Please You, Draw Near: Autobiography, 1922–1968* (London: Cassell, 1969), p. 85.

13. S.P. Mackenzie, *The Home Guard: The Real Story of "Dad's Army"* (Oxford: OUP, 1995), p. 38. He cites sources on p. 37, stating that between 40 and 75 percent of the force were veterans, and he concludes it was probably around 35 percent in 1940.

14. Graves, *The Home Guard*, p.13. This emphasis on the veteran membership in the Home Guard led to a pointed interjection in a debate in the House of Commons on 23 July 1940, when Colonel Arthur Evans MP asked for it to be borne in mind "that ex-Servicemen of the last war are also serving with the *regular* army in this war." Hansard, Parliamentary Debates, vol. 363, col. 576, emphasis added.

15. Winston Churchill, *The Second World War. Volume I: The Gathering Storm* (London: Reprint Society, 1950 ed.), p. 393. Letter from the First Lord to the Home Secretary, 7 October 1939. Churchill was suggesting at this early date that a Home Guard should be formed, as he was anxious about morale on the home front.

16. The full quotation is "Old Soldiers never die; they simply fade away." Anonymous, British soldiers' song, c. 1914–1918, see H.L. Mencken, ed., *A New Dictionary of Quotations* (New York: Alfred A. Knopf, 1962); and John Bartlett, ed., *Familiar Quotations* (London: Macmillan, 1968).

17. Hansard, Parliamentary Debates, vol. 365, cols. 1928–1932, Edith Summerskill's contribution to Adjournment Debate, 19 November 1940. For a full account of the pressure group activities of women determined to take an equal part in home defense, see P. Summerfield, "'She Wants a Gun Not a Dishcloth!' Gender, Service and Citizenship in Britain in the Second World War," in G. DeGroot and C. Peniston-Bird, eds., *A Soldier*

and a Woman: Sexual Integration in the Military (Harlow: Pearson Education, 2000), pp. 119–134.

18. For evidence of women joining informally and also forming their own Women's Home Defence organization, see Penny Summerfield and Corinna Peniston-Bird, "Women in the Firing Line: The Home Guard and the Defence of Gender Boundaries in Britain in the Second World War," *Women's History Review* 9, 2 (2000): 231–255.

19. Hansard, Parliamentary Debates, vol. 376, col. 1373, 9 November 1941.

20. Ibid., vol. 365, cols. 1928–1932, Adjournment Debate, 19 November 1940.

21. See, for example, the government releases *Citizens Army* (1940), *Home Guard* (1941), *One Man, Two Jobs* (1944).

22. See, for example, *Punch* cartoon, June 1940, in Mackenzie, *The Home Guard*, Illustration 2, in which a butler lays an LDV brassard on his master's bed, saying, "I've laid your uniform out, My Lord."

23. For example, a cartoon showing men dressed as medieval archers, armed with pikes and long bows, with the caption spoken by one military type to another, " ...and then, before the enemy has recovered from his surprise," *Punch*, 24 July 1940, p. 107.

24. S. P. Mackenzie, *The Home Guard* (Oxford: OUP, 1995), p. 40. David K. Yelton, "British Public Opinion, the Home Guard and the Defence of Great Britain, 1940–1944," *Journal of Military History* 58 (July 1994): 472.

25. Ex-Home Guards (men) expressed resentment at this (interviews by Corinna Peniston-Bird with Cecil Halford, 28 October 1999); Ray Atkins, 23 March 2000; interview by Penny Summerfield with Andrew Bridges, 1 October 1999 (who mentions it three times). The difference in the belts was also used for plot development in the wartime film *Waterloo Road* (1944).

26. See P. Summerfield, "'She Wants a Gun Not a Dishcloth!' Gender, Service and Citizenship in Britain in the Second World War," in Gerard DeGroot and Corinna Peniston-Bird, eds., *A Soldier and a Woman: Sexual Integration in the Military* (Harlow: Pearson Education, 2000), pp. 124–132.

27. Graves: *The Home Guard*, p. 12, repeated in MacKenzie, *The Home Guard*, p. 40, without post-comma addition.

28. Interchange between Woodburn and Eden, 16 July 1940. Hansard, Parliamentary Debates, vol. 363, cols. 4–5.

29. *Punch*, 19 August 1942. Used with permission.

30. Winston S. Churchill in a speech 14 May 1943 in Robert Rhodes James, *Winston S. Churchill: His Complete Speeches*, vol. VI (New York: Chelsea House Publishers, 1974), p. 6772.

31. See, for example, S. Evelyn Thomas, ed., *Laughs with the Home Guard* (London: George G. Harrap, 1942), pp. 46 and 47. D. Langdon cartoon of two Home Guards confronting each other in an exercise: "'Hey, you're dead!' 'No, I'm not. I'm just sort of staggering forward, weak with loss of blood and exhaustion, to recapture our position'"; cartoon by Giles showing a diminutive Home Guard pointing his gun at the back of a very large soldier, concurrently worsting two other Home Guards. The soldier turns his head and says to the small Home Guard, down his nose, "Did I understand you to say *you've* killed *me?*"

32. We explore this issue in an as yet unpublished paper, "Gender Instabilities in the Home Guard in the Second World War," given at the Institute of Contemporary British History Annual Conference on Gender in July 2000. Ex-members of the Home Guard whom we interviewed evoked the tension between the army and the Home Guard in a variety of ways. For some the unfairness of the Home Guard's inferior reputation still rankled. For example, one Home Guard who worked long hours as a farm laborer commented: "I mean the regular Army, they had the one job. They weren't, they weren't working in agriculture were they? They had that one job, the Army." Interview by Corinna Peniston-Bird with Lee Roper, 29 November 2000.

Chapter 6

Violence in the Military Community

Deborah Harrison

INTRODUCTION

Violence comes from the word "violate," to which the *Oxford Dictionary* attributes at least three meanings that are relevant: (1) to treat irreverently; to desecrate, dishonor, profane, or defile; (2) to interfere with by appropriation; (3) to treat without proper respect or regard. One meaning of *violence* itself is "undue constraint applied to some natural process, habit, etc., so as to prevent its free development or exercise." Although based on empirical work, this chapter is mainly a conceptual effort to link the above definitions of violence with the socially constructed genderedness of the military community and to examine the consequences for military wives of military combat readiness. It argues that capturing the essence of the situation of military wives necessitates using a conceptualization of violence that is broad enough to incorporate physical abuse, psychological abuse, and economic vulnerability.

I begin with a description of our empirical research, including its underlying feminist epistemology. From there I move to an analysis of the ways military combat readiness organizes the gendered work experiences of military wives, a description of some of Canadian military wives' recent acts of resistance, and some provisional conclusions.

METHODOLOGY

Between 1990 and 1993 Lucie Laliberté[1] and I conducted a national study of Canadian military wives.[2] The first stage of our research consisted of traveling to Canadian military communities in Ontario, Québec, New Brunswick, Nova Scotia, Alberta, and Germany, interviewing in an oral-historical open-ended way, confidentially and anonymously, 112 English- and French-speaking wives and former wives representing all ranks and service elements.[3] These interviews provided us with a wealth of detail about military wives' lives, which enabled us to frame their routine activities as work and to supplement existing sociological knowledge of domestic labor, corporate wives, woman abuse, and older women, pensions, and poverty.

These interviews also gave us a solid sense of the standpoint of the military wife insofar as this standpoint could be theorized as a unitary entity. By standpoint of the military wife I mean the situation of the woman who marries a man and by so doing simultaneously subjects herself to the control of the military institution.

We assumed that the military wife's personal and economic well-being—her health, safety, and ability to exercise some control over her life—was distinct from the well-being of the military institution. Indeed, our interviews showed us how in asserting its necessary control over its members, the Canadian military asserts analogous control over their wives.

Our research was informed by the feminist sociological methodology of institutional ethnography as developed by Dorothy E. Smith.[4] Institutional ethnographer's methodology builds on Karl Marx's theory of alienation—his understanding that those who have been excluded from "the making of ideology, knowledge, and culture" find themselves caught up in systems that define, without reflecting, their own lived experiences. An institutional ethnographer's first task is to discover disempowered persons' lived experiences in order to fashion these experiences into the ethnography's intellectual starting point. Its second task is to attempt to understand how these experiences reflect social relationships that though not superficially visible, comprise an important segment of the social formation's "relations of ruling."[5] One among many of these relationships of ruling is constituted by the social formation's military apparatus.[6]

Like many feminist methods, institutional ethnography rejects positivism's assertion that there is a detached position, uncontaminated by experience, from which social phenomena can be scrutinized. Institutional ethnographers follow the critique of positivism in asserting that since human beings are a part of what they observe, every observation is inevitably rooted in the observer's (or some other human being's) limited experience. Every investigation begins with particular assumptions, and these assumptions shape the investigation's results. Every investigation thus begins from a determinate place. No observer can avoid the responsibility of making a human choice about where this place shall be. The institutional ethnographer's human choice is to begin his or her research from the standpoints of the actualities of his or her subjects' lives. Needless to say, this epistemological stance is relativistic. From it one might be tempted to conclude that what the institutional ethnographer discovers is neither more nor less "true" than what is found by a researcher using traditional methods: Each perspective is equally valid. Yet, until recently women's perspectives have been so excluded from sociological research that institutional ethnographies should be valued for the enormous significance of the knowledge vacuums they fill.

Our quest to determine how the military asserts its control over wives was not confined to our interviews with the 112 wives. In order to understand the relationship of wives' work to the military organization, we needed to understand how wives' work contributes to the military, how the military makes sure that wives' work is done, and the overall place of wives' work within the military's structures and goals. Hence, after carrying out our interviews with wives, we reformulated their accounts as issues that we problematized during our subsequent interviews with forty-eight Canadian military members and civilian staff of military facilities. In the second stage of our research we interviewed military members in the same confidential, anonymous, open-ended, oral-historical way in which we had interviewed the wives. We obtained members' perspectives on the problems identified by the wives. We also learned what members' work means to them. We then continued to ascend the military hierarchy, interviewing, in a more focused and policy-oriented manner, military supervisors, social workers, padres (ministers), doctors, family support personnel, program administrators, high-ranking generals and, finally, the Deputy Chief of Defence staff. During this third set of interviews we learned about the Canadian military's priorities and forms of organization, and about how the military's priorities and forms of organization structure the way the military treats wives, tries to control wives, and benefits from wives' unpaid work. By the end of our research, we had made some specific discoveries about how military relationships of ruling are embedded in the everyday work experiences of Canada's military wives. The aspects of military organization that are highlighted in this chapter are therefore selective in the sense that they are the aspects of military organization that we found to be most relevant to the experiences of Canadian military wives.

MILITARY COMBAT READINESS

Accordingly, let us consider military organization. We begin with the imperative of combat readiness, which is the military's organizational job. Although components of combat readiness include equipment and skills, we will confine ourselves to its motivational side. To achieve and maintain combat readiness, the military must turn ordinary human beings into the kind of people who at any time can be mobilized to make war.[7] It must also motivate the wives of these people—the Canadian military is 90 percent male—to provide the necessary backup support.

The military's most important method of achieving these objectives is control. Human beings are not born to be combat ready, and despite being to varying degrees "pro-military," the civilian environment is not equipped to create combat readiness. Combat readiness must be nurtured in a total-institution environment,[8] where military recruits are segregated from civilians. During the eight weeks of basic training (seven weeks for officers), recruits exchange their old identities for the military uniform, haircut, and daily routines. They are humiliated, derogated, and emptied of the achievements of their previous lives by being told repeatedly that nothing they did prior to coming to boot camp was important. The vacuum created in recruits' self-esteem by this harassment is then filled with the new "combat-ready" identity that the military wishes to provide. Gradually, drill instructors replace verbal abuse with morsels of positive feedback until, at graduation, the recruits have learned to be proud of themselves in a whole new way. They have acquired a new set of skills and a new support system. They have also embarked on a distinctive new life that has begun to capture their most deeply rooted personal loyalties.

After basic and trades training, the total-institution environment continues in more diluted form as single members merge home with work by living in barracks on the base and many married members live on the base in Permanent Married Quarters (PMQs). Most Canadian members are also posted to a new location every several years to ensure that they will not establish strong civilian roots. Members participate in the military's distinctive rituals and traditions, such as parades and initiation rites. They wear a distinctive uniform. They consult military priests, doctors, lawyers, and social workers, rather than their civilian counterparts. They are taught to believe that civilians are incapable of understanding the military life, and they are encouraged to become more or less insular within the military world.

Encouraging military members to fraternize exclusively with one another relates to perhaps the most important mechanism of military control—combat bonding or combat unit cohesion. From the point of view of combat, if a member were to desert his unit when it was under fire, everyone else in the unit might die. Combat unit bonding exists to make sure that such a catastrophe could not happen, to make each military unit so cohesive that under the stress of combat its members would be psychologically prepared literally to die to save one another's lives.[9]

Bonding is crucial to the military culture and ethos. It is constructed and maintained by the military's separateness from civilians, its member-only social functions, its member-only absences for weeks or months on end (on courses, exercises, peacekeeping missions, or real combat), its rigid hierarchy, its insistence on blind obedience to superiors, its denial of such civic rights as union membership or political participation, and its general antipathy toward the civilian way of life. It is cemented by the expectation that unit members will drink together, by initiation rituals, and by celebrations of the characteristics that unite the members of the unit (and converse denigrations of categories of persons who are different) in preparation for the combat exigency of needing to denigrate and dehumanize the enemy. Cultural pluralism is considered hostile to the objectives of the combat unit. In the words of one member:

We had such a hassle over the Sikh coming in, because uniformity is the key....If you are not part of the team, you are not part of the team. It's nothing directed personally at you, it's just the way the unit operates—you are a part of us or you don't exist....And when you go to boot camp—same uniform, same haircut, same routine, same style—you are part of it. The best is having the same color, the same haircut, the same religion, the same color of eyes, the same height, the same weight. Because everybody outside of that—we don't like difference. (Interview 86)

The principle of exclusivity unites the members of a combat unit by dehumanizing members of so-called socially subordinate groups in preparation for dehumanizing the enemy. This dehumanization tendency accounts for the racist dehumanization rituals that "get out of hand" (such as the Somalia murder of Shidane Arone in 1993 by members of the Canadian Airborne Regiment). The exclusivity culture of the combat unit condones vicious treatment of certain categories of people because of the perceived contribution of in-group solidarity to bonding and combat readiness.[10] One of these categories of people is women. Like other gendered organizations, the military community takes for granted the naturalness of the patriarchal notion of a masculine-feminine polarity, or the idea that men and women[11] are fundamentally different. Relatively few members of this community question the patriarchal dichotomy between "tough warrior" men and supportive "dependent" women. The military uses its socially constructed polarity between masculine and feminine in order to use masculinity as the cementing principle that unites "real" military men in order to distinguish them from non-masculine men and women. During basic training, male recruits are challenged to become "real men" by proving that they are not women. Instructors encourage stereotypically masculine behaviors from recruits by using female-associated words to derogate them. Male recruits who perform well gradually earn the right to be addressed as "men," and it is the relief of having earned this right that often crystallizes their organizational loyalty. Excluding and derogating women are important aspects of combat unit bonding. The members of especially macho units celebrate their shared maleness by objectifying women, viewing pornography films, and joking about making women the targets of violence. Some of these "macho" unit members report deriving a similar pleasure from raping women to the pleasure they derive from killing.[12] Dehumanizing women and members of ethnic minority groups while celebrating white masculinity simultaneously draws members of combat units together and facilitates the characterization of members of the dehumanized groups as "the enemy," whenever this characterization becomes necessary or convenient. Combat readiness is believed by military commentators to be enhanced by these social psychological processes.[13]

Although military combat units are perhaps the most obvious examples of men in groups bonding together to condone violence against women, they are merely illustrative of a masculine phenomenon that is more general. Research on the influence of male peer support on men's abuse of women indicates that many non-military organizations in which men bond together closely, including fraternities and sports teams, also provide peer support to men who contemplate abusing and derogating women.[14]

Bonding unites the members of a combat unit. In a looser way bonding links present military members with the military members of the past, especially those who died in combat.[15] In the military's view, the risk of dying in combat is the major life circumstance that separates military members from civilians and bonds military members, past and present, tightly together. As one member puts it:

We are a society unto ourselves, and we do what we want. I don't have to go to a civilian doctor, dentist, lawyer or—and that's to make you look inward. You know what I am saying? Everything I need is in the armed forces, therefore I think of nothing outside. I mean, your thinking is nothing else.... It's the way we do things, it's parades, it's the Mess. It's all done that way to make the bonding this closely. The higher the risk job, the greater the call for the bonding. (Interview 86)

Although military authorities state otherwise when describing official policy, almost any practice is unofficially considered acceptable whose likely outcome is the solidification of bonds among combat unit members, the enhancement of their collective motivation to annihilate a foe, and the increased likelihood that under combat conditions they would stick together sufficiently to survive. Militaries all over the world have resisted integrating gays and women into their combat units because they have been afraid of the destabilizing effect that such integrations might have on the exclusivity that is the essence of combat bonding.[16]

Military organization is partially predicated on the derogation of women. The military nevertheless extends its principle of combat unit bonding to wives and children to extend its control to the members of military families and to condition these family members to cooperate and coordinate with the bonding among the men.[17] The well-bonded military unit takes the form of a patriarchal family, in which the commanding officer is called "The Old Man," his wife is called "The Mother Hen," and junior unit members are called "The Kids." Well-bonded units socialize together frequently, their wives and children become friends, and the families support one another during difficult times. Few civilians have experienced the speed and efficiency with which military units take up collections, provide home-cooked food, re-route planes, send flowers, visit hospitals, or mobilize limousines during an illness or other family crisis.

Wives are drawn in to their husbands' units through the social life, the hard times togetherness, the military's various family support programs, and the military rank structure, which encourages wives to participate in a parallel social system in which every wife's place relative to the other wives mirrors her husband's place in the ranked world of the men. Wives are also drawn into military bonding by default, since they too have been posted every several years, they too have not put down meaningful civilian roots, and they too have been encouraged to depend on the military community for their identities and often their paying jobs.

Wives are drawn into the military social world so that they themselves can be controlled by the military and can indirectly contribute to combat discipline among the men.[18] Military philosophy and three decades of military-sponsored social scientific research, especially in the United States, indicate that wives who are well integrated into the military community are less likely to complain, less likely to be a burden when their husbands are away on deployments, and more likely to contribute their efforts to the efficient functioning of the military system.[19] A Canadian general uses the example of a regimental wives' function to explain how wives are mobilized to facilitate the integration of other wives and to manage other wives' anxieties when their husbands are deployed. He summarizes:

The corporals' wives are there. And if they're doing their job properly and they get to know each other, there isn't too much turbulence. And you get to know them on a first name basis by these little groups and associations that these good units and stations and bases are running. When she has a problem she won't be afraid to phone Mary whatever-her-name-is, who's the master warrant officer['s wife].... And she'll get all kinds of tips and counseling from them. That is a very important contribution. (Interview 145)

Wives are primarily drawn in to the military by their labor. An important part of the military community's genderedness is the community's appropriation of the patriarchal ideology that the gendered division of labor is natural. Gendered labor is a cornerstone of the Canadian military community, in which it is taken for granted that every military wife will (1) assume 100 percent of the couple's domestic work and childcare responsibilities during the several months of the year her husband is away on deployments; (2) counteract the domestic destabilizing effects of her husband's absences by not seeking, or awarding high priority to, her own paid employment; (3) relinquish her own paid employment every time her husband is posted to a new place; (4) do most of the unpaid work associated with each new posting, such as packing, unpacking, house-hunting, and helping each of her children adjust to a new neighborhood, school, and peer group; (5) fill the vacuum created by her weak affiliation with the labor market by performing cheap—and often volunteer—work on military bases; and (6) in the case of senior officers' wives, devote a significant amount of time to entertaining, mentoring other wives, and representing the military in civilian charity work. The same general summarizes the vicarious dedication to the military effort that the Canadian military expects of wives:

Oh, spouses are in the military! If a person in the military marries somebody that doesn't understand that they are part of the military in the sense that they're going to have to move, and they're going to have to do a whole bunch of things that they normally wouldn't have to do if they married somebody who wasn't in a uniform, either the marriage breaks up or they're going to have to change their views. Because you're marrying an institution here! (Interview 145)

As a result of their frequent moves, military wives do not participate in the labor market on an equitable basis with their civilian counterparts. Their geographic mobility forces a disproportionate number of them into part-time or low-waged jobs and makes it difficult for the professionally qualified among them (e.g., teachers, nurses) to acquire seniority. Most military wives endure periods of involuntary unemployment and fail to make significant contributions to employer pension plans.[20]

However, the military regards much more favorably wives who contribute their volunteer efforts to military family support programs than it regards wives who secure well-paying jobs off the base and raise a ruckus when their husbands are transferred. The military heartily approves of wives who forego opportunities for good jobs off the base in order to donate their labor to the base community. As a Canadian army officer puts it:

I often say that there are several types of military wives. There are those wives that can't cope, never will be able to cope. There are those wives who couldn't cope and came up with a way to cope, which usually was to go out and remove themselves, start another career, move out of PMQs or whatever, and they generally learned how to cope and do not offer anything as a solution to the problem. And there are those women who have learned how to cope, who offer the solutions to the problems. (Interview 96)

From the military's perspective, then, many military wives do "offer the solutions to the problems." At enormous cost to themselves, they become and remain loyal to the military, they become well-bonded members of the military community, and they concede to the military's demands for their unpaid and cheap work.

OTHER ASPECTS OF MILITARY CONTROL

Combat bonding is not the only form of control exercised by the military over its members that has implications for civilian wives. Two other relevant forms of military control are the zero-sum nature of combat and the significance of combat morale.

Combat is predicated on a zero-sum model of control according to which success means assuming control over others in order to kill them or save their lives. The effectiveness of a military unit is often measured by its commander's ability to "take control." In the military's eyes, an order provided by a person in authority is often exactly what it takes to pull a whole unit out of life-threatening jeopardy. As a Canadian navy member explains:

In the Falklands, a ship got hit—got whacked. And the shock was so great, even though the guys weren't killed. I mean, you are talking maybe 600 or 900 pounds of explosives hit the ship—just picked the ship out of the water. And what they immediately did—they found later on—they took an executive officer, an engineer, and flew him over from the other ship, 'cause the guys were just in a daze. And then as soon as somebody got on there, started issuing orders, everybody immediately came back. And that's where the drill comes by, okay? "Somebody is in charge—I am going to be all right." (Interview 86)

Most persons who are abused by their intimate partners describe these abusers as obsessed with control. Although many abuse perpetrators who are obsessed with control are not members of the military, clearly the military is one of the organizational sites where controlling behavior is valued.

The military community is also a place where a member who is perceived to be unable to "control his wife" is threatened with loss of face. Obsession with control supplements the misogynist character of military bonding in helping to account for the relatively high frequency of woman abuse within the military community.[21] In addition, in the units that are operationally closest to combat, a shared cavalier attitude toward violence is considered necessary in order to convince each unit member that the others would be trustworthy enough not to flinch during the real thing.[22] A ganglike violent act is the occasional horrific outcome. We need only think of the murder of Shidane Arone in Canada or the collective sexual assault of women members at the American Tailhook military convention in 1991 in the United States. Family violence is another frequent situational spillover. A recent issue of the *New York Times* reports that in the United States one spouse or child dies each week at the hands of a military member relative. It cites data from a survey that indicate that one out of every three U.S. Army families has experienced domestic violence.[23] A recent U.S. study, which compared thirty army with thirty civilian couples, found that 23 percent of the military wives reported being battered, as opposed to only 3.0 percent of the civilian wives in the control group.[24] Other U.S. studies indicate that the rate of wife battering is especially high among military members in the combat-related trades.[25] During our interviews we heard so many shocking stories from women survivors of violent military marriages that we have every reason to believe that the Canadian situation is similar.[26]

Morale is considered important in the military; military morale is believed to vary positively with the degree to which the persons who give orders are perceived to merit the trust of the persons who obey. Consequently, covering up superiors' mistakes is often considered operationally justifiable. Military culture is rife with anecdotes about covering up: covering up for your buddy's mistakes (which recruits learn to do during basic training), covering up for your superior's mistakes, covering up for the military's mistakes, not letting the side down, appearing—to the external world—to be flawless. Like most other aspects of military culture, the flawless appearance imperative is linked with the military's preoccupation with control. As Mary Edwards Wertsch has observed:

A good military outfit is one that is prepared to control any situation, no matter what the variables. And, of course, a good military outfit should look and act at all times as if it is in tune with that mission. It's as though, in their polished appearances and rehearsed behavior, the warriors were saying, "Observe how we control ourselves, and you'll know we can control the enemy."[27]

Some of the most important aspects of military warfare are indeed psychological. In this context, the perfect appearance is crucial. The uniform that is

perfectly creased, the shoes that are perfectly shined, the tiny parts of the perfectly coordinated brigade that march in the parade square in perfect rhythm,
assembling soundlessly to confront and intimidate the foe. This perfect appearance, the coordination of 5,000 people raising their guns in unison, is choreographed to destroy the enemy's will. In military discipline, whatever needs to
be concealed to create that perfect appearance usually will be concealed because
like the cohesive combat unit, the perfect appearance is believed to be largely
responsible for saving combatants' lives. A navy member uses the example of
the 1991 Oka standoff between Canadian First Nations residents and military
personnel to explain how a formidable appearance is targeted at the enemy's
self-confidence:

Oka, okay? You show up with 5,000 troops—a brigade. Okay? What are you doing?
You are destroying their determination, their will to fight. . . . That's what you're doing.
That's sort of the reverse of self-esteem. That's what we are talking about. You show
up—overwhelming force. "You haven't got a chance." You just destroy their will.
(Interview 86)

Covering up to create this perfect appearance begins at boot camp, where
if one person in the squadron makes a mistake, everyone is punished, such
that it rapidly becomes clear to each squadron member that it is in his interests to cover up for the mistakes of his peers. Recruits subsequently learn to
cover up for the mistakes of their superiors. They have no choice in any case
because in a dispute between two versions of the same story, it is the superior's version that is believed. On one occasion we encountered during our
interviews, a non-commissioned member learned that his own child had
been sexually abused; he was forced to cover up for the officer who had done
it. On another occasion an air captain was commanded to do whatever it took
to get members to attend an unpopular dance so his colonel would not lose
face for having planned it. On another, a navy member who received a brain
injury from a superior during a brawl was told to keep quiet about the matter or face discharge.

According to Canadian military philosophy, persons who give orders must
appear infallible so their orders will be obeyed. This socially constructed infallibility is considered essential to the maintenance of unit morale and to the prevention of outbreaks of mutiny. A senior officer explains:

It's very important that you have confidence in your superiors because one day they
may ask you to do something very dangerous. And we train for war, we don't train for
peace. And so the whole thing, if you carry it far enough, it's all done because one day
you're going to need to call on that trust and confidence in your people. (Interview 26)

It is secrecy that largely preserves this constructed infallibility. This consideration helps to account for the military's organizational tendency to close
ranks after abuses have occurred. Analogously, each military member learns
that any problem with his personal life, if disclosed, might reflect negatively on

the external appearance and the internal morale of his unit. Despite the military's official stance that it "needs to know," members are discouraged from coming clean about their personal problems unless they are perceived to be falling down on the performance of their jobs. Hence, the member who is an alcoholic or who abuses his wife has every incentive to make sure that his wife keeps quiet.

Shame, fear of worse beatings, or her often accurate perception that no one in the community wants to listen gives the alcoholic's or abuse perpetrator's wife her own motivations not to tell. Such a wife is often a person who has moved every several years with the military member, has lost touch with her old civilian friends, and has come to believe that the military community and her husband's paycheck represent the only security she has. Such a wife may also realistically fear for her life. The wife who overcomes these fears and is courageous enough to seek help on the base often receives little help from military padres or social workers. These personnel have their own career motivations for keeping military bonding strong and continuing to support the member. Many of them also lack knowledge of woman abuse dynamics.[28] If the wife calls an off-base civilian professional, that person often refers her back to the military. Certainly one of the highest quality-of-life costs of combat readiness is the psychological isolation and physical vulnerability of the military wives who are abuse survivors.

ECONOMIC VULNERABILITY

Not all military wives are targets of woman abuse, of course. However, almost all military wives are made economically vulnerable by the vicissitudes of the military lifestyle. The military's often-successful efforts to encircle wives within combat bonding (described above) lull wives into the false sense of security of believing that the military will always look after them and that they will always belong to the military family. While married, the wife is encouraged to relax and settle into the predictable comforts afforded by the military community: fellowship, housing, built-in social life, and the sharing of a common world. She reckons that the risks involved in following her husband will be minimal because at every stop the military will provide continuity, familiarity, and a pre-selected circle of new friends. She feels that she can "go with the flow" because as a result of being free to do his job, her husband will be promoted, the family will benefit, she will be regarded as a career "asset," and the military will supply the rest. She is lulled into believing that what she is doing is not work or sacrifice but merely her bit for a community that is also doing its bit for her.

Within this mythical construction of "military as family," the military man is one of the country's heroic protectors whose job of "keeping Canada safe" is the most important job there is. His wife is his cherished consort who is honored to do her part, to put up with his six-month absences, put her own life on hold, follow him from posting to posting, and cope with the academic and emotional fallout of her children's continually changing schools and parting with friends. She is encouraged by the military to be proud of herself for not complaining and to find her own identity in the military community, rather than in the civilian world.

She is encouraged to believe that her commitment to playing a military support role should be as boundless as her husband's commitment to sustaining Canada's defense.

The Canadian wife whose marriage ends experiences a rude shock, however. Relative to civilian wives in the same predicament, she experiences phenomenal downward economic mobility, especially since during her marriage she is unlikely to have kept up her marketable skills or acquired any of her own assets or superannuation. Although she has made numerous sacrifices for the military, the separated wife is treated as if she had never worked for the military at all, as if she had been rendering a mere personal service to some ordinary inconsequential man.[29] At the moment of separation, military bonding reaches out to re-encircle the member at the same time as it conversely slams the door on his wife. A non-commissioned navy officer summarizes the military's attitude toward separated and divorcing wives:

We will actually try—if we know. We'll bend over backwards for you—for the wife. A guy's wife comes up and she's got a problem—her husband has to go to the Middle East—okay! We'll go out and shovel her sidewalks. We'll go and do all sorts of things— at least at my base. But if she was to be divorced, or separated, or leave, then she's left the mob. She's left the family. Boom! Bingo! That's the way it works. Because we look inward. I told you, we look inward. (Interview 86)

All militaries have been slow to recognize that the unpaid support work wives provide to the military is indeed work, that separated and divorced military wives deserve to be compensated for the military work they have done (and the opportunities for civilian work they have lost), and that a pension is deferred remuneration for both partners' work rather than property that belongs exclusively to the member.[30] Militaries have also been slow to acknowledge that a wife whose social anchor for years was the military community is, at the moment of her separation, a person who has been cruelly cut adrift. A former Canadian army wife summarizes how she felt when her marriage ended:

I had no identity. I wasn't me. I was somebody's something. Mrs. Chief Warrant Officer. You know? And I didn't realize. I thought that was what I was supposed to do. I really thought that was what I was supposed to do. Then suddenly I wasn't required any more. And I was wrapped up in the newspaper and put out like fish bones. (Interview 14)

The situation of the separated or divorced military wife vividly exemplifies the military's exploitative appropriation of wives' work.

MILITARY WIVES' RESISTANCE

Needless to say, there is a profound conflict between the imperative of combat readiness and the well-being of military wives. So unsurprisingly, despite the social isolation of the military community, the impact on husbands' careers, and the military's sophisticated methods of intimidation and control, some Canadian wives have found ways to overcome their alienation and resist.

Wives' methods of resistance have included challenging postings, privileging their own education and job prospects, persuading their husbands to request release from the military, opting out of military socializing, and mustering the courage to leave a husband who is an alcoholic or abuse perpetrator. At a more public level, the wives of some of the members deployed to the Persian Gulf tried to get their husbands' extra wartime pay allotted to them to help them keep their families functioning during a period of heightened stress. Some Canadian wives working at military family resource centers have tried to prioritize the actual needs of families over the military's desire to retain tight control over its family support programs.

Organized resistance among military wives has been rare. After all, wives are moved so often that strategic affiliations among them have little time to develop. The competitive structures of rank also incorporate wives and inhibit their potential alliances. Finally, most wives are so exhausted from the work of coping with the military lifestyle that they lack the energy required to become activists. Despite these obstacles, two recent rebellions of Canadian wives can be considered social movements in the sense of being collective, organized, public, and sophisticated in their use of communications media.

The first such movement, at CFB (Canadian Forces Base) Calgary in 1979, was prompted by the military's decision to stop charging members a flat rate for PMQ occupancy and to tie PMQ rents to local economies. PMQ occupants in Calgary were hit especially hard because the city's oil boom was producing inflated prices. Wages did not keep up with the rent hikes. A number of Calgary military members were pushed below the poverty line, which at the time was defined as needing to spend more than 61 percent of one's income on basic necessities.[31] Some members became eligible for welfare.

Despite fear of reprisals from the military, many wives mustered enough courage to complain to the media, and over 95 percent of the wives living in PMQs signed a petition that was sent to the minister of defense. As a result of the well-publicized protests against the Calgary rents, the military instituted an accommodation assistance allowance in areas of Canada that had a high cost of living. But the military took care to post the wives who had spoken out (and their husbands) away from Calgary almost immediately and did not send any two of them to the same place. The military also took full credit for the accommodation assistance allowance.

The most sustained instance of Canadian wives' organized resistance has been the Organization of Spouses of Military Members (OSOMM).

OSOMM originated in 1984 at CFB Penhold, where a group of wives began meeting informally to discuss how they might lobby for a family dental plan (until then, only armed forces members were covered), day care, pensions, and a safer traffic intersection. The wives believed that these improvements would help every family on the base, and they assumed the military would agree. After the wives had distributed their first newsletter about dental care, traffic intersections, and school lunchrooms, however, the base commander invoked the "political activity"[32] regulation and prohibited them from meeting on the base. His action was corroborated by a letter from the minister of defense. The wives were amazed, especially when they realized that base facilities were being used for a retired members' group lobbying for Ronald Reagan's Star Wars. These conservative women, who had always considered themselves part of the military "family," suddenly found themselves transformed into the enemy. When they threatened to continue distributing their newsletter without permission, military officials threatened to arrest them and evict them from their homes.

Contrary to its original intentions, the wives' group became a movement. Calling itself OSOMM, it responded to the letter from the defense minister by obtaining a Secretary of State Women's Program grant to establish off-base headquarters. OSOMM subsequently mushroomed into a national organization, received considerable notoriety in Parliament and the national media, and sponsored by LEAF (Legal Education and Action Fund), sued the Department of National Defence under the Freedom of Association and Equality sections of the Charter of Rights and Freedoms.

As part of their suit, the wives claimed that their inability to make decisions on issues that affected their daily lives amounted to discrimination on the basis of sex and marital status.

Many wives resigned from OSOMM because of the pressure the military put on their husbands. Nevertheless, the civilian publicity OSOMM received brought results. The wives eventually obtained a dental plan for dependents, a safer traffic intersection near Penhold, and a slightly relaxed definition of political activity on bases (Advisory Group to the Minister of National Defence, 1987).[33] Considering the tremendous insularity of the military community, as well as the military wives' then isolation from civilian feminists, the Penhold wives' accomplishment was immense.

In 1987 OSOMM established a special new chapter comprised of ex-wives who had lost, or were in danger of losing, their earned share of pension benefits. In 1990 OSOMM and four of the members of this chapter filed a second Charter of Rights and Freedoms suit against the Department of National Defence, alleging that certain provisions of the Canadian armed forces pension plans discriminated against spouses on the basis of sex and marital status. OSOMM's first lawsuit was dropped in 1991, when the military implemented a national Military Family Support program. But OSOMM's pension lawsuit is still going forward. OSOMM has continued to be a viable organization, which meets regularly, publishes pamphlets, raises funds, and maintains a national network of information and emotional support.

CONCLUSION

Military members readily admit that combat readiness is the ultimate reason for most of the policies that militaries implement and practice. Combat readiness requires militaries to exercise control over their members and to take organizational steps to ensure that they have secured their members' obedience and loyalty. We were guided to extract this information from Canadian military members by the experiences that had been related to us by their wives.

Militaries' control over their members is deemed to rely on a combination of military hierarchy, members' military organizational loyalty, and finally, on the deep personal bonding that happens within military units, especially the units devoted to combat. An important prerequisite of strong military bonding is believed to be cultural homogeneity; hence the fulfillment of this requirement often devolves into racism and sexism. An important characteristic of military community genderedness is combat units' celebration of masculinity and their converse denigration of women.

Control represents the military's main approach to its members; control is also the essence of what the military does. The zero-sum model of control practiced by the military provides positive rewards to military members who successfully exercise control over difficult situations; one such situation is an "uppity wife." Hence, in units devoted to combat, violence against women is specifically tolerated and fostered.[34] Despite its misogynistic tendencies, the Canadian military also expects organizational loyalty and bonding behavior from wives.[35]

The results of this expectation include the loyalty of many wives to the military, the enjoyment by many wives of the camaraderie of the military community, and the consequently greater difficulty experienced by abused wives who attempt to solicit military community support. In the military, obsession with unit morale often translates into the cover-up of problems; this consideration makes it difficult for survivors of violence to approach military human services personnel.

By "violence" we usually mean physical or psychological abuse. However, the inclusion of "appropriation" and "constraint" in the definition of *violence* that opened this chapter reminds us that our conceptualization of military family violence must be broader. The economic vulnerability of military wives and the economic plight of most separated and divorced military wives also qualify as violence, in the sense of appropriation or of constraints being "applied to some natural process" in order to "prevent its free development or exercise." The military lifestyle prevents most wives from earning a living in a manner commensurate with their abilities. Although the same economic vulnerability is true of many married women, the combination of the geographical mobility of the military, the isolation of the military community from the civilian world, and the quantity of unpaid services that the military extracts from wives makes the vulnerability of military wives extreme.

The recent resistances of Canadian military wives provide hope. However, unless militaries are forced to take responsibility for their violence toward members' wives, the organizational secrecy around this problem will prevail, and abused military wives will continue to suffer in intolerable isolation. The interest shown in the 1990s Somalia Inquiry demonstrated that the public finds unacceptable the Canadian military's view that its shortcomings are no one else's business. The aftermath of Somalia has subjected the actions of the Canadian military to renewed public scrutiny. If an opportune time ever existed to take action on woman abuse and other forms of violence inflicted on civilians in the Canadian military community, that opportune time exists right now.

ACKNOWLEDGMENT

This chapter originally appeared in Lori G. Beaman, ed., *New Perspectives on Deviance: The Construction of Deviance in Everyday Life* (Scarborough: Prentice-Hall, 2000), pp. 246–262. Reprinted with permission by Pearson Education Canada Inc.

NOTES

1. Lucie Laliberté, co-founder of the Organization of Spouses of Military Members (OSOMM), is a partner in the Ottawa law firm Gahrns & Laliberté, who practices in the areas of pensions and family law. She was a military wife for thirty years and is the mother of five children. Laliberté and I jointly collected all the data for this project, and she was the co-author of our book.

2. Our research was funded by the Social Sciences and Humanities Research Council Women and Work Strategic Grants Program (No. 882–91–0004). Former Minister of National Defence Hon. Kim Campbell gave us permission to interview several high-ranking members of the Canadian military. Former Associate Minister of National Defence Hon. Mary Collins and her assistant Deborah MacCulloch also provided advice and support. This article reworks some of the data we collected. See Deborah Harrison and Lucie Laliberté, "How Combat Ideology Structures Military Wives' Domestic Labour," *Studies in Political Economy* 42 (Autumn 1993): 45–80; *No Life Like It: Military Wives in Canada* (Toronto: James Lorimer and Co., 1994); and "Gender, the Military, and Military Family Support," in Laurie Weinstein and Christine White, eds., *Wives and Warriors: Women and the Military in the United States and Canada* (Westport, CT: Greenwood, 1997).

3. Approximately 60 percent of the spouses we interviewed were (or had been) married to non-commissioned members; 40 percent were (or had been) married to officers.

Approximately 40 percent of the members to whom our interviewees were (or had been) married were (or had been) in the army; 40 percent were (or had been) air element members; and 20 percent were (or had been) members of the navy.

4. See Dorothy E. Smith, "Institutional Ethnography: A Feminist Method," *Resources for Feminist Research* 15, 1 (1986): 6–13, and *The Everyday World as Problematic: A Feminist Sociology* (Toronto: University of Toronto Press, 1987).

5. Dorothy E. Smith, "Feminist Reflections on Political Economy," in M. Patricia Connelly et al., eds., *Feminism in Action: Studies in Political Economy* (Toronto: Canadian Scholars' Press, 1992), pp. 1–21.

6. C. Wright Mills, *The Power Elite* (New York: Oxford University Press, 1956).

7. lt. col. Dave Grossman, *On Killing: The Psychological Cost of Learning to Kill in War and Society* (Boston: Little, Brown and Co., 1995), p. 13.

8. In his *Asylums: Essays on the Social Situation of Mental Patients and Other Inmates* (New York: Doubleday, 1968), Erving Goffman defines a "total institution" as "a place of residence and work where a large number of like-situated individuals, cut off from the wider society for an appreciable period of time, together lead an enclosed, formally administered round of life."

9. Grossman, *On Killing*, pp. 148–155.

10. Ibid., pp. 156–170.

11. Cynthia Enloe, *Does Khaki Become You? The Militarization of Women's Lives* (Boston: South End Press, 1983); *The Morning After: Sexual Politics at the End of the Cold War* (Berkeley: University of California Press, 1993); *Maneuvers: The International Politics of Militarizing Women's Lives* (Berkeley: University of California Press, 2000).

12. Grossman, *On Killing*, pp. 136–137.

13. See David H. Marlowe, "The Manning of the Force and the Structure of Battle: Part 2, Men and Women," in Robert K. Fullinwider, ed., *Conscripts and Volunteers: Military Requirements, Social Justice, and the All-Volunteer Force* (Totowa: Rowan and Allanheld, 1983), pp. 189–199; F.H.K. Krenz, "Maclean's, Women in the Canadian Armed Forces," in *Final Report: The Army and the Nation, 1–2 October 1998* (Oromocto, N.B.: Canadian Forces Base Gagetown Combat Training Centre, 1999); and Major J. R. Near, "The Army's Self-Image–Actual and Potential," in *Final Report: The Army and the Nation, 1–2 October 1998* (Oromocto, N.B.: CFB Gagetown Combat Training Centre, 1999).

14. See M. Morris, "By Force of Arms: Rape, War, and Military Culture," *Duke Law Journal* 45 (1996): 651–781; and M. D. Schwartz and Walter S. DeKeseredy, *Sexual Assault on the College Campus: The Role of Male Peer Support* (Thousand Oaks, CA: Sage, 1997).

15. See Department of National Defence, *1994 Defence White Paper* (Canada: Minister of Supply and Services, 1994), in which Canada's refusal to continue to provide a combat-ready force to NATO was characterized as a betrayal of the "more than 100,000 Canadians [who] have died [over the past eighty years], fighting alongside our allies for common values" (p. 13).

16. The Canadian armed forces have always resisted changes in the composition of military personnel, or in military family structure, that would move toward greater

liberalism. The recognition of women in combat roles (1989), common-law marriages (1991), and gays and lesbians (1992) has occurred as a result of successful legal challenges under the Canadian Human Rights Act (combat) or the Charter of Rights and Freedoms (common law; gays and lesbians).

17. See Harrison and Laliberté, "Gender, the Military, and Military Family Support."

18. Enloe, *Does Khaki Become You?* p. 40. Also Harrison and Laliberté, *No Life Like It*, chap. 2.

19. See, for example, Seth Spellman, "Utilization of Problem-Solving Resources among Military Families," in H. I. McCubbin et al., eds., *Families in the Military System* (Beverly Hills: Sage, 1976), pp. 174–206; Frank Montalvo, "Family Separation in the Army: A Study of the Problems Encountered and the Caretaking Resources Used by Career Army Families," in McCubbin et al., *Families in the Military System*, pp. 147–173; Jerry L. McKain, "Alienation: A Function of Geographical Mobility among Families," McCubbin et al., *Families in the Military System*, pp. 69–91; Duncan M. Stanton, "The Military Family: Its Future in the All-Volunteer Context," in Nancy Goldman et al., eds., *The Social Psychology of Military Service* (Beverly Hills: Sage, 1976), pp. 135–149; H. I. McCubbin et al., "Family Policy in the Armed Forces: An Assessment," *Air University Review* 29, 6 (September-October 1978): 46–57; Dennis K. Orthner, *Families in Blue: A Study of Married and Single Parent Families in the Air Force* (Washington, DC: Department of the Air Force, 1980); R. Szoc, *Family Factors Critical to Retention* (San Diego: Naval Personnel Research and Development Center, 1982); Janet A. Kohen, "The Military Career Is a Family Affair," *Journal of Family Issues* 5, 3 (1984): 401–18; E. W. Van Vranken et al., *The Impact of Deployment Separation on Army Families*, Report NP-84–6 (Washington, DC: Walter Reed Army Institute of Research, 1984); Mady W. Segal, "The Military and the Family as Greedy Institutions," *Armed Forces and Society* 13, 1 (1986): 9–38; Dennis Orthner et al., "Family Contributions to Work Commitment," *Journal of Marriage and the Family* 48 (1986): 573–581; Joe Pittman et al., "Predictors of Spousal Support for the Work Commitments of Husbands," *Journal of Marriage and the Family* 50 (1988): 335–348; Gary Bowen et al., "Organizational Attitude toward Families and Satisfaction with the Military as a Way of Life: Perceptions of Civilian Spouses of U.S. Army Members," *Family Perspective* 23, 1 (1989): 3–13; Dennis K. Orthner et al., *Building Strong Army Communities*, Research Note 90–110 (Alexandria, VA: United States Army Research Institute for the Behavioral and Social Sciences, 1990); D. Bruce Bell et al., *The Army Family Research Program: Origin, Purpose and Accomplishments*, Army Project Number 2Q263731A792 (Alexandria, VA: United States Army Research Institute for the Behavioral and Social Sciences, 1991); Charlotte H. Campbell et al., *A Model of Family Factors and Individual and Unit Readiness: Literature Review*, Research Note 91–30 (Alexandria, VA: United States Army Research Institute for the Behavioral and Social Sciences, 1991); and Standing Committee on National Defence and Veterans Affairs, *Moving Forward: A Strategic Plan for Quality of Life Improvements in the Canadian Forces* (Ottawa: Department of National Defence, 1998).

20. Harrison and Laliberté, *No Life Like It*, chaps. 5 and 7; and Department of National Defence Canada Directorate of Social and Economic Analysis, *Operational*

Research and Analysis Project Report 712, Military Spousal Employment and Loss of Income (Ottawa: Department of National Defence, 1995).

21. See W. A. Griffin and A. R. Morgan, "Conflict in Maritally Distressed Military Couples," *American Journal of Family Therapy* 16, 1 (1988): 14–22; M. Thompson, "Armed Forces: The Living Room War," *Time* 143, 21 (23 May 1994): 48–51; C. Cronin, "Adolescent Reports of Parental Spousal Violence in Military and Civilian Familes," *Journal of Interpersonal Violence* 10, 1 (1995): 117–22; and R. E. Heyman and P. Neidig, "A Comparison of Spousal Aggression Prevalence in U.S. Army and Civilian Representative Samples," *Journal of Consulting and Clinical Psychology* 67, 2 (1999): 239–242.

22. P. D. Starr, "Military Socialization in the University: The Role of Subcultures in Navy-Marine ROTC," *Human Organization* 41, 1 (1982): 64–69.

23. See "Military Struggling to Stem an Increase in Family Violence," *New York Times* (23 May 1994).

24. Griffin and Morgan, "Conflict in Maritally Distressed Military Couples."

25. M. M. Brown et al., "Abusers of Clients of Women's Shelter: Their Socialization and Resources," *Journal of Sociology and Social Welfare* 8, 3 (1981): 462–470; Starr, "Military Socialization in the University"; P. H. Neidig, "Domestic Violence in the Military. Part II: The Impact of High Levels of Work-Related Stress on Family Functioning," *Military Family* (July-August 1985): 3–5; L. Baron and M. A. Straus, "Four Theories of Rape: A Macrosociological Analysis," *Social Problems* 34 (1987): 467–489; A. Shupe et al., *Violent Men, Violent Couples: The Dynamics of Domestic Violence* (Lexington, MA: Lexington Books, 1987); Z. Solomon, "The Effect of Combat-Related Posttraumatic Stress Disorder on the Family," *Psychiatry* 51 (1988): 323–29; L. J. Maloney, "Post Traumatic Stresses on Women Partners of Vietnam Veterans," *Smith College Studies in Social Work* 58, 2 (1988): 122–143; E. W. Gondolf et al., "Wife Assault among VA Alcohol Rehabilitation Patients," *Hospital and Community Psychiatry* 42, 1 (1991): 74–79; and Heyman and Neidig, "A Comparison of Spousal Aggression Prevalence in U.S. Army and Civilian Representative Samples."

26. See Muriel McQueen Fergusson Centre for Family Violence Research (University of New Brunswick) and RESOLVE Violence and Abuse Research Centre (University of Manitoba), *Report on the Canadian Forces' Response to Woman Abuse in Military Families* (submitted to the Minister of National Defence, May 2000). If, however, they were knowledgeable about woman abuse issues, military supervisors would be in a structural position to exercise a beneficial influence on the men who work under them. See Stephen J. Brannen et al., "Understanding Spouse Abuse in Military Families," in L. Martin et al., *The Military Family* (Westport, CT: Praeger, 2000), pp. 169–183.

27. Mary Edwards Wertsch, *Military Brats: Legacies of Childhood inside the Fortress* (New York: Random House, 1991), p. 34.

28. See *Report on the Canadian Forces' Response to Woman Abuse in Military Families*.

29. Dorothy E. Smith, "Women, Class and Family," in Varda Burstyn et al., *Women, Class, Family and the State* (Toronto: Garamond, 1985), pp.1–44; and M. A. Burke et al., "Falling through the Cracks: Women Aged 55–64 Living on Their Own," *Canadian Social Trends* 23 (1991): 14–17.

30. For a detailed discussion of the usual pension entitlement of the separated or divorced military wife, see Harrison and Laliberté, *No Life Like It,* chap. 7. After the book went to press, the regulations accompanying the new Pension Benefits Division Act were made public. As a result of lobbying by the Organization of Spouses of Military Members, they were subsequently modified to make the situation slightly more favorable for separated and divorced military spouses.

31. See "Troops on March to Welfare," *Calgary Herald,* 19 October 1979.

32. According to Queen's Regulations and Orders, Article 19:44, military members are not permitted to engage in "political activities," which include campaigning for political parties, displaying political signs during election campaigns, or signing political petitions. The definition of political activity is largely left to individual base commanders.

33. Under the new rules, meetings that the base considers "political" may now be held inside individual PMQs, but not anywhere else on the base.

34. See especially M. Morris, "By Force of Arms: Rape, War, and Military Culture."

35. See Harrison and Laliberté, "Gender, the Military, and Military Family Support."

Chapter 7

Masculinity in Work and Family Lives: Implications for Military Service and Resettlement

Samantha Regan de Bere

INTRODUCTION

This chapter is based on the view that naval personnel relate to naval institutions to the extent where military discourses may be used as personal frames of reference in everyday life. Such discourses may influence personal and group attitudes and behaviors and, therefore, experiences of both service life and resettlement into civilian worlds. More specifically, the chapter is concerned with the ways in which elements of naval discourse are consistently informed and maintained through underlying notions of a distinctively military masculinity, as well as the ways in which naval identity informs particular notions of what it is to be masculine. The analysis presented is drawn from the findings of research carried out on a sample of naval leavers in Plymouth between the years 1995 and 1998, as well as ideas generated by related literature.[1]

Literature has long focused on the identity-producing nature of work organizations and careers;[2] the relationship between masculinity and identity is one of central importance in cultural and identity studies.[3] The research presented here was originally designed to capture experiences of coping with resettlement and career change among naval leavers,[4] but masculine identity arose consistently as a central concern for both servicemen and their wives.

Discussions about joining and remaining in the navy focused heavily on "masculine" identity formation and personal pride, and this was paralleled in discussions about leaving. It would appear that naval life offers men a sense of identity and personal fulfilment, regardless of personal social backgrounds or employment histories. Although interviews highlighted variations between men's motivation for joining and remaining with the navy, one theme was constant: being a naval man. Moreover, the naval man identity was invariably saturated in notions of military masculinity and, more specifically, the idea of the macho serviceman positioned against the less masculine civilian.

So how exactly are masculine naval identities created? What processes affect their maintenance or transformation, and what implications does this have for the experience of the service career and the process of resettlement into civilian life?

DISCOURSES, IDENTITIES, AND MASCULINITY IN THE MILITARY

In discussing masculine identity formation and transformation in military cultures, we are concerned with the role of meaningful ideas and practices in a distinctive area of social life. Depending on the social context within which we find a man, he may be a serviceman or he may be a father, a sportsman, a husband, and so on. The identity of a man is contingent on the social situation and the particular type of social discourse that assigns meaning of "being" to him at that particular moment in time.[5] Put plainly, compatible ideas, values, and ideologies may be articulated into various discursive frameworks or "interpretative repertoires" that help inform identities in different ways, at different times, and in different contexts.

Howarth (1995) refers to discourses as "systems of meaning" that "shape the way people understand their roles in society and influence their activities... the concept of discourse involves all types of social and political practice, as well as institutions and organisations within its frame of reference."[6] People's attitudes and behaviors in different situations are directed by knowledge and practices derived from particular institutionalized discourses, that is, systems of meaning or frames of reference. Many career situations provide this wider frame of reference, constructing identities and appropriate attitudes and behaviors around the work role.

Janowitz (1960) remarks that a form of "doctrination" to military organizational discourses occurs in the military, effected through the "daily routine of military existence" and resulting in the formation and maintenance of military identities.[7] The military has its own institutions for training and continuous socialization, in which the person's work is felt to be his or her whole life,[8] and where the "presenting self" of new recruits is effectively destroyed as they are immersed in the naval routine and separated from the outside world. Many servicemen come to value this separation and develop a sense of pride and self-esteem in their new and different role. Indeed, it is this separation and symbolic differentiation that helps to maintain naval identities both in work and out.

This argument is adopted by Morgan in his exposition of hegemonic military masculinity, where he suggests that "the informal cultures that elaborate in the course of military training and beyond... are linked to strong and hegemonic definitions of masculinity."[9] Here, certain notions of masculinity are dominant in military culture, excluding, for example, the interests and acceptability of women and homosexuals. Morgan proposes that hegemonic masculinity is strengthened by two key factors: boundedness (from wider civilian society) and the pervasiveness of military values (into civilian society).

In relation to the former, he refers to the boundedness of the military in terms of Goffman's "total institutions."[10] Indeed, the British armed services may appear to share some common features with total institutions whereby institutional members are isolated from the wider society, although this definition refers mainly to army communities. Certainly, all military institution are bounded to varying degrees by their very nature: The need for an element of secrecy and, often, safety to members of the public mean military facilities and civilian society are kept at arm's length both socially and geographically.

However, to say with confidence that the various military represent total institutions as Goffman defines them is problematic. Recent developments in relation to the civilianization of some traditionally military tasks, and the introduction of civilian personnel to military organizations, has had some impact on the boundedness of the military, as has the trend toward household owner-occupation in civilian areas.[11] Access to the outside civilian world, though sometimes difficult, is hardly restricted in a total sense, although the exception is perhaps the time spent on ships at sea in the Royal Navy. Nevertheless, the high degree of isolation of service personnel is important in terms of socialization and the internalization of service culture, and, as such, boundedness does have some resonance here.

The issue of pervasiveness relative to Britain's armed forces is perhaps less straightforward. In militaristic societies, military cultures will be visible to all and relevant to military personnel and civilians alike. However, in British society, pervasiveness is less extensive. Despite recent media coverage and fly-on-the-wall documentaries of military life, military institutions remain something of an unknown quantity to many in civilian life, even in towns with a strong military presence.[12] Nevertheless, pervasiveness does appear to be highly relevant in terms of the extension of military discourses to the private sphere of families and kinship-friendship networks.

The British military forces are organized around predetermined schedules, codes, and disciplines that inevitably extend into the private worlds of their members to the extent where the boundaries between work and home are often indistinguishable. The military career, along with its associated discourses, is extended into many different aspects of servicemen and women's lives, often at the cost of their personal privacy and freedom. It is therefore pertinent to consider that discourses represent controlling aspects of military culture and organization.[13]

Foucauldian critical discourse analysis is concerned precisely with the ways in which discursive formations refer to systematic bodies of ideas that claim to produce valid knowledge about the world.[14] In so doing, discourses present a particular reality that serves the interests of those who formulate or direct them (in this case, promoting the hegemony of the military institution over its members). This is a persuasive argument when the demanding nature of the military organization is taken into account, even more so when its members may be required to put their lives on the line for it. It also holds support for Morgan's notion of hegemonic masculinity, where distinctive notions of masculinity are used to inform and direct particular attitudes and behaviors at the expense of other, less appropriate ones.

The relevance of hegemonic masculinity cannot be overstated here. The very notion of the warrior in classical militarism provides us with a key symbol of masculinity, one that endures despite social, political, and technological developments in modern warfare and peacekeeping. The integration of women, the acceptance of homosexuals, and the aforementioned civilianization of the military may have changed certain aspects of military culture, but there is little real evidence to suggest that the traditional links between masculinity, combat, and protection have been completely severed.

Fallowes (1981), calling for "ethical reform" and "rededication to military values," highlights the importance of controlling military discourses to the very survival of the military.[15] Fallowes' perspective is germane not just in terms of values, discourses, and hegemony. He also relates military effectiveness to traditional notions of male camaraderie, hierarchy, social usefulness, male career centrality (prioritized over the careers and familial roles of service family members), and social networks, all of which have masculine overtones. Along with Parker,[16] Jolly, and many other writers, Fallowes emphasizes the battlefield context in discussing naval identity, socialization, and military hegemony.

The relevance of the battlefield context to this argument is that many battles are fought exclusively by men. The organizational structures of the military services make for difficult integration of women into their various branches, and some do not allow women at all.[17] Several works have portrayed the military as being deliberately "masculinist,"[18] and the very notion of war is one loaded with masculine conceptions, where fighting and masculinity are terms often used interchangeably.[19] Enloe (1983) suggests that combat is often perceived as the ultimate test of man's masculinity.[20]

Of course, in wider civilian society men often engage in, and enjoy, a masculine image. However, servicemen have been perceived as particularly notorious in the popular imagination. Goldman and Stites (1982) explore the origins of such imagery, pinpointing the camp followers of past times and the continuing organized provision of prostitution.[21] Bunyard (1995) discusses the ways in which servicemen "prove themselves" in their participation in brothel visits and strip-shows,[22] whereas Hearn and Parkin (1993) note the masculinity boasted of in war chants.[23] Feminists argue that these processes serve to maintain and perpetuate an environment built on male autonomy, saturated with images of masculine identity.[24] Others, such as Parker or Fallowes, argue that masculine cultures and identities are essential to military effectiveness.

According to much literature, then, the masculine culture of the military is based on its organizational structure, determined through military objectives, and masculine identities are necessary products of naval occupational socialization. Notwithstanding these contentions, it is clear that masculinity and masculine identities are as embedded in military life as strategies, tactics, and technology, and efforts must be made to analyze servicemen's perceptions, feelings, and behaviors in terms of the masculine military discourses within which they occur. To this end, the author has reviewed interview data derived from 60 interviews with service personnel and their partners.[25]

MILITARY MEN AND THEIR RELATIONSHIP WITH NAVAL DISCOURSE

Various symbolic characteristics have been assigned to the military, including isolationism, conservatism, collectivism, loyalty, discipline, hierarchy, and traditionalism.[26] Articulation of these elements unifies a series of ideological, political, economic, and social elements, each having no essential meaning to military life on its own, into a military discourse. Therefore, through years of practice by Royal Navy service members, a particularly naval discourse may become normalized, providing a naval discursive framework to which personnel and their families are able to refer in the course of their everyday lives.

In terms of my own research findings, it is possible to identify a naval discourse that informed identities and gave men a sense of who they were, who others were, and how they should interact with others. Respondents referred to the processes of initiation and training that had helped them to develop their naval identities, and most had clearly gained some sense of pride in belonging to a particularly naval group, identifying themselves through their difference from civilian others. There appeared to be a particularly naval way of approaching life, with specific emphasis on military masculinity and personal pride.

Respondents described what they held to be typical naval ideas and approaches to life, and several themes recurred throughout the research: loyalty and camaraderie, status and hierarchy,[27] rules and regulations, order and effectiveness, male-centered social lives, demonstrations of machismo, traditionalism, and an "us and them" perspective toward civilian men. Underlying all these themes were constant references to masculinity and male identity. We can view such ideas as representing elements of a particularly naval discourse through which naval life can be understood and conducted in the "appropriate" manner.

For example, men explained how male-centered tribalism and loyalty were important in maintaining the collectivism or camaraderie imperative to their organization. Isolationism, or the "us and them" perspective, valued by many members, helped sustain collectivism and attitudes toward appropriate male identities, and "male bonding sessions"[28] enhanced this. Moreover, patriarchy, essential in maintaining the centrality of the service career to men's families as well as the extension of hierarchy into the family sphere, was bolstered by the machismo and male-centered social elements of naval discourse.

Conservatism and traditionalism made it possible for men to close off from alternative discourses, protecting masculine discourse from radical change despite change in circumstance. For example, where men considered the more recent changes in the global political climate and no longer viewed themselves as protectors or warriors, many derived their pride from the fact that they were now useful in their capacity as peacekeepers, still providing what they viewed as a masculine role within society.

Masculinity in naval discourse, then, includes peacekeeper/warrior or "socially useful" identities, physical fitness and stamina, breadwinner status in hierarchical, patriarchal family formations, and macho social lives based on all-male company, pseudo-aggression toward other ranks and civilians, sexually laden banter and frequent alcohol binges. All this, within the overall context of a hegemonic masculinity that prompts negative attitudes toward civilianization and female integration.

Day-to-day training resulted in a "layering on" of masculine ideas and meanings, this process being reinforced through both naval organizational protocol and symbolic social etiquette. Put more crudely, masculine principles of naval discourse were exposed, internalized, and eventually viewed as natural reactions to service life. The concept of the masculine naval man was therefore naturalized over time, and interview data show how, for many respondents, this resulted in the internalization of certain attitudes and behaviors that became routinized in everyday life. Indeed, many respondents were unable to remember the origins of certain attitudes and behaviors until prompted by their wives or partners.

This analysis does not, therefore, lend itself to the argument that service personnel draw consciously on naval discourses. Although it does appear that distinctly naval discourses are made available, their deployment is not necessarily deliberate. It might be suggested that personnel more accepting of naval discourses had practiced some form of cognitive dissonance, whereby inconsistencies between previous attitudes and the realities of service life were reconciled by switching to alternative "naval" attitudes. That is, it could be argued that men and families used discourses as a way of rationalizing their dependence on the navy and that therefore such discourses were less attractive to them personally, yet they provided a useful way of explaining their own (controlled) behavior once in service.

Of course, the naval contract does force adherence to naval discourse to some extent. However, its influence was enhanced where men personally found discourse relevant to their own lives. Indeed, variability occurred throughout the interview accounts, and levels of dependence on naval discourses varied among different groups of individuals within my sample.

So, although socializing practices may have been played out on servicemen and their families, not all were successfully or completely institutionalized. Consistency and inconsistency were evident in all people's lives, but what is of relevance here are the ways in which they were used as argumentative or rhetorical strategies through reference to various discourses. It was clear that almost all the respondents had drawn on masculine naval discourse as a frame of reference through which to conduct their work, but some embraced it more enthusiastically than did others. Some individuals drew heavily on masculine discourse, whereas others drew more extensively on alternative gender discourses. For these men, reference to masculine discourse had led to the development of strong male naval identities.[29]

"It's all very male...very macho...it's the perfect environment for it."

I guess I felt a bit of a hero...serving Queen and country...thought it made me a man, would get me the girls!"

"It draws you in and makes you someone...gives you a sense of pride."

Where key elements of such discourses had been internalized, men employed them in order to understand their lives, inform decision making, and justify action. Those drawing most heavily on naval discourse were able to adapt most comfortably to service life. These were commonly men whose lives were conducted around the central naval breadwinner role, and whose involvement with the navy, both inside and outside working hours, was high. Many of these men had very little contact with civilian life in any sense. Most of the single men surveyed were located in this group. Others were married to women who felt personally involved in the navy and who, in some cases, had developed their own female service identities as service wives.[30] Therefore, both men and women in these more involved groups embraced naval family and gender discourses with a certain enthusiasm and expressed more satisfaction with service life in general. It was these individuals who often felt the naval career offered everything they required in life.

Yet, there were men who drew less on masculine discourse, developing strategies for drawing on different discourses in their day-to-day lives. These individuals were typically more exposed to civilian life than those in the involved groups. They were more likely to have a mixture of service and civilian friends, as well as more gender-balanced social lives, and to reside in mainly civilian localities and not in naval quarters. Further exposure to contemporary gender attitudes resulted from wives' participation in civilian labor markets.

"It's not really nice for wives to put up with ... especially if they've got their own jobs to think about."

"I think younger wives are demanding better treatment these days."

Since this less-involved group conducted part of their lives, at least in a social sense, with civilian contemporaries, they had become familiar with contemporary gender discourses and had drawn on them to make sense of certain features of their lives. However, incompatibility between masculine discourse and more civilianized lives within the less-involved group soon became clear. In particular, the problems posed by naval discourse in directing life in the private sphere of the family had resonance for the experience of service life as a whole.

GENDERED NAVAL DISCOURSE AND FAMILY LIVES

Military organizations are able to exercise a considerable element of control through discourses about military families. Military life is one that has been viewed as traditional, conservative, and patriarchal, where wives are expected to derive pride and fulfilment from their own involvement in service life. However, developments toward greater social equality and dual-career households in civilian society have had some impact on the attitudes of service wives toward their own naval roles. Although there are many practical benefits to be gained from the service lifestyle, women have begun to question traditional military family roles, and conflict between the military career and the family is often the result.[31]

Reviewing the research findings, it became evident that the naval career extended quite considerably into men's family and personal lives. Some families had come to view themselves as naval families, demonstrating the impact of naval life on the identities of other family members. Although accounts differed, several key characteristics of a "perfect naval wife" became evident, including: an ability to complement and support the husband in his position, observance of rules and codes in relation to dress and self-presentation, the capacity to effectively manage domestic arrangements made more difficult by frequent husband absence, the ability to act as two parents during separation and to allow the serviceman to resume his role on return, and the forming of naval friendships with other service personnel, particularly their wives.

"There are certain ways a naval wife should act."

"Naval wives should complement their husbands."

Because of the required centrality of the naval role, family members were accorded different identities and positions in the household, and the importance of the naval identity enabled men to maintain considerable status within a gender-based hierarchical family network. Men's participation in the domestic sphere was minimized by their naval breadwinner status,[32] whereas women's participation came solely to represent the role of housewife and, in most cases, mother. A number of women had withdrawn from labor markets in order to accommodate their housewife and mother identities. Both husbands and wives tended to naturalize such arrangements, and , in many cases doing so did reinforce normative gender service wife and serviceman identities.

"There's no room for two careers...I wouldn't have time, what with this lot and him to look after!"

"You need to have a wife who can handle domestic management competently."

"We've settled into this way of life...you undoubtedly think that sexist, but it works for us."

Gender discourses also permeated families' social networks. Although the macho elements of naval culture did not always sit comfortably with family life, men were often expected to socialize with "the boys," even when they had just returned from long periods of absence. Male-centered friendship networks appeared to be influential in maintaining a sense of belonging to a naval group and in defining and perpetuating the "naval way" among some servicemen and families.

Husband: "They arrange something the first night back after three months away...but you want to be with your family."

Wife: "You get called a few names for not going."

Levels of belonging, however fostered, will differ. It is not simply a case of those who accept and those who don't: A complex of issues is pertinent here. Jolly argues that many wives do not wholly embrace the traditional image of the archetypal service wife and family.[33] Jessup explains: "It would be wrong to say that this pattern of social assistance was entirely voluntary. Beneath the spirit of altruism and the undeniable mutual benefits lurked also the anxiety that failure to participate would damage the careers of service husbands."[34]

This contention was borne out by my research findings. Adherence to naval discourses and the development of fully naval identities were by no means consistent among the sample. Once again, two broad family types emerged from the data: those who had been more involved with service life and drew more extensively on gendered naval discourse, and those who had maintained more links with civilian life and according discourses. Furthermore, the involved families were generally more able to adapt successfully to the military way of life than their less-involved counterparts.

"It's easier if you just accept it...there's a lot there for the taking, if you want it."

"It's like a bigger family...it's all men together...and there's stuff for the women while the men are away."

"When you see him on passing-out parades you feel so proud...you feel part of it yourself."

Where naval discourse had been dominant in involved families, there tended to be fewer antagonisms. A particularly gendered lifestyle had often become naturalized, where differential identities became organized according to different gender characteristics in a hierarchical context. Women's internalization of

naval gender discourse appears to have resulted from their involvement with
the navy in the capacity of proud naval wives Although wives' identification is
arguably based on the more social aspects of naval life, this may nonetheless
represent the internalization of naval gender discourses by other members of
servicemen's families, making easier men's reference to, and realization of,
naval notions of masculinity.

"Naval wife was pretty much my whole identity."
"It's like being a serviceman, but without doing the job!"

By contrast, the centrality of the service career over family life was often
problematic for less-involved families. Many less-involved men found that
their identity as full-time servicemen was not compatible with their identities
as husbands and, particularly, fathers. Their subsequent withdrawal from male-
centered social life and service-centered networks caused problems for some
men in other aspects of their life because in failing to demonstrate sufficient
levels of male-centered camaraderie and independent macho behavior, they
were viewed as being less loyal.

"You have to ... stand up and take the flack for it ... it's not macho to wanna be with the
wife now, is it? Well, it is for certain things, I suppose!"

Many less-involved wives found it difficult to identify with traditional naval
gender discourses, objecting to familial and social relationships that were hierarchically organized around male interests, and this had implications for stability in family life. Often compromise was the answer, but in some cases these
problems were irreconcilable. Men were often forced to choose between their
careers or their wives-partners.

Furthermore, changing parenting discourses had begun to challenge more
traditional notions of masculinity that had emphasized the role of the detached
father and justified intermittent absence and immersion in naval adult male social activities. Some men described how they had applied "naval principles" to
parenting their children, assuming primary responsibility for discipline and en-
forcing what they themselves perceived as over-disciplinarian regimes in the
family. Separation was increasingly viewed as clashing with most efforts to
fulfil what men saw as natural father identities.[35] For some, incompatibility
between military and father identities generated antagonisms that became in-
surmountable. "Unnatural" and "old-fashioned," naval parent identities were
cited often by those leaving service voluntarily.

It is fair to conclude that for all the antagonistic features of naval and civilian
discourses, most were managed through well-developed coping strategies, but
combining gendered naval and parenting identities represented an issue that was
for many individuals problematic, and for some irreconcilable. Notwithstanding
these issues, when faced with career change and resettlement, almost the entire
sample found leaving service life a difficult, and often traumatic, process.

MEN, CAREERS, AND FAMILIES: MASCULINITY AND CHANGE

We have seen how the naval career may involve subordination of the self to the requirements of military life. If this is the case, then what happens when a service leaver departs military service? What are the implications for masculine identity in becoming a civilian? Most military leavers have access to high-quality resettlement training and advice on housing needs, financial matters, and job search. Retraining is plentiful for those who wish to avail themselves of the opportunity,[36] and psychological counseling is often included. However, little is said about the impact that leaving the military institution has on masculine identity.

The adaptation of identity to a new employment, or unemployment, situation is imperative to successful resettlement. The consequent rebuilding of an appropriate alternative self-image is not a straightforward process, however. It involves a transformation of the multiplicity of elements that together make up an individual's identity. The maintenance of identity relies on particular perceptions of life; of self-image, of work and family relationship, of behavior, attitudes, and responsibilities.[37] Redefinition of internalized notions of self is complex and has often been regarded as synonymous with struggle, whereby identities must disengage from the previous situation before embarking on another.

For every serving man and woman, much time, energy and money is given over by the military to create and sustain a military persona. This research demonstrates that the military persona is built upon notions of masculinity; we could therefore expect that when a person leaves the service, this masculine self-image is inevitably eroded. But there is no assistance with discarding this military persona, nor any help in building the necessary new social identity. If this task is to be accomplished, it is to be accomplished only by the servicemen or women themselves, as well as, perhaps, by their families and friends.[38]

This is an important point, particularly when the ritualistic and symbolic nature of naval life and discourse is taken into account. Men had regarded rituals and ceremony as the symbolic confirmation of the usefulness of their own masculine role. For this reason, some were confused and others exhibited feelings of self-doubt. Some interviewees also felt frustrated, disappointed, or resentful about the absence of any rite of passage, especially when they had viewed ceremony as a valuable feature of service life that bolstered firm, proud masculine identities. It is worth pointing out that the erosion of self-worth, confusion, and disappointment or resentment appeared to hinder successful adaptation.[39]

"I've got used to being a naval man...it's not just a change of job."

"You're losing your whole identity...an identity which makes you feel proud...and then some scrawny young wren hands you your ID papers and you're not what you were...it's not good."

"I felt that I had outlived my usefulness and was being dumped."

Reflecting previous studies,[40] leavers attempted to secure employment that was compatible with the discourses on which they had previously drawn, and they clustered into three main areas: management,[41] engineering, and the emergency services. This can perhaps be explained as the transference of technical skills to similar work. However, selection of employment types appeared, at least in part, attributable to similarities in a social and cultural masculine sense. If we look at the types of employment men sought—such as emergency services, the coast guard, probation services, the nursing profession, and teaching—it becomes clear that these are jobs that provide a service to the general public, rather than individualistic careers in the much-talked-about rat race.

What is important here, in terms of the social and cultural aspects of work, is that the service-centered segments of the labor market represent sectors that are based on values, and not profit. It is understandable that service leavers sought such work, particularly when we consider the masculine pride they had always derived from their naval values, camaraderie, and perceptions of social usefulness, not to mention the often-cited masculine appeal of a dress uniform.

"The navy fills an important role ... it gives you self-worth ... I won't find that again."

"There's something about a sailor that fills you with pride ... that will change."

"I know he'll be the same person out of uniform ... but it wouldn't be so special."

Other leavers felt able to make more conscious changes in their lives. This tendency appeared to be more characteristic of the less-involved interviewees. At the extreme, there were interviewees who had never been able to relate successfully to naval discourse, and most of these individuals felt confident about resettlement. Less-involved individuals had also demonstrated more willingness to change what they interpreted as masculine values and to redefine their sense of worth in this respect, albeit to varying degrees. Six months after leaving the navy, men were generally beginning to redefine their masculinity according to their new roles. However, many interviewees described suffering what they perceived as identity crises, commonly characterized by an inability to disengage and resocialize to new masculine identities.

"I'm not sure who I am ... let alone what I'm supposed to do!"

"It's hard for the guys who eat navy, drink navy, sleep navy ... and then they're not navy ... but they still are in a sense, because they can't let go."

Let us consider such crises. In order to make sense of civilian life, some effort has to be made to change discourses and related behaviors.[42] Since masculine discourses had been so heavily sedimented and naturalized, it is not always possible to recover their origins and overwrite them. New discourses and redefinitions of identity have to be learned or internalized over time. The service leaver stands on the frontier of military and civilian discourses, attempting to draw on elements of both, but not sure to which he should refer and how he should refer to them in order to understand the changes taking place in his life.

Not all the men had been able to resocialize and assume a new masculine identity from new civilian roles. It appeared from interviews that those still perceiving themselves as naval men had faced more problems; for some, re-forming identities had become an extended period in the life cycle. Many reported struggling to come to terms with their perceived emasculation, and threats to masculinity were the most often cited aspects of identity crisis. These were particularly marked where leavers were forced to confront changes in the family lives that had for so long been influenced by the naval career. Adaptation of naval families to civilian life required extensive and complex change on social, psychological, and practical levels.

First, established masculine (and, to a lesser extent, feminine) identities often came under attack, particularly where men and women had adapted to identities that were organized through naval discourse. Once out of the navy, most men found that their new employment required less centrality, involved less or no absence, and, as a consequence, enabled family roles to be renegotiated through more contemporary notions of gender.

"I try to do more around the house now. It's not so much fun for me, but I've no doubt she likes it!"

"I have more time because I'm not out with the boys all the time ... if they could see!"

"Well, why should she do it all now the career is gone?"

Many men had left precisely in order to spend more quality time with their families. On return to the family home, however, some expressed feelings of dissatisfaction and sometimes frustration. Positions began to be redefined based on the new, non-naval situation, and adapting involved re-defining the acceptable in terms of gender attitudes and behaviors. Where behaviors resulting from reference to old naval discourses were not wholly incompatible, they appeared to be accepted. However, where particularly gender-based naval attitudes and behaviors were inappropriate for civilian family or life, they required adaptation. Many men described facing some form of identity crisis as they struggled to define their new masculine role within the family.

"I felt like a bit of a spare dick ... well, I did, I felt excluded sometimes."

"I expected to have a little more authority and respect, but I realized that I had to earn it first."

Crises were particularly common where women had been able to return to work and become breadwinners as well as housewives and mothers. Men described how they had experienced a sense of disappointment and emasculation through losing or sharing their previous identity as a provider. This is important when it is considered that most men reported downward occupational mobility on leaving the navy.[43]

"I felt insecure at not providing...it's probably my age, but that's what a man does...or what he feels he should do...and it's definitely what 'men in blue' do."

"I'm not 'the man' of the house anymore, am I? She can cope without me, and I don't bring in the money...well, we both do now, but it's not the same."

Men expected adaptation to civilian parenting to come easily, with little effort, and they expressed much disappointment here, as well as confusion over their masculinity. This is an important point, considering that it was the father role that men found most difficult to adapt to their naval identities, and the reason that most offered for their leaving. When they had given up their careers, it was parenting issues that had reaffirmed their decisions to leave and provided a sense of confidence in their choice. Where adapting to their children was a difficult task, men were clearly upset and spoke again of emasculation.

"I've been a bit macho about it all in the past...I think it's good in some ways because it makes them more outgoing, but I can't be like that now...I have to be (how do you put it?)...more touchy...touchy-feely [laughs]...yeah, touchy-feely...it doesn't come easily!"

"I have always been the proud father, but a bit distant, if you know what I mean. That doesn't work now, which I feel slightly bitter about."

"I've had to change my attitudes to what a father is...mmm...what he does...what I do...I've been less authoritarian...and I suppose I've had to work for more respect from the kids by being with them more...like she does."

In most cases, although certainly not all, this stage was temporary as men began to draw on alternative, more contemporary parenting discourses. Most expended more efforts on developing deeper relationships with all members of their families. In contrast to the detached disciplinarian father, masculinity in parenting often became associated with close, open relations. Within six months of leaving most men reported an increased closeness to their children. Many expressed the feeling that rather than being an emasculating experience, higher levels of participation in their children's lives enhanced their feelings of masculinity in their new civilian worlds.

In addition to changing family-based notions of masculinity, men began to adapt to new jobs and careers, learning new occupational discourses. Gradually they began using them to come to terms with change and develop new, perhaps different, perceptions of masculinity with which they could identify in civilian organizations. Fears of the unknown were often slowly replaced with a confidence that came from realization of the transferability of skills learned in naval careers, enhancing notions of usefulness, professionalism, and personal pride.

Many also found that involvement in new pursuits, in particular what they viewed as masculine sports and hobbies, softened the blow metered by resettlement, and this helped ex-servicemen to deal with various aspects of their identity crises. Although rates of adaptation differed considerably, particularly among those individuals who were more or less involved in naval life, most leavers ultimately viewed resettlement as the beginning of something new, rather than as purely an end to something better.

SUMMARY

The argument that military personnel are exposed to particularly masculine military discourses through which they are able to make sense of service life is a persuasive one, and it appears to be supported by the research outlined here. Hegemonic masculinity does appear to be a factor in service life, one that is central to the smooth running of the navy. Military discourses may be used to inform masculine identity, to understand the demands of the military contract, and to justify the more personal, social, and cultural sacrifices made by service personnel. They may also serve to bolster traditional biological notions of gender at work and at home for both men and their wives.

However, it is important to consider the sense of agency exercised by military personnel, whether conscious or otherwise, in drawing on such discourses. For some servicemen and women, they may be intrinsically meaningful, for others less so: military communities, like other groups in society, are not entirely homogenous. The research outlined demonstrates how discourses are not merely controlling devices used against passive recruits to bolster military hegemony. Control may be one consequence of the military discourse in which masculinity plays a central role. However, the internalization of military representations of masculinity relies on their persuasiveness in certain contexts, and service members are active in deciding whether or not they have the necessary validity for adoption. Certain interpretations of masculinity must appeal to the majority.

So, although the Royal Navy and the wider military may offer particular representations of masculinity to their members, a representation will be accepted only if personnel and their families find it suitable. It is clear that other compatible elements of military discourses have helped bolster military masculine identities, but recent problems with retention levels and family breakdown serve only to draw attention to the increasing need to review these discourses in what might be termed a postmodern society.[44]

This argument, of course, challenges perspectives that are founded on purely structural accounts of military organizations. Studying military discourses helps us to understand the place of masculinity in directing service life, yet also demonstrates its variable adoption and its transformation or maintenance in times of crisis and occupational change. In studying masculinity and identity, we can comprehend more clearly the complexities of service life and in so doing find ourselves better placed to provide advice and support where needed. The research documented in this chapter demonstrates that such support is essential, not just for men and women making sense of the more troublesome aspects of service life but also for those coming to terms with the change from military service to more civilian lifestyles, as well as for the families that help them through it.

NOTES

1. S. Regan de Bere, *Military Identities: Men, Families and Occupational Change* (unpublished Ph.D. thesis, University of Plymouth, 1999). The research used three sets of qualitative interviews with twenty couples, within a longitudinal framework, and a larger questionnaire survey of 250 men leaving the service. The project was originally designed to assess the impact of resettlement on a sample of service leavers; issues surrounding notions of masculinity were extrapolated from the wider findings.

2. E. Goffman, *Encounters: Two Studies in the Sociology of Interaction* (Indianapolis: Bobbs Merrill, 1961); E. Goffman, *The Presentation of Self in Everyday Life* (London: Penguin, 1969); M. Wetherell, ed., *Identities, Groups & Social Issues*, 1st ed. (London: Sage, 1996); S. Clegg and C. Hardy, eds., *Studying Organisation: Theory and Method* (London: Sage, 1999); N. Elias, *The Established and the Outsiders*, 1st ed. (London: Sage Publications, 1994); L. Ingram, *The Study of Organizations: Positions, Persons and Patterns*, 1st ed. (Westport, CT: Praeger Publishers, 1995); and C. Moskos, *The Military: Just Another Job?* (London: Brassey's, 1988).

3. B. Pease, *Recreating Men: Postmodern Masculinity Politics* (London: Sage, 2000); N. Edley and M. Wetherall, "Jockeying for Position: The Construction of Masculine Identities," in *Discourse and Society* 8, 2 (1997); R. W. Connell, *Masculinities* (Cambridge: Polity, 1995); J. McKay, *Masculinities, Gender Relations and Sport* (London: Sage, 2000); and L. Segal, *Slow Motion: Changing Men, Changing Masculinities* (London: Virago, 1990).

4. Since female service career cycles are vastly different to those of men, and numbers more limited, comparative analysis was beyond the scope of this study, although it is acknowledged that similar study can be of benefit to understanding the diversity of military careers. As female integration is more widely practiced, it will become possible to explore the implications of, and for, dominant masculine discourses.

5. U. Eco, *Semiotics and the Philosophy of Language* (Houndmills: Macmillan, 1984); R. Barthes, *The Elements of Semiology* (New York: Hill and Wang, 1967); G. Houston, *Being and Belonging: Group, Intergroup and Gestalt*, 1st ed. (Chichester: Wiley & Sons, 1993); M. Foucault, *The Archaeology of Knowledge*, 1st ed. (London: Routledge. 1972); J. Derrida, "Form and Meaning: A Note on the Phenomenology of Language," in *Speech and Phenomena* (Northwest University Press, 1973a); J. Derrida, *Speech and Phenomena* (Northwest University Press, 1973b); H. Garfinkel, *Studies in Ethnomethodology* (Englewood Cliffs, NJ: Prentice-Hall, 1967).

6. D. Howarth, "Discourse Theory," in D. Marsh and G. Stoker, *Theory and Methods in Political Science* (London: Macmillan Press. 1995), p. 115.

7. M. Janowitz, *The Professional Soldier: A Social and Political Portrait* (New York: Free Press, 1960).

8. R. Jolly, *Changing Step: From Military to Civilian Life: People in Transition* (London: Brassey's, 1996); and M. Edmonds, *Armed Services and Society* (Leicester University Press, 1988).

9. D. Morgan, "Theater of War: Combat, the Military, and Masculinities," in H. Brod and M. Kaufman, eds., *Theorizing Masculinities* (California: Sage, 1994), p. 167.

10. E. Goffman, *Asylums: Essays on the Social Situation of Mental Patients and Other Inmates.* (Harmondsworth: Pelican, 1968).

11. de Bere, *Military Identities.*

12. S. Regan, D. Mason, and L. Bryant, *Career Change, Job Search and Family: Naval Leavers in Plymouth* (Report to the Royal Navy: University of Plymouth, 1996).

13. The relationship between discourse, identity, and power is explored fully in the following works: S. Zizek, *The Sublime Object of Ideology,* 1st ed. (London: Verso, 1989); M. Foucault, *Discipline and Punish* (Harmondsworth: Penguin, 1977); M. Foucault, *Power/Knowledge* (New York: Pantheon, 1980); and A. Gramsci, *Selections from the Prison Notebooks,* 1st ed., ed. Q. Hoare and G. Norwell-Smith (London: Lawrence and Wishart, 1971).

14. M. Foucault, *Madness and Civilisation* (Tavistock, 1987); M. Foucault, *The Birth of the Clinic* (Tavistock, 1976); M. Foucault, *The Order of Things* (Tavistock, 1986); M. Foucault, *Discipline and Punish* (Harmondsworth: Penguin, 1977); M. Foucault, *Power/Knowledge* (New York: Pantheon, 1980).

15. J. Fallowes, "9 to 5 and Home for Dinner: The Civilianization of the Army," in *Atlantic Monthly,* February 1981, pp. 98–108.

16. T. Parker, *Soldier, Soldier* (London: Heinmann, 1985).

17. J. Chandler, L. Bryant, and T. Bunyard, "Notes and Issues: Women in Military Occupations," in *Work, Employment and Society* 9, 1 (1995): 123–135.

18. See particularly C. Enloe, *Does Khaki Become You? The Militarisation of Women's Lives* (London: Pluto Press, 1983).

19. M. Van Creveld, *On Future War* (London: Brassey's, 1991).

20. Enloe, *Does Khaki Become You?*

21. N. Goldman and R. Stites, "Great Britain and the World Wars," in L. Goldman, ed., *Female Soldiers—Combatants or Non-combatants? Historical and Contemporary Perspectives* (Westport, CT: Greenwood Press, 1982).

22. T. Bunyard, *Personal and Occupational Career Aspirations of Young Recruits to the Royal Navy* (unpublished M. Phil., Department of Applied Social Science, University of Plymouth, 1995). Quoted with author's consent.

23. J. Hearn and W. Parkin, *Sex at Work: The Power and Paradox of Organizational Sexuality,* 1st ed. (New York: St Martin's Press, 1987).

24. W. Parkin, "The Public and the Private: Gender, Sexuality and Emotion," and J. Hearn, "Emotive Subjects: Organisational Men, Organisational Masculinity and the (De)construction of Emotions," both in S. Fineman, *Emotions in Organisations,* 1st ed. (London: Sage, 1993); and B. Gutek, "Sexuality in the Workplace: Key Issues in Social Research," in J. Hearn et al., *Gender in Organisations* (London: Sage, 1989).

25. Interviews took place with twenty couples drawn from a sample representative of different ranks and ratings, as well as ages. Three interviews were conducted with each couple over the space of two and a half years, although three couples were lost during the period of the fieldwork through our inability to contact them. Interviews took place in family homes and lasted roughly one to one-and-a-half hours. It was noted that male responses dominated the interviews, even where schedules were redesigned (as a consequence) in the second stage of interviewing to encourage more female response. It is interesting to note that when women were questioned directly in the second- and third-stage interviews, they often deferred to their husbands or checked for confirmation that their answers were correct.

26. Moskos, "The Military: Just Another Job"; Janowitz, "The Professional Soldier"; Edmonds, *Armed Services and Society*; J. Hockey, *Squaddies: Portrait of a Subculture* (Exeter: Exeter University Press, 1986); M. Janowitz and J. Van Doorn, eds., *On Military Intervention*, 1st ed. (Rotterdam: Rotterdam University Press, 1971); S. Huntington, *The Soldier and the State: The Theory and Politics of Civil-Military Relations* (Cambridge: Harvard University Press, 1957); M. Shaw, *Post Military Society.* (Cambridge: Polity Press, 1991); M. Janowitz, *Essays in the Institutional Analysis of War and Peace* (London: Sage, 1975); C. Dandeker, *Surveillance, Power and Modernity*, 1st ed. (Cambridge: Polity Press, 1990); British Military Studies Group, *The Future of British Military Cultures: Social and Legal Change in Britain and Europe; The Personnel Implications for the Armed Forces of the 21st Century* (8 October 1997).

27. Whereby personnel are accorded different status depending on their position within the naval occupational hierarchy (for example, with commissioned officers being accorded more prestige than non-commissioned officers, non-commissioned officers being accorded more than ratings, and so on).

28. This is a commonly referred-to social activity, with particular emphasis on drinking substantial quantities of alcohol.

29. This may differ from other interpretations of masculinity within and between the Tri-services (Royal Navy, British Army, and RAF), although available literature suggests that there are underlying similarities. See Enloe, *Does Khaki Become You? Militarisation of Women's Lives*, and Hockey, *Squaddies: Portrait of a Subculture.*

30. This differs from the identity construction of women in service in the Royal Navy and refers to identities constructed specifically around the role of service wife or partner, a theme currently being developed in further research.

31. de Bere, *Military Identities.*

32. Intermittent absences further reinforced male breadwinner and female housewife and mother roles.

33. Jolly, *Military Man, Family Man: Crown Property?* (London: Brassey's, 1989).

34. Jessup, *Breaking Ranks: Social Change in Military Communities* (London Brassey's, 1996).

35. Here men most often referred to more contemporary, and less military, notions of fatherhood. This appeared to be the one aspect of naval discourse that could not be incorporated into servicemen's own approaches to service life.

36. TRSO (Tri-Services Resettlement Organisation), *Useful Facts and Figures about People leaving the Services* (Marshall Tanous plc, March 1996).

37. R. Jenkins, *Social Identity* (London: Routledge, 1996); C.W. Mills, *The Sociological Imagination* (London: Oxford University Press, 1959); E. Laclau, *The Making of Political Identities*, 1st ed. (London: Verso, 1994); G. Mead, *Mind, Self and Society: From the Standpoint of a Social Behaviorist* (University of Chicago Press, 1934); and R. Merton, "Bureaucratic Structure and Personality," in R. Merton, ed., *Social Theory and Social Structure* (Glencoe, IL: Free Press, 1957).

38. See also Jolly, *Changing Step.*

39. Regan, Mason, and Bryant, *Career Change, Job Search and Family;* Jolly, *Changing Step.*

40. Regan, Mason, and Bryant, *Career Change, Job Search and Family;* and S. Regan, *Naval Careers and Household Formations: The Case of Military Leavers* (unpublished M. Sc., University of Plymouth, 1995). It was the findings of these studies that prompted the research on which this chapter is based.

41. Higher-ranking individuals placed themselves in managerial positions; other ranks found employment in engineering and the emergency services.

42. de Bere, *Military Identities;* Jolly, *Changing Step.*

43. The majority of the sample had found securing employment in higher levels of local labor markets problematic. Most reported having to accept jobs for which they were overqualified in terms of technical expertise and work experience.

44. Where individualism, pluralism, egalitarianism, and the fragmentation of identity take center stage.

Chapter 8

The State and Military Masculinity

John Hopton

INTRODUCTION

I was born in England in 1956 and have lived there all my life. I have never seen any form of military service and have never worked for the Ministry of Defence. I have never lived in or even visited a military base. Indeed, the closest I have ever come to military culture is learning how to march and drill when I was in the junior section of the Boys' Brigade for three or four years. Furthermore, because all Britain's wars during my lifetime have been fought entirely on foreign soil, I have no firsthand experience of warfare of any kind. Nevertheless, although I have strong sympathies with pacifist politics and am repulsed by warmongering politicians, I am fascinated by military culture and admit to sometimes admiring soldiers for some of the work they are expected to do. I am also impressed by the actions of soldiers and other armed forces personnel who distinguish themselves in battle. Furthermore, I am aware that some of my own ideas about what it means to be masculine, to be a man, have been shaped by ideologies of militarism. Yet, those aspects of military culture that celebrate the use of lethal violence and glamorize war disturb me. In this chapter I explore the cultural influences that have informed my contradictory attitudes toward militarism and discuss how those cultural influences may be beginning to change. There are four central themes to this chapter. First, militarist ideals represent the most extreme expression of the values of what Connell terms hegemonic masculinity.[1] Second, although state militarist policies are most evident in saber-rattling foreign policy, there are also more subtle militarist influences on public policy that are particularly evident in debates about law and order. Third, state militarist policies have traditionally played a major role in promoting and reinforcing ideologies that shape popular conceptions of what it means to be masculine and manipulate such ideologies to gain support for use of violence by the state. Fourth, the 1990s represented a turning point in the relationship between masculinity and militarism as women service personnel became better integrated into the culture, structure, and role of the armed services while the collapse of the Soviet bloc and new technologies transformed the nature of warfare.

MILITARISM AND THE INSTITUTIONALIZATION OF MASCULINITY

Writers who have developed critiques of masculinity suggest that there is a form of masculine identity (hegemonic masculinity) that boys and men are generally encouraged to aspire to.[2] This form of masculinity is characterized by the interrelationship of stoicism,[3] phallocentricity and the domination of weaker individuals,[4] competitiveness and heroic achievement.[5] Thus, men who exemplify this model of masculinity tend to be accorded a higher social status than those who do not.[6] By publicly demonstrating that he has at least the potential to conform to this model of masculinity, a boy or man may have his masculinity affirmed. Military organizations, military successes, military pageantry, and rituals such as the "passing out" parades for successful recruits to the armed forces represent the public endorsement of such values and their institutionalization in national culture. Certainly, there exist other manifestations of this process of celebrating masculinity, but uniquely the exploits of the military are always openly and aggressively celebrated in the public sphere. Indeed, there are echoes of militarism in everyday language. For example, "Dunkirk spirit"[7] is a shorthand term for expressing admiration for someone's unwillingness to accept defeat; whereas someone who is finally defeated after a lengthy struggle may be said to have "met their Waterloo."[8] Furthermore, boys encounter many militarist influences during their childhood and adolescence.

Although there are exceptions to the rule,[9] uniformed youth organizations for boys tend to explicitly reflect military culture. For example, the organization, uniforms, and culture of the Boy Scout movement reflect the military background of its founder, Robert Baden-Powell. Similarly, from the very beginning, military-style drilling was a core activity of the Boys' Brigade to the extent that its founder, William Smith, originally introduced wooden dummy rifles into these activities. Whereas the use of wooden rifles was abandoned relatively early on in the Boys' Brigade's history, drilling remained a core activity within a military structure of brigade, battalions, and companies together with a quasi-military hierarchy of officers and non-commissioned officers retained to this day.[10] More explicitly, the various army, air, and sea cadet forces in Britain, which offer young people opportunities to participate in many adventure activities and sports at low cost,[11] are supported by the Ministry of Defence. These and other similar organizations have played a key role in exporting a culture equating masculinity and militarism from the public schools, where the link between militarism and masculinity first became institutionalized,[12] to boys from the middle and working classes.[13] Although not all boys and men will ever have any connection with uniformed youth organizations such as the Boy Scouts or the Boys' Brigade, most will be aware of the cultural values such organizations promote. For example, they will probably develop social and professional relationships with men who have been associated with such organizations and internalized at least some of the values they promote. Thus, a shared understanding of masculinity will be influenced by these values.

This valorization of military values is also reflected in other ways. One of the most commonly cited examples is the toys with which boys have traditionally been encouraged to play by their peers and their parents. Typically, these may include toy tanks, toy guns, toy warplanes, and toy soldiers. Indeed, even many of the fantasy figure toys that have become popular over the last twenty years are armed with what are clearly meant to be lethal weapons. Links between militarism and masculinity are also evident in printed matter and other media aimed at the youth market. For example, during the 1960s, British boys' comics such as *The Valiant* and *The Victor*, whose very titles reflected military culture, celebrated the heroic exploits of both fictional and non-fictional soldiers. During the 1980s, television series such as *The A Team*, *Airwolf*, and *Magnum*—some of which were aimed at adults as much as children—attributed the astuteness, strength, self-reliance, and sexual attractiveness of the central male characters to their military backgrounds; and during the 1990s many video and computer games featured violence and had explicitly militarist themes. Such cultural constructs are a powerful influence on how children and young people interpret the world around them and their place within it,[14] and they may lead to them equating manliness with military ideals.

THE RECIPROCAL RELATIONSHIP BETWEEN MILITARISM AND MASCULINITY

Historically, there is a reciprocal relationship between militarism and masculinity. On the one hand, politicians have utilized ideologies of idealized masculinity that valorize the notion of strong active males collectively risking their personal safety for the greater good of the wider community,[15] gaining support for the state's use of violence, such as wars in the international arena and aggressive policing in the domestic situation. On the other hand, militarism feeds into ideologies of masculinity through the eroticization of stoicism, risk–taking, and even lethal violence. This can be detected in populist fictional and non-fictional books about war and weapons and in newspaper coverage of military actions.[16]

Whatever the intentions of the authors, the attraction of these books could be described as pornographic.... The page-after-page of photographs are, in fact, pin-ups, but instead of pictures of young women...they are pictures of soldiers and their weapons and equipment....Whereas the traditional pin-up celebrates and endorses heterosexuality, these soldier pin-ups celebrate...a tough warrior masculinity. [17]

The reciprocal relationship between militarism and masculinity may be illustrated using the First World War as an example. In the earlier part of the 1914–1918 war, recruitment of volunteer soldiers owed much to Victorian ideologies that defined masculinity in terms of strength, courage, determination, and patriotism. In turn, this image of masculinity was reinforced by wartime propaganda that glamorized military culture and military success and tacitly encouraged brutality toward war resisters and those males, such as Jewish refugees from Eastern Europe, who were ineligible for military service.[18]

In the British context, a more recent example of this process is the media obsession with the Special Air Service Regiment (SAS)—an elite special forces regiment that is part of the British Army—which began with the Iranian embassy siege of 1980.[19] Geraghty, himself a journalist, has neatly encapsulated the media image of SAS trooper as the epitome of socially constructed masculinity: "The essential qualities needed for weeks and perhaps months in isolation were initiative; self-discipline; independence of mind; ability to work unsupervised; stamina; patience; and a sense of humour...they cling to the tribal security of a four man patrol with total loyalty."[20]

The deployment of the SAS in situations that might arguably have been more appropriately handled by the civil police, and the subsequent media coverage of such events, is particularly interesting in the context of the relationship between masculinity and militarism. Whether the victims of such intervention are Iranian or Irish terrorists or protesting prisoners,[21] the message remains the same: The dissidents may be displaying the masculinist virtues of aggression, domination, and endurance, but glory and respect[22] can belong only to the fighting men whose aggression is controlled and regulated by the state and used to uphold the authority of the state. This message was reinforced in the case of the Gibraltar shootings when the makers of the *Death on the Rock* documentary were castigated by the government and sections of the press for exposing the fact that SAS troopers shot dead unarmed members of the Provisional Irish Republican Army (Provisional IRA), an illegal paramilitary organization committed to an armed struggle for the independence of Northern Ireland from the British state. In this situation the state celebrated the aggression and determination of its super-masculine soldiers while those who condemned the soldiers' actions were portrayed as ineffectual men and untrustworthy women.[23] One British newspaper, *The Sun*—reflecting Frank Mort's analysis of sexualities considered to be dangerous[24]—even went as far as to inaccurately claim that the testimony of one female witness was unreliable because of an (inaccurate) allegation that she had once been a prostitute.[25]

Lynne Segal has shown how in addition to celebrating "heroic" exploits of aggression and competitiveness, the ideology that links maleness with rugged individualism may also play a role in promoting intensely conservative politics and values.[26] The link between militarism and masculinity reaches beyond the eroticization of masculinism, however, through the glamorization of military culture and military actions,[27] and it can be detected in the law-and-order policies of British governments during the 1980s and 1990s. The most obvious manifestation of this glamorization is the increased use of paramilitary tactics by the police.[28] It may also be seen in penal policy. Police cavalry charges and similar paramilitary approaches to riot control throughout the 1980s and 1990s have been extensively documented.[29] Taken in isolation such policies seem to have no direct bearing on the politics of sexuality. If the main purpose of such actions is taken to be the suppression of dissent,[30] however, they may be interpreted as a public spectacle wherein the forces of law and order appropriate the symbols and ritualized behavior of eroticized masculinity—military language, helmets, combat dress, special weapons, and tactics[31]—to enforce the authority of a government that systematically reinforced ideologies of the patriarchal family[32] and attacked alternative sexualities.[33] The sexual-political undertones here are that these masculinist symbols and ritualized behaviors are associated in "commonsense" assumptions with the exercising of legitimate power and authority.

Within the penal system militarism has, from time to time, been reflected in ideas about the rehabilitation of young offenders. For example, young offenders' institutions have sometimes adopted regimes based on military drill and army-style physical training in the belief that this will prepare young male offenders for law-abiding manhood.[34] Here, the motive seems to be to deny the possibility that young men's "crimes" may represent political protest or reaction to social disadvantage and, instead, to view their antisocial behavior as arising from destructive biological urges,[35] which military style discipline will enable them to control. Such policies seem to be rooted in an ideology that regards militarism as the ultimate form of disciplined masculinity,[36] an ideology that at the same time ignores the contradiction that militarism in many ways celebrates the most extreme forms of violence.

If the reciprocal relationship between masculinity and militarism is weakened, so too is the power of the state to manipulate public support for its right to use violence to pursue its policies at home and abroad, as well as to encourage young men to join the armed forces. Thus, the state has a vested interest in maintaining strong ideological links between militarism and masculinity.

THE MILITARIZATION OF WOMEN

To summarize the argument thus far: Militarism is the major means by which the values and beliefs associated with ideologies of hegemonic masculinity are eroticized and institutionalized. Although there are alternative contexts in which traditional masculine virtues are valorized and eroticized, they lack the potential to link masculinity with the political concerns of the state. This is not to say that women are innately pacifist. Indeed, both male and female pacifists have been known to renounce pacifism when faced with hideously brutal political regimes or genocidal armies.[37] Furthermore, throughout history women have actively participated in military life in a variety of roles.[38]

The willingness of some women to join the armed forces and even assume combat roles may be used to refute an essentialist position in relation to feminist pacifism.[39] Nevertheless, until recently militarism has tended to work against the interests of women, often in ways that directly benefit men. For example, both Julie Wheelwright[40] and Barbara Rogers[41] have shown how military organizations that openly incorporate women have sometimes contrived to prevent them from enjoying benefits, privileges, and advantages equal to those enjoyed by the men in those organizations; Vera Brittain[42] and Cynthia Enloe[43] have documented how the military throughout modern history has regulated and controlled the sexuality, social roles, and labor of women in the interests of patriarchal states.

Since the early 1990s, however, there has been increased emphasis on developing policies that give female armed forces personnel equal rights with their male counterparts, for example, allowing women in the British armed forces to take maternity leave (whereas previously, female personnel who became mothers would not have been allowed to continue their careers) and allowing them to assume full combat roles.[44] This new approach might simply reflect growing concern to genuinely promote equal opportunities and change the culture within the armed forces, yet there may be alternative explanations. For example, the emergence of a view of masculinity that refuses to equate militarism with manliness[45] has presented the masculinist-militarist power elites with a potential labor shortage that could partly be offset by allowing an expansion of the role of women in the armed forces. Whatever the rationale, though, clearly the relationship between militarism and masculinity is changing. The question is whether the essence of militarism has been transformed by the sexual politics of the last thirty years or whether an increased presence of women in the armed services has just modified its superficial appearance.

1991: A TURNING POINT

The 1991 Gulf War seems to represent a turning point in the relationship between militarism and masculinity. On the one hand, the traditional relationship between masculinity and militarism is clearly evident in the political rhetoric used to justify the war.[46] On the other hand, a weakening of the link between the traditional preoccupations of hegemonic masculinity and militarism is also evident in the build-up to the war, the defeat of Iraq, and the aftermath of the war. First, notwithstanding the contradictory attitudes sometimes shown toward such women, female armed services personnel involved in the war were given a high profile. Second, as the war reached its conclusion, notions of a new world order and new forms of military intervention began to emerge—although these were also contradictory.

It is highly probable that the 1991 war against Iraq was an avoidable event deliberately started by Western governments—principally those of the United States and the United Kingdom—who had previously ignored Iraq's poor record on human rights.[47] In this context, the rhetoric of the new world order, which accompanied the promotion of the war, may be interpreted as an attempt by mostly male politicians in the West to capitalize on the political changes in Eastern Europe—and the resultant demise of the Warsaw Pact military alliance, which might otherwise have kept their ambitions in check—to justify the further pursuit of militaristic policies and to act out the masculinist fantasy of becoming "heroes-hunters-competitors-conquerors"[48] on a global scale. This interpretation is reflected in the views of some U.S. politicians and generals who saw the Gulf War as an opportunity, in the words of George Bush Sr., to "put paid to the Vietnam Syndrome once and for all." Some commentators have taken this to have meant not only to demonstrate America's military might in the international arena but also to reaffirm the authority of a government that promotes those traditional values of patriarchy and masculinity[49] that were challenged at the time of the Vietnam protests.[50]

Nevertheless, the presence of 40 000 female personnel among the U.S. military force in Saudi Arabia during the war represented a change in the relationship between women and the military.[51] Historically, the militarization of women's lives has involved the regulation and control of women serving the needs of male military personnel in the roles traditionally ascribed to women in patriarchal societies, namely, as wives, cooks, laundresses, prostitutes, secretaries, and the like.[52] During the Gulf War, though, women were serving as soldiers, marines, air force personnel and sailors in support units close to and even within combat zones.[53] Although, on a superficial level, this seems to have signaled a radical change in the relationship between militarism and social constructions of femininity, this new relationship was contradictory.

Press coverage of female military personnel during the buildup to the Gulf War, the war itself, and its aftermath tended to highlight those female soldiers who were also mothers of young children. One article in a British newspaper, for example, was accompanied by a picture of U.S. Army Captain Jo Ann Conley in full combat dress with a photograph of her two-and-one-half-year-old daughter fixed to her helmet.[54] Such imagery implicitly challenges the view that the violence of war is inextricably linked to men's violence against women. When a female U.S. soldier was captured by the Iraqis, however, fears that she might be raped by her captors or that female soldiers who were mothers might be killed, and that such events might adversely affect the morale of male troops, were expressed openly.[55] Thus, despite a clear message that war and other military intervention is no longer to be a strictly gendered activity, there is tacit recognition that the casual misogyny that pervades military culture may lead to male sexual violence against women becoming an integral part of war.[56]

Since the conclusion of the Gulf War there have been major changes in the politics of war, the role of the armed forces of the major world powers, and in the case of some nation-states, the role of women within the armed forces. Although the observation by some commentators that the new world order emerging in the wake of the Gulf War heralded the retreat of militarism has proved to have been mistaken,[57] there have been many changes in the politics of war, the nature of militarism, and the sexual politics of militarism.

The most obvious change in the politics of war since the Gulf War has been in the tendency of Western governments to claim humanitarian motives for any military intervention beyond their own borders. Whereas similar arguments may be advanced to justify Britain's declaration of war against Nazi Germany in 1939, Western military interventions during the 1990s were inconsistent and ambiguous. For example, there were large-scale United Nations and NATO intervention in the Balkans, Somalia, and Iraq, but little attempt was made to intervene militarily in similar situations in Rwanda and other Third World countries.[58] Notwithstanding such inconsistency, though, after 1991 there was a steep increase in United Nations peacekeeping activities, "which in 1993 cost about $3bn [billion]. In 1994 almost 80, 000 'Blue Helmets' were deployed around the world, most based in 'South' countries and without the consent of one or other of the parties in the conflicts."[59] By the late 1990s, though, politicians were using the same logic they had used to justify the deployment of ground troops to protect humanitarian aid convoys and act as peacekeepers to justify aerial bombing raids on Iraq and Serbia.[60] Significantly, the politicians who sanctioned these bombing raids justified their action with a rhetoric of "determination," "courage," and euphemistic references to "diminishing and degrading" Saddam's nuclear and chemical weapon stocks or "attacking the heart of Milosevic's security structure." Although clearly both Saddam and Milosevic are leaders whose regimes have committed crimes against humanity, such rhetoric is reminiscent of traditional masculine-militaristic political posturing, disregards the reality that some bombing raids resulted in civilian casualties, and overlooks the futility of such a strategy as a means of dislodging despotic and cruel political regimes.

Paradoxically, though, a softening of the link between the values of hegemonic masculinity and militarism has taken place alongside the emergence of this new contradictory politics of war and human rights. For example, between 1992 and 1994, Britain's Women's Royal Army Corps, Women's Royal Naval Service, and Women's Royal Air Force became fully integrated with the British Army, the Royal Navy, and the Royal Air Force (RAF), respectively; and in 1995 the first women qualified as an RAF combat-ready Tornado bomber pilot.[61] Although a minority of branches and trades within the armed forces remains closed to women—for example, service in commando units and submarines—a British Army recruiting advertisement in the late 1990s emphasized the integration of women in the armed forces and, significantly, linked this to the growth in the army's peacekeeping role. The film shows a woman cowering in the corner of a building as the commentary intones, "She's just been raped by soldiers. The same soldiers murdered her husband. The last thing she wants to see is another soldier—unless that soldier is a woman." Then, as the advertisement concludes, an armed female soldier in full battle-dress enters the room. Thus, notwithstanding the persistence of militaristic posturing by certain politicians, there are signs that the relationship between militarism and masculinity may be changing.[62]

CONCLUSIONS

Traditionally, the casual sexism, competitiveness, and celebration of aggression and the domination of others so characteristic of hegemonic masculinity has been explicitly and unambiguously reflected in military culture.[63] Similarly, militarism—that is, the celebration of military culture in national politics and popular culture—has represented an affirmation of the legitimacy of hegemonic masculinity. Conversely, men who reject militarism have often been portrayed as effeminate, naive, untrustworthy, or even politically dangerous.[64] Thus, there are clear links between militaristic attitudes, male self-esteem, and sexual charisma.[65]

Although this established relationship was evident in the events leading up to, during, and immediately following the 1991 Gulf War, that war and its aftermath also represented a turning point in the relationship between militarism and masculinity. First, there was an expansion of the role of the women in the armed services and full integration of separate women's services into the army, navy, and air force. Second, there was a shift in the political discourses around military intervention away from traditional masculine preoccupations with power, dominance, and territoriality toward issues of human rights and peacekeeping. Yet, some male politicians continued to behave in stereotypically masculinist-militarist fashion, pursuing overtly militaristic foreign policy and justifying their actions in language reflecting both traditional masculinist-militaristic concerns and a newer rhetoric of promoting human rights and political stability. In this context, it is probably worth noting that books by Gulf War veterans have played a significant role in promoting the public obsession with the SAS as national heroes, as "warrior supermen, capable of taking on overwhelming odds to accomplish the most dangerous of tasks in the most inhospitable terrain."[66]

Thus, developments since the Gulf War have been contradictory. On the surface, the fuller integration of women in the armed forces and increased emphasis on using the military in peacekeeping roles and humanitarian interventions seem to indicate a weakening of the links between the values of hegemonic masculinity and militarism. At the same time, the public fascination with the derring-do of SAS troopers is little different from the Victorian public's obsession with military heroes and military success; meanwhile, politicians continue to imply that being prepared to sanction military intervention is a sign of moral courage and strong government. Given these conflicting trends, it is too early to determine whether the integration of women within the armed forces will lead to an erosion of the misogyny that pervades military culture; whether there truly is a shift toward concerns with the protection of human rights and peacekeeping as the *raison d'être* for military intervention; or whether these new aspects of militarism may ultimately lead to the development of a new hegemonic masculinity that is more tolerant of pacifist sensibilities. For the time being, though, it is probably safe to assume that the reciprocal relationship between masculinity and traditional forms of militarism will continue to shape boys' and men's perceptions of themselves and will continue to influence politicians' ideas about what constitutes appropriate foreign policy.

NOTES

1. R. W. Connell, *Gender and Power* (Cambridge: Polity, 1987).

2. Ibid.; Myriam Miedzian, *Boys Will Be Boys* (London: Virago, 1992); Ian M. Harris, *Messages Men Hear* (London: Taylor & Francis, 1995).

3. Richard Bradley and Mark Phillips, "Behind Every Wild Man Is a Happier Woman," *The Independent*, 20 January 1992.

4. Barbara Rogers, *Men Only* (London: Pandora, 1988); John Stoltenberg, *Refusing to Be a Man* (New York: Meridian, 1990); Liz Stanley and Sue Wise, *Georgie Porgie* (London: Pandora, 1988); Arthur Brittan, *Masculinity and Power* (Oxford: Basil Blackwell, 1989).

5. Brittan, *Masculinity and Power*; Miedzian, *Boys Will Be Boys*; Harris, *Messages Men Hear*.

6. Connell, *Gender and Power*.

7. Ironically, the term "Dunkirk spirit" in many ways reflects some of the contradictions explored in this chapter. Although Dunkirk remains an important source of British national pride sixty years later, it was, in fact, one of the most humiliating military defeats in history. Nevertheless, the willingness of the British people to support the war against Germany in the wake of this defeat—possibly a reflection of the macho pride so frequently critiqued in studies of masculinity—ultimately led to the defeat of one of the most brutal, genocidal political regimes in the history of the world. Thus, even the most committed pacifist or radical feminist would find it difficult to suggest a viable alternative to the overtly militarist stance that Winston Churchill adopted during the Second World War.

8. A reference to Napoleon's defeat by the Duke of Wellington at the 1815 Battle of Waterloo.

9. The Woodcraft Folk, founded in 1925, has a uniform in the form of a green shirt or pullover that has always been used for both sexes; the group emphasizes cooperative activity, is organized democratically, and is explicitly not militaristic.

10. Donald M. McFarlan, *First for Boys: The Story of the Boys' Brigade, 1883–1983* (London: Boys' Brigade, 1983).

11. Although in recent years girls have increasingly been encouraged to join the cadet forces, they were originally all-male organizations. There were smaller organizations for girls, such as the Girls Training Corps and the Women's Junior Air Corps, which merged in 1964 to form the Girls Venture Corps (now the Girls Venture Corps Air Cadets). This organization now receives no government funding and has only informal links with the other cadet forces.

12. In Britain, *public school* refers to an exclusive fee-paying private school, not to a school funded by the government.

13. Jeffrey Weeks, *Sex, Politics and Society* (London: Longman, 1981); Harry Brod, *The Making of Masculinities* (London: Allen & Unwin, 1987).

14. Eric Berne, *What Do You Say after You Say Hell?* (London: Corgi, 1986).

15. Lynne Segal, *Slow Motion: Changing Masculinities, Changing Men* (London: Virago, 1990); Anthony Barnett, *Iron Britannia* (London: Allison & Busby: 1982); Steve Platt, "Casualties of War," *New Statesman & Society* 4, 139 (1991): 12–13.

16. Simon Shepherd, "Gay Sex Spy Orgy," in S. Shepherd and M. Wallis, *Coming on Strong* (London: Unwin Hyman, 1989), pp. 213–230.

17. John Newsinger, *Dangerous Men* (London: Pluto Press, 1997), p. 80.

18. Richard Taylor and Nigel Young. *Campaigns for Peace* (Manchester: Manchester University Press, 1987); Showalter, Elaine, *The Female Malady* (London: Virago, 1987).

19. Tony Geraghty, *Who Dares Wins* (Glasgow: Fontana/Collins, 1980); Philip Warner, *The SAS: The Official History* (London: Sphere, 1983).

20. Geraghty *Who Dares Wins*, p. 262.

21. Warner. *The SAS: The Official History*, pp. 271–273; Tony Dawes et al., "How the Spanish Police and SAS Kept Track of Suspects," *The Times*, 8 March 1988; Phil Scraton, Joe Sim, and Paula Skidmore, *Prisons under Protest* (Milton Keynes: Open University Press, 1991).

22. See Elizabeth Stanko, *Everyday Violence* (London: Pandora, 1990).

23. Jolyon Jenkins, "Truth on the Rocks," *New Statesman and Society* 2, 34 (27 January 1989): 10–11.

24. Frank Mort, *Dangerous Sexualities* (London: Routledge & Kegan Paul, 1987).

25. Jenkins, "Truth on the Rocks."

26. Segal, *Slow Motion.*

27. As Newsinger (1997) has shown, the eroticization of militarism has an explicit form inasmuch as there is a pornography of war that fetishizes weapons, uniforms, and other military equipment and is freely available in news agents without any of the restrictions that apply to sexual pornography.

28. Tony Jefferson, *The Case against Paramilitary Policing* (Milton Keynes: Open University Press, 1990).

29. Jim Coulter, Susan Miller, and Martin Walker, *State of Siege* (London: Canary Press, 1984); Paddy Hillyard and Janie Percy-Smith, *The Coercive State* (London: Fontana, 1988); "Tony," "Sticks and Stones," *New Statesman & Society* 3, 95 (1990): 10–11.

30. Hillyard and Percy-Smith, *The Coercive State*.

31. See Stoltenberg. *Refusing to Be a Man*, p. 117, on pornography and male supremacy. See Mike Macnair, "The Contradictory Politics of SM," in S. Shepherd and M. Wallis, *Coming on Strong* (London: Unwin Hyman, 1989), pp. 147–162, on the politics of sadomasochism.

32. Jane Millar and Caroline Glendinning, "Gender & Poverty," *Journal of Social Policy* 18, 3 (1989): 363–381; Ruth Lister, "Women, Economic Dependency & Citizenship," *Journal of Social Policy* 19, 4 (1990): 445–467.

33. Shepherd and Wallis, *Coming on Strong*.

34. John Muncie, "Failure Never Matters: Detention Centres and the Politics of Deterrence," *Critical Social Policy* 10 (Summer 1990): 53–66.

35. Brittan, *Masculinity and Power*. See also Roger Scruton, "The Case against Feminism," *The Observer*, 22 May 1983.

36. Brittan, *Masculinity and Power*.

37. Sybil Oldfield, *Women against the Iron Fist* (Oxford: Basil Blackwell, 1989); Tonci Kuzmanic et al., "An Open Letter to Peace Movements," *Peace News* 2382 (September 1994), p. 6.

38. Julie Wheelwright, *Amazons and Military Maids* (London: Pandora, 1989).

39. Segal, *Slow Motion*.

40. Wheelwright, *Amazons and Military Maids*.

41. Rogers, *Men Only*.

42. Vera Brittain, *Lady into Woman: A History of Women from Victoria to Elizabeth II* (London: Dakers, 1953).

43. Cynthia Enloe, "The Women in 'America's Backyard,'" *Trouble and Strife* (1986): 15–23; Cynthia Enloe, *Does Khaki Become You?* (London: Pandora, 1988).

44. Peter Almond, "Combat Role for Women in RAF," *Daily Telegraph*, 17 December 1991; Terence Shaw, "Servicewomen in Maternity Leave MOD Turnaround," *Daily Telegraph*, 17 December 1991.

45. Stoltenberg, *Refusing to Be a Man*.

46. Victoria Brittain, ed., *The Gulf between Us* (London: Virago, 1991).

47. Marcel Farry, "Iraqi Women's League Speak Out," *Spare Rib* 223 (1991): 14–17; Jan Melichar, "Indecent and Indelicate," *The Pacifist* 29, 4 (1991): 3, Cale Kirsten, "Kuwait Was Never the Issue," *Living Marxism* 30 (1991): 12–15. Alexander Cockburn and Andrew Cohen, "The Unnecessary War," in V. Brittain, ed., *The Gulf between Us* (London: Virago, 1991), pp. 1–26.

48. Brittan, *Masculinity and Power*.

49. Mike Freeman, *The Empire Strikes Back: Why We Need a New Anti-war Movement* (London: Junius Publications, 1993).

50. Stoltenberg, *Refusing to Be a Man*.

51. Carol Ann Douglas, "Dear Ms Woolf, We Are Returning Your Guineas," *Trouble and Strife* 21 (1991): 21–22.

52. Enloe, *Does Khaki Become You?*

53. Susan Ellicott, "America Faces Dilemma over Female Role," *The Times*, 1 December 1991.

54. Ibid.

55. Kate Muir, "Bridging the Gender Gulf," *The Times,* 5 February 1991.

56. R. McGowan and J. Hands, *Don't Cry for Me Sergeant Major* (London: Futura, 1983); Klaus Theweleit, *Male Fantasies* (Cambridge: Polity, 1987); Enloe, *Does Khaki Become You?;* Joan Smith, *Misogynies* (London: Faber & Faber, 1989).

57. Martin Shaw, *Post-military Society* (Cambridge: Polity, 1991).

58. Frank Richards, "Behind the West's Humanitarian Mask," *Living Marxism* 52 (February 1993): 18–22; Friends Committee on National Legislation (Washington, DC), "Somalia: Not Just Drought, Famine and War," *Peace News* 2362 (January 1993): 8–9; John Gittings,. "UN Intervention: Too Little, Too Late," *Red Pepper* 9 (February 1995): 20–21.

59. Florence Assie, "United Nations?" *Peace Matters* 10 (Summer 1995): 6–9.

60. Jon Swain, Matthew Campbell, and Tom Rhodes, "War and Impeachment," *The Sunday Times,* 20 December 1998; Simon Jenkins, "Stone Age Strategy," *The Times,* 18 December 1998; Patrick Wintour, "War in the Balkans," *The Observer,* 4 April 1999.

61. Rachel Cooke, "Tired of Women in Fatigues," *The Sunday Times,* February 26 1995.

62. Gerard J. de Groot, "Women: A Force for Change," *The Guardian,* 14 June 1999.

63. Aaron Hicklin, *Boy Soldiers* (Edinburgh: Mainstream Publishing, 1995); Christian Jennings and Adrian Weale, *Green-Eyed Boys* (London: HarperCollins, 1996).

64. Taylor and Young, *Campaigns for Peace.*

65. Philip Warner, *Auchinleck: The Lonely Soldier* (London: Sphere, 1982); Hicklin, *Boy Soldiers.*

66. Newsinger, *Dangerous Men,* p. 5; Hicklin, *Boy Soldiers.*

Chapter 9

Conscientious Objectors in the Great War: The Consequences of Rejecting Military Masculinities

Lois Bibbings

INTRODUCTION

This chapter[1] analyzes dominant constructions of English masculinity during the First World War.[2] Wartime is often characterized by crude dichotomies; the extremes of a national emergency tend to lead to rapid shifts in and the polarization of conceptions and attitudes, in the definitions of "us" and "them."[3] Unsurprisingly, then, the First World War brought with it particular and temporary reconstructions of notions of appropriate and inappropriate masculinity that drew upon pre-existing clusters of ideas about manhood. One pivotal binary in this period is examined here, namely, that of the military man versus the conscientious objector (CO) to military service.[4] Depictions of these cultural categories are described and discussed using contemporary portrayals of and attitudes toward these men. The objector in this period has been studied before, but neither specifically in relation to masculinity nor in contrast to the contemporary image of the military man. As such, this chapter forms part of a larger project that examines manhood and conscientious objection to military service.[5]

WARTIME MANHOOD AND THE INTRODUCTION OF COMPULSION

From the outbreak of war in August 1914 until early 1916, the sole method of recruitment in England was volunteerism.[6] Initially, then, those who signed up to serve were volunteers, and they signed up in huge numbers[7] despite the unpopularity of the military as a career, particularly within the working classes, in the years prior to the Great War.[8] Swiftly, manhood came to be redefined "in terms of soldiering."[9] Recruitment drives and the jingoistic elements in the press sought to call out the manhood in men and utilized pre-existing exemplary images of military men to do so.[10] Among other things, the recruitment machine drew upon the Victorian revival of the Arthurian tradition and its gentlemanly (Christian) cult of chivalry.[11] There were also the stories for boys and the patriotic adventure stories of empire, which had enjoyed great popularity from the latter half of the nineteenth century. Adventure stories came to be part of the very myth of empire, "the story England told itself as it went to sleep at night."[12] The military man was variously portrayed: for example, as a knight (in the case of the officer classes); a romantic hero; a saintly, godly man—a Christian soldier—and a good-hearted and loyal Tommy (in the case of the working classes). Such glorious images of an attainable English or British manhood—all a man had to do was wear a uniform—were fortified by the assumption that this would be a speedily and victoriously concluded war; so the sacrifice of service, if it was considered to be a sacrifice, would be brief, and the rewards great.[13] In contrast, those who failed to enlist without such excuses— for whatever reason, but particularly on the grounds of conscientious objection—came, as we shall see, to be despised and rejected by society.

Despite the statistical evidence that so many men were coming forward to serve and suffer, there was a pervasive perception that many were inexplicably shirking their responsibility, benefiting from their own cowardice and prolonging the war. In particular, young, able single men who failed to sport a uniform were frequently challenged, harangued, and castigated in the press and in streets, shops and sitting rooms around the country. There was a steadily growing pressure to make these men do their patriotic duty, to which the coalition government of late 1915 eventually yielded.[14] In 1916 the Military Service Act (the Act) introduced military compulsion for all able-bodied men, initially single, deemed to be fit and of military age, initially 18–41.[15] Men to whom it was applicable were liable to serve in the military once they were called up. Prime Minister Asquith justified the measures by stating that subjecting men to conscription simply "deemed in law ... what every man recognised to be their duty as a matter of moral and national obligation in the time of greatest stress in all our history."[16]

The Act was seen as a universalist measure that allowed for some exceptions and exemptions, but the latter were kept to a minimum to ensure the legitimacy of the legislation; excluding too many men from its ambit might have appeared discriminatory and might have increased resistance to the measure. Surprisingly, however, alongside exceptions for the ministers of religion, men who were medically unfit, and some provision for workers in essential industries, the Act provided for the exemption of those who professed a genuine conscientious objection to combatant service.[17] This provision, by which an essentially illiberal measure included limited recognition of autonomy, was part of the compromise with those in government who opposed military compulsion.[18] Consequently, in theory the Act allowed some of those hated men who had refused to enlist voluntarily to avoid the military. Critics felt this "conscience clause" recognized cowardice and represented a shirkers' charter and, hence, potentially undermined the universality and legitimacy of conscription.

Those who wished to claim exemption on conscience grounds had to argue their case in front of a tribunal system that considered all claims for exemption from or postponement of call-up.[19] Those the tribunal regarded as being genuine could, under the Act, be granted absolute, partial, or conditional exemption, although, there was initially some doubt as to whether absolute exemption was available to an objector.[20] Absolute exemption meant that the man concerned was completely absolved from the recruitment process. Partial exemption directed the individual to non-combatant duties within the military, and exemption could also be granted on the condition that the applicant undertake or continue in a particular field of labor, often in essential industry or agriculture.

If an applicant on conscience grounds was refused exemption or was granted a level of exemption he refused to accept, he would subsequently be deemed to be enlisted in the military. If he refused to report for duty, he would be arrested, fined in the magistrate's courts, and handed over to the military.[21] At this point an objector would be subject to the harshness of military rules and discipline that applied to all soldiers. His continued refusal to put on a uniform and obey orders would, therefore, result in military punishment, court martial, and military detention or imprisonment. Initially, no provision was made for dealing with men who persisted in their refusal. Subsequently, however, the government allowed for their transfer to civilian prisons.[22] It became common for COs to receive multiple terms of military and civilian incarceration; for each time they were released, they were returned to the military and again refused to obey.

In civilian prisons COs endured a harsh regime under the rule of silence and with minimal food or human contact; the latter could be further restricted, since disobedience would frequently be punished by solitary confinement. In addition, the use of straitjackets was not uncommon. If objectors refused to eat, they could be roughly force-fed, as those other gender dissidents, the suffragettes, had been before them.[23] Yet it should be remembered that in the military and in prison they were subject to the same harsh systems faced by others at this period of time. Thus the harshness they experienced was not necessarily a wholly unique experience, although they may have been especially unpopular with the authorities.

When incarcerated objectors persisted in their defiance, provision was made for their claims to be re-examined and for those adjudged to be genuine, if they were willing, to be released from the military and prison onto the Home Office Scheme, which sent them to hard-labor camps around the country.[24] The offer of release from the military onto this scheme was hardly an improvement, as conditions were often primitive and the local inhabitants often strove to make their lives as unpleasant as possible.

For those individuals who campaigned for peace or publicized the COs' cause, there was always the possibility of being hounded by the authorities and prosecuted under the Defence of the Realm Acts.[25] In fact, a number of supporters were. For example, those who worked with the No Conscription Fellowship, one of the organizations that supported COs throughout the war, or helped produce *The Tribunal*, its newspaper, were often arrested; some were charged and prosecuted with criminal activity.[26] Even after the war, once even those objectors in prison had been eventually released and dishonorably discharged from the army, the discrimination against them continued. The Representation of the People Act, 1918, which granted the vote to some women and many men for the first time, took away their franchise for a period of five years after the official end of the war.[27] Objectors also continued to find difficulty in employment for some time after the war, although a growing belief in peace meant that this lessened to some extent.[28]

IMAGES OF THE CONCHY

At the beginning of the war about 15,000 men had declared themselves to be conchies, as objectors came to be known.[29] Over the course of the war about 16,100–16,500 men objected in various ways to the terms of the Military Service Act.[30] This figure represented 0.33 percent of the 4,970,902 men who volunteered or were conscripted into the military.[31] Once compulsion was introduced, probably about 14,000–16,500 COs argued their claim for exemption in front of a tribunal.[32] Some of these applicants were undoubtedly not genuine objectors but were seeking a way out of the war; some changed their stance,[33] but 5,944 of their number obstinately refused to accept the exemption granted to them or the refusal of a certificate of exemption, and 985 were absolutists who refused to accept any alternative service even when it was offered to them under the Home Office Scheme.[34]

Objectors came from a range of social, economic, and educational backgrounds and based their objection on varied grounds. For some, their stance came from the tenets of their religion or their own religious beliefs. These included Quakers, Christadelphians, Plymouth Brethren, Jehovah's Witnesses, Methodists, Anglicans, and Catholics, as well as at least one Buddhist and members of small religious sects. Others based their beliefs on moral, political, or humanitarian grounds, sometimes alongside religious beliefs. For example, some were followers of Tolstoy and some, as socialists, saw themselves as part of an international brotherhood of workers who should unite rather than fight each other. The nature of these men's objections also varied greatly: There were the absolutists in prison who refused to accept the state's authority to direct them, and there were those who were happy to accept a role in the military in the Non-Combatant Corps—or "No Courage Corps," as it came to be popularly known.

Conscientious objections to various forms of compulsion had been know before in relation, for example, to the old militia ballots, to oath swearing, and most recently to the vaccination of children.[35] However, the context of the First World War and the advent of universal conscription meant that COs to military service were popularly regarded in a distinct way from their forebears. These men represented identities that sounded a particularly audible discord with the dominant ideas of the period.

DESPISED AND REJECTED

"In general society you could scarcely mention their existence, much less claim acquaintance with an individual COs [sic], so great was the disgust and abhorrence called forth...some families expelled the conscientious objector members from their midst, so keenly did they feel the disgrace of the connection."[36]

The Great War fervor, or perhaps fever, seemed to spread rapidly through British culture. There was a sense that the war was a joint sporting enterprise.[37] It was for some a festival celebrating national greatness, to which everyone should contribute either by helping with the preparations or by taking part in the festivities themselves.[38] Even in the days before war was declared, accounts record a wave of "mass hysteria." On 3 August 1916 in London "[a] vast procession formed in the streets...everyone waving flags and singing patriotic songs."[39] On the next day "[a]ll of London was awaiting Germany's reply to our Ultimatum, the excitement was intense, and it was plain that a large Majority were in favour of war" and a "seething mass' of men crowded round the Great Scotland Yard recruiting offices seeking to join up and join in.[40]

This was a carnival of war, a ritual of reversal, where the normal perceptions of existence shifted dramatically; killing, normally forbidden and unlawful, became compulsory, whereas refusing to kill suddenly became the most reprehensible stance for a man to hold. Thus one tribunal member asked a CO applicant, "Do you really mean to say you wouldn't kill anybody?" When the applicant agreed that this was the case, the interrogator responded, "What an awful state of mind to be in!"[41] As a result, during the war many COs were held in the same prisons that housed "ordinary" murderers.

In this context, COs who refused to be implicated in the war effort were perceived as wilfully excluding themselves from a great celebratory endeavor. They were likely, at the very least, to be misunderstood, misinterpreted, and maligned. But the depths to which jingoism was to sink, with its stories of Germans eating babies, cutting off boys' hands, and committing other such pagan atrocities, meant that responses to the idea of conscientious objection were likely to be far more vehement and violent. Jingoism at its worst operated as "[a] coarse patriotism fed by the wildest rumours and the most violent appeals to hate and the animal lust of blood."[42] This blood lust was to be directed toward both the Hun and the conchy in the war years. Although the intensity of hatred for COs fluctuated, its depth depending in part upon the success of the military, they were at the very least unpopular for the duration of the war and to some extent after peace was declared. Objectors were often shunned and sometimes hounded by those who sought to verbally attack them or persuade them to give in, and in some cases they were beaten by mobs of concerned citizens.[43] Indeed, they received a great deal of attention, given that they numbered so few, although it may have been assumed that they were everywhere. What seemed to be important was what they supposedly symbolized.

Thus, conscientious objectors to military service in the Great War were frequently portrayed and treated as the worst of men—assuming it was accepted that they had any claim to manliness, or even to humanity. If the volunteer was the most exemplary of men and the conscript was at least doing what he was told, the CO was effectively publicly and shamelessly rejecting his very identity as an English man. Thus, in the extreme polarities of wartime England, the conchy embodied a dominant conception of deviant, marginal masculinity; he was seen as the antithesis of the volunteer, as a complete anathema. If he was to be portrayed at all, he had to be described in the most negative of lights to discourage others from following him or conceiving of him as a martyr. The objector for a brief period became the epitome of a new, dangerous masculinity.

If the military man was brave, loyal, patriotic, self-sacrificing, and true, the CO had to be cowardly, disloyal, unpatriotic, selfish, and traitorous. Indeed, many representations or descriptions of the objector drew upon images of the military man to contrast with the supposed qualities of the CO. Each, therefore, was represented as a type, with the despised category *conchy* conflating all the very different men into one hated common identity; although from surviving accounts it is possible to argue that among these the religious and particularly the Quaker objector was more likely to be viewed more sympathetically.[44]

Religion often figured in the contrasting depictions of the soldier and the CO. For example, the soldier was frequently depicted as a shining Christian knight or as "a type of crucified Christ."[45] Dominant notions of Christianity propounded the idea of fighting as a noble, just, and necessary act; war was justified by the teachings of Christ, and "we" were fighting for him. Further, there was a feeling that because God was on "our" side, he would protect "us." The transformation of the short story "The Bowman," by Arthur Machen,[46] into the myth of the Angel of Mons and, thence, purportedly into fact was an extreme but not unrepresentative example of this feeling.[47] Moreover, Christ was, after all, British, as one tribunal member noted when an applicant began to explain the meaning of a New Testament passage in the Greek: "Greek, you don't mean to tell me that Jesus Christ spoke Greek. He was British to the backbone."[48] In contrast, the Christian conchy, in particular, was often portrayed as a heretic who failed to see or wilfully ignored the true teachings of the Bible. His refusal to fight was to "turn Christianity upside down,"[49] as "the very essence of Christianity is to fight."[50] One member of a Lancashire tribunal told an applicant: "I think you are exploiting God to save your own skin....It is nothing but deliberate and rank blasphemy."[51] Indeed, the CO was also often castigated for his refusal to fight against evil (Prussianism) and the devil (the Kaiser).[52]

The construction of the CO also drew upon and became part of the fears of the degeneration of British manhood.[53] This idea, which was linked to eugenic and Darwinian thought, reached its peak during the Boer War when many recruits failed their medical examinations. Such concerns about physical fitness even led to the setting up of an Inter-Departmental Committee on Physical Deterioration, which reported in 1904.[54] The Muscular Christianity movement and organizations such as the Boys' Brigade and the recently formed Scouting movement perceived a physical and moral degeneration of manhood that were often conceived of as being linked. They consequently sought to address their concerns, to reassert and reproduce true manliness, through the provision of sometimes militaristic physical training and to some extent moral education for boys. Healthy activity was generally prioritized over the unhealthy potential of introspection and self-absorption.[55] Portrayals of COs as pathetic physical specimens drew upon and resonated with these concerns. One CO, for example, was described at his tribunal hearing as "a shivering mass of unwholesome fat."[56] In another example, an applicant at Holborn Tribunal seemed to have been refused exemption because of his failure to take healthy exercise and his supposedly unwashed appearance. One member stated, "Yours is a case of an unhealthy mind in an unwholesome body."[57] An applicant's presumed moral degeneracy and cowardice or laziness was also often noted in the tribunals and the country.[58] In contrast, the image of the soldier was one of physical prowess and stoicism; in the recruitment posters of the day the military man was always the finest of physical specimens and was unquestionably morally upstanding merely because he wore a uniform.

Masculinity was perceived to be in decline or in crisis in a number of respects in the late nineteenth century. There were, for example, the challenges posed by the New Woman, the female suffrage movement and the Suffragettes. In addition, the Naughty Nineties and the trial of Oscar Wilde had raised concerns about upper-class decadence. often linked to the idea of degeneracy, and "the love that dare not speak its name."[59] The newly categorized homosexual was beginning to be associated with the effeminacy and aestheticism of the dandy that Wilde had epitomized. Thus, as Sinfield has described, Wilde was beginning to represent unhealthy and unspeakable desires in men; the idea of effeminacy as a cultural term was changing; it was gradually recoded after the trial and was coming to denote a liminal category.[60]

Representation of the CO drew upon these fears. He was often described as a snivelling, pathetic, morally lacking, inadequate, sometimes with the suggestion of sexual inversion. In one telling cartoon from *John Bull* in May 1918, he was represented as a dandified figure, bearing a passing resemblance to Wilde, slouched lazily in an armchair, hands in pockets and smoking. In the background "Happy Families" playing cards depict his father, brother, and uncle in the army, a cousin in the navy, his mother as a nurse, and even a sister in uniform. The caption reads, "This little piggie stayed at home." All the other members of his family, even the women, are doing their bit, while he lazes smugly, presumably protected by the "shirkers' charter." Consequently, he is an unnatural man, a pointless man; an aberration who is not only unmanly and possibly an invert but also less than a woman.

Resonating with elements of the portrayal of the CO in the popular imagination, the idea of the parasite had some cultural currency at the *fin de siècle*.[61] Thus, some descriptions of COs seemed to tap into fears of loss of control, atavistic degeneration, and the figure of the vampire. Conchies' very masculinity was parasitic; they were prepared to stand by and watch others fight for them, and they could profit from the manpower shortage caused by others joining up. Scavenging at the margins of society, such men were "the most awful pack that ever walked the earth."[62]

In addition to being considered pathetic specimens who were unmanly and degenerate, conchies were often viewed as posing a threat to the war effort by their very existence. Pacifism, it was feared, could spread. To some Britons, objection and lack of patriotic fervor was an indication that COs were spies, supporters of the Kaiser. Thus, the *Daily Express* described objectors as traitors who were helping to stab the army in the back and were "fighting for Germany."[63] If they were actually working for Germany, then the risk they posed to the country was far greater than a merely anti-war stance. Objectors and their supporters were subjected to state surveillance and police raids throughout the war.[64] The Home Office kept files on pacifist agitators and "Anti-Recruiting and Peace Propaganda."[65] The secret state monitored them just as it sought to monitor the decadent establishments in London, which were viewed as potential nests of spies.[66] But one category of CO came to be feared more than other objectors. The anarchic tendencies of a minority of such men led some to predict the danger of a Bolshevik revolution in England. Thus the militant objectors who were housed in Dartmouth Gaol following its "deprisonization" and renaming as the Princetown Work Centre under the Home Office Scheme were perceived to pose a particular threat.[67] A CO strike at the center, following the death of one of the men from diabetes, brought a new wave of public hostilities against objectors.[68] Such men were very different from the supposedly more honorable religious and moral objectors in that they strove to create confusion and chaos for the authorities.

As noted briefly above, despite the conscience clause, the CO could be categorized as a civilian or military criminal if he refused to comply with the authorities. Beyond this, he was widely conceived of as deviant, as the most heinous "cultural criminal." In this respect his criminality lay not so much in his legal status as in his outsider and outlaw masculinity. His disobedience and lawlessness was committed against the laws of duty, patriotism, and manliness; he represented a dissident masculinity. There was then a form of informal or *de facto* criminalization of the conchy that the panic tendencies of a nation in crisis created and amplified.[69] All COs, regardless of their exemption status, were perceived of as the worst of criminals precisely and merely because of their stance. Objection was perhaps one of those acts that Nicola Lacey suggests might already be criminal, irrespective of whether it was formally so defined.[70] Indeed, it has been argued that "[n]early all [tribunals] agreed in regarding conscience as an unpatriotic offence which must be visited by penalties."[71] Certainly, there is evidence of objectors being bullied during their hearings.[72] Indeed, "a great many of the tribunals seem[ed] to take delight in heaping scorn and insults upon the applicants."[73] In addition, objectors were often silenced and dismissed without a hearing once the grounds of their application was known; by claiming to be COs, they spoke their own guilt. H. E. Stanton's tribunal appearance on 8 March 1916 before the Luton Tribunal lasted less than three minutes, and Harold Bing's application was dismissed once the tribunal realized he was only 18 years old and thus, unlike the boys of 18 and under who volunteered, was too young to possess a conscience.[74] Indeed, some tribunal members seemed to see it as their patriotic duty to give objectors as hard a time as possible. They were "blackguards"[75] and a "pack of animals"[76]—in short, they deserved to be punished by nothing short of death.[77] In this context, prison was often regarded as too safe and hard labor as too soft.

The need for COs to be punished or forced to conform was a common theme in their treatment. Some people undoubtedly saw them as degenerates whose disobedient masculinity meant that they required masculinization. In the military a proportion of objectors were ordered to obey or suffer the consequences if they refused. The military view in May of 1916 was that "once a man is handed over to the military authorities as a soldier...the clear duty of every commanding officer [is] to do his best with the legitimate means at his disposal to make every man who is handed over to him an efficient soldier."[78]

Those who were not considered genuine should, in the words of Major General Sir Wyndham Childs. "be broken to discipline under the military machine."[79] In extreme cases objectors were subjected to bizarre tortures that seemed to fall well beyond the use of legitimate means in attempts to secure obedience. At Atwick Camp near Hull, Private John Gray was stripped and, with a rope tied around his waist, was pushed into a pond and dragged out again—this was repeated eight or nine times. He had also been frog-marched and punched.[80] At South Sea Camp, Cleethorpes, Private James Brightmore was kept in solitary confinement in a waterlogged pit measuring five or ten feet deep and three feet in diameter.[81] A number of objectors were also sent to the front in France, where they would face death for further disobedience. None were shot, for although a number were sentenced to death, their punishment was subsequently commuted to penal servitude.[82] Of course, some of the techniques employed to make a CO a soldier or to enact punishment upon him were not dissimilar from the general horseplay and realities of military discipline for the ordinary soldier. There is some evidence to suggest, however, that these punishments were more severe and more inventive in the case of COs.[83]

After the war the temporary disenfranchisement of COs was seen as both a punishment and a deterrent by MPs; objectors had given up their right to citizenship,[84] whereas fighting men and working women had earned this right. The various discriminatory practices against COs in employment during and after the war were also seen as deserved penalties.[85] In addition, for some time after peace was declared, their war record—or lack of a proper one—was treated as if it were a criminal record.[86]

As a stark contrast to such evidence of torture and alongside images representing the CO as a threat, a dangerous masculinity, there was also a tendency to ridicule objectors, thus belittling their stance. The *Daily Sketch*, for example, followed the progress of "Percy" the CO in the military, portraying him as a nonsensical figure grinning maniacally while sporting an army blanket, implicitly emasculated by his refusal to wear a uniform.[87] Publicly portraying the conchy as the fool was far safer than taking him too seriously. In addition, it would have been difficult in the case of some devoutly religious objectors to conceive of them as threatening. These men may have seemed foreign from the standpoint of establishment Anglicanism, but they were also often the most law-abiding and inoffensive of men.

A further means of dealing with COs and their supporters was to seek to conceal or silence them. Certainly, the decision to transfer objectors into civilian prisons was a means of hiding them away. Similarly, the prosecutions under the Defence of the Realm Act amounted to censorship. Segregating objectors often had a similar effect; for example, in civilian prisons they were initially forbidden paper, they were bound by the rule of silence, which meant it was difficult to converse with anyone, and they were allowed few visitors. Further, the provisions in the Representation of the People Act meant that after the war their political voices were officially suppressed. Perhaps one reason for this need to conceal and silence lay in official concerns that COs should not get too much sympathetic publicity. A prominent legal academic of the time, A.V. Dicey, voiced concerns about martyrdom and fears that COs might command popular sympathy; he argued that reform should be instituted in order to diminish the reality or appearance of injustice to objectors.[88] Some of the surviving records in the Public Records Office reveal similar anxieties. One such file records discussions among the Home Office, the War Office, and the Law Society. The latter wished to strike off a conscientious objector, Scott Druckers, from the roll of solicitors for calling the profession into disrepute by his unpatriotic stance. The Law Society was seeking the temporary release of Druckers from prison to enable them to proceed against him. War and Home Offices decided that the president of the Law Society was to be strongly discouraged from this course because a disciplinary hearing would draw attention to the objector and might risk making him a martyr to the pacifist cause. Far better that he remain incarcerated and hidden.[89]

CONCLUSION

To many Britons in the First World War, COs and their supporters were a "suspect community." This notion is by no means a new one,[90] but here we see it as a historical phenomenon: There are such groups around "us" all the time but who "they" are changes. Objectors were imagined to embody a range of despised traits and were depicted as the antithesis of the soldier. They represented rogue and subversive masculinities and were to some degree segregated (within prisons and the Home Office Scheme camps) as a means of controlling and silencing them. It was as if their disease had to be contained lest the contagion spread or, if possible, cured so they could be reintegrated into manhood.

Yet, this is only a part of the picture. The images and treatment of the CO were not so uniformly negative. Equally, the soldier sometimes failed to live up to his idealized image. Nevertheless, the dominant portrayal of the CO maintained a sharp distinction between him and the exemplary military man. In this cultural-historical context, military masculinities ruled supreme.

REFERENCES

Arnold-Foster, H. O., "The Army and the Government," *19th Century* (1898) XLIII: 346.

Bibbings, L., "State Reaction to Conscientious Objection," in I. Loveland, ed., *The Frontiers of Criminality* (London: Sweet and Maxwell, 1995), pp. 57–81.

Bibbings, L., *Dishonourable English Men: Masculinity and Conscientious Objection to Military Service in the Great War* (forthcoming, 2002).

Braithwaite, C., "Legal Problems of Conscientious Objection to Various Forms of Compulsion under British Law" (1968) *Journal of the Friends Historical Society* 2–18.

Braithwaite, C., *Conscientious Objection to Various Compulsions under British Law* (York: William Sessions, 1995).

Brockway, F., *The No Conscription Fellowship: A Souvenir of Its Work during theYears 1914–1919* (London: NCF, 1919).

Chrisp, P., *Conscientious Objectors: 1916 to the Present Day* (London: Tressell Publications, 1988).

Clarke, M. J., "Mobid Introspection" in W. F. Bynum, R. Porter, and M. Shepard, eds., *The Anatomy of Madness: Essays in the History of Psychiatry,* vol. III: *The Asylum and Its Psychiatry* (London: Tavistock Publications, 1988).

Dawson, G., *Soldier Heroes: British Adventure, Empire and the Imaging of Masculinities* (London: Routledge, 1994).

Dicey, A. V., "The Conscientious Objector" (1918) *Nineteenth Century,* February: 357–373.

Druckers, S., *Handed Over* (London: Daniel, 1917).

Fussell, P., *The Great War and Modern Memory* (Oxford: Oxford University Press, 2000 ed.).

General Annual Reports of the British Army for the period from 1 October 1913 to 30 September 1919, Cmd. 1193, 1921.

Girouard, M., *The Return to Camelot: Chivalry and the English Gentleman* (New Haven: Yale University Press, 1981).

Graham, *Conscription and Conscience: A History, 1916–1919* (London: George Allen and Unwin, 1922).

Green, M., *Dreams of Adventure, Deeds of Empire* (London: Routledge and Kegan Paul, 1980).

Greenslade, W., *Degeneracy, Culture and the Novel, 1880–1940* (Cambridge: Cambridge University Press, 1994).

Hearnshaw, F., "Compulsory Military Service in England" (1916) *Quarterly Review* April: 416–437.

Hillyard, P., *Suspect Community: People's Experience of the Prevention of Terrorism Acts in Britain* (London: Pluto, 1993).

Hoare, P., *Wilde's Last Stand: Decadence, Conspiracy and the First World War* (London: Duckworth, 1997).

Hobhouse, S., "An English Prison from Within" (1918) *Quarterly Review* July 21–38.

Hobhouse, S., and Brockway, F., *English Prisons To-Day* (London: Prison System Enquiry Commission, 1922).

Hobson, J. A., *The Psychology of Jingoism* (London: Grant Richards, 1901).

Lacey, N., "Contingency and Criminalisation," in Loveland, *Frontiers of Criminality* (London: Sweet and Maxwell, 1995), pp. 1–27.

Leed, E., *No Man's Land: Combat and Identity in World War I* (Cambridge: Cambridge University Press, 1979).

Mitchel, D., *Women on the Warpath: The Story of the Women of the First World War* (London: Jonathan Cape, 1966).

Nevinson, H. W., "The Conscientious Objector" (1916) *Atlantic Review*, November: 686–694.

Playne, C., *Britain Holds On, 1917–18* (London, George Allen and Unwin, 1933).

Powell, E. C., Reminiscences, Imperial War Museum PP/MCR/37.

Rae, J., *Conscience and Politics: The British Government and the Conscientious Objector to Military Service, 1916–1919* (London: Oxford University Press, 1970).

Reader, W. J., *At Duty's Call: A Study in Obsolete Patriotism* (Manchester: Manchester University Press, 1988).

Russell, B., "Some Psychological Difficulties of Pacifism," in J. H. Bell, ed., *We Did Not Fight, 1914–1918: Experiences of War Resisters* (London: Cobden Sanderson, 1935).

Showalter, E., *Sexual Anarchy: Gender and Culture at the Fin de Siècle* (London: Virago, 1992).

Sinfield, A., *The Wilde Century: Effeminacy, Oscar Wilde and the Queer Moment*, (London: Cassell, 1994).

Snowden, P., *British Prussianism: The Scandal of the Tribunals* (Manchester, National Labour Press, 1916).

Tate, T., *Women, Men and the Great War: An Anthology of Stories* (Manchester: Manchester University Press, 1995).

Taylor, A.J.P., *English History, 1914–45* (Harmondsworth: Penguin, 1975).
Williams, B., *Raising and Training the New Armies* (London: Constable, 1918).

NOTES

1. I would like to thank Dave Cowan for commenting on a draft of this chapter.

2. Although this chapter centers upon Englishness in particular, it considers Englishness and Britishness as one because of the tendency to conflate the two terms or use them interchangeably.

3. See, for example, P. Fussell, *The Great War and Modern Memory* (Oxford: Oxford University Press, 2000 ed.), Chap. III; B. Russell, "Some Psychological Difficulties of Pacifism," in J. H. Bell, ed., *We Did Not Fight, 1914–1918: Experiences of War Resisters* (London: Cobden Sanderson, 1935), p. 329; C. Playne (on war psychosis), *Britain Holds On, 1917–18* (London, George Allen & Unwin, 1933), p. 303.

4. *Conscientious objector* is used here to describe those men who raised an objection to military service, non-combatant military service, and/or compulsory war work consistently and from the outset. However, even this definition is not satisfactory, as some objectors were not visible since some, for example, were protected by their work in an essential occupation and others were already in the army. On the problem of definition see J. Rae, *Conscience and Politics: The British Government and the Conscientious Objector to Military Service, 1916–1919* (London: Oxford University Press, 1970), pp. 68–71.

5. I am currently completing a monograph to be entitled *Dishonourable English Men: Masculinity and Conscientious Objection to Military Service in the Great War.*

6. For a different view of the military tradition see F. Hearnshaw, "Compulsory Military Service in England" (1916) *Quarterly Review,* April, pp. 416–437.

7. Two and a half million men and boys signed up in the first sixteen months of the war prior to conscription coming into effect: General Annual Reports of the British Army for the period from 1 October 1913 to 30 September 1919 (Cmd. 1193), 1921, p. 9.

8. For example, in 1898 H.O. Arnold-Foster, the secretary of state for war, stated that "[n]o tradition is more deeply rooted in the minds of the poorer classes...than that which represents enlistment as the last step in the downward career of a young man." "The Army and the Government," *19th Century* (1898) XLIII: 346.

9. T. Tate, *Women, Men and the Great War: An Anthology of Stories* (Manchester: Manchester University Press, 1995), Introduction, p. 5.

10. W. J. Reader describes this reconstruction of the image of soldiering through existing cultural ideas in *At Duty's Call: A Study in Obsolete Patriotism* (Manchester: Manchester University Press, 1988), see especially chap. 6.

11. On the cult of chivalry in the nineteenth and early twentieth century see M. Girouard, *The Return to Camelot: Chivalry and the English Gentleman* (New Haven: Yale University Press, 1981); chap. 18 focuses upon the Great War.

12. M. Green, *Dreams of Adventure, Deeds of Empire* (London: Routledge & Kegan Paul, 1980), p. 3. See also G. Dawson, *Soldier Heroes: British Adventure, Empire and the Imaging of Masculinities* (London: Routledge, 1994), chap. 3. P. Fussell describes this

myth and the romanticized language used to talk about the war as echoing such sources: A horse was a "steed" or "charger'; the enemy was "the foe"; danger was "peril"; to conquer was "to vanquish"; to die was to "perish"; the blood of young men was, in the words of Rupert Brooke, "the red/Sweet wine of youth." *The Great War,* pp. 21–22 and generally.

13. For example, the accompanying text to Army Form B212 (the wartime enlistment form) promises this.

14. Although their yielding was probably more about manpower management than obtaining more recruits for the military: "The army had more men than it could equip, and voluntary recruitment would more than fill the gap, at any rate until the end of 1916," A.J.P. Taylor, *English History, 1914–45* (Harmondsworth: Penguin, 1975), p. 53.

15. Subsequent measures refined and extended the scope of conscription to married and older men.

16. HC 5 col. 961, 5 January 1916.

17. Military Service Act, 1916, s.2(1)(d).

18. See J. Rae, *Conscience and Politics,* chap. 2.

19. Military Service Act, 1916, s.2(7), scheds. 2,3 and Military Service Regulations (Amendment) Orders SR&I 1916 No. 53.

20. Ibid., s.2(3).

21. Ibid., s1(1)(b).

22. Army Order X (AO 179, 1916) directed that any CO found guilty of an offense against discipline should be sentenced to imprisonment rather than detention and after court-martial should be sent to a civil prison.

23. Two prominent objectors, Stephen Hobhouse and Fenner Brockway, became active in the prison reform movement after the war as a result of their experiences. See S. Hobhouse, "An English Prison from Within" (1918) *Quarterly Review,* July, pp. 21–38; S. Hobhouse and F. Brockway, *English Prisons To-Day* (London: Prison System Enquiry Commission, 1922).

24. For a discussion of the scheme see, for example, Rae, *Conscience and Politics,* chap. 8.

25. Defence of the Realm Consolidation Act, 1914, and Defence of the Realm (Amendment) Act, 1915.

26. See, for example, the report of Bertrand Russell's conviction as author of a Fellowship leaflet, *The Tribunal,* 8 June 1916; for an account of the hounding and prosecutions see Graham, *Conscription and Conscience: A History, 1916–1919* (London: George Allen and Unwin, 1922), pp.190–204. Also see below.

27. S.9(2). The Act provided that COs who had been exempt from all military service or who had been court-martialed were disqualified unless they could prove they had undertaken work of national importance. Disqualification ended on 30 August 1926 because the war was not legally included until 31 August 1921.

28. For more detailed accounts of objectors' treatment see especially Graham, *Conscription and Conscience,* and Rae, *Conscience and Politics.*

29. See Graham, *Conscription and Conscience,* p. 344.

30. Ibid., pp. 348–349, and Rae, *Conscience and Politics,* p. 71.

31. Cmd. 1193, 1921, p. 9.

32. This can only be an estimate, since full records did not survive (see PRO, MH 47/3, 8 November 1921, for the instruction to destroy tribunal papers.). Some COs were not prepared to appear before a tribunal because doing so would have entailed accepting the state's authority to categorize them; others fled the country, were deemed to be medically unfit, were able to argue for exemption on other grounds, or joined an organization such as the Red Cross or Friends Ambulance Unit and, hence, avoided conscription. See Rae, *Conscience and Politics*, pp. 68–70, and, for example, http://www.pro.gov.uk/leaflets/ri2016.htm.

33. See Rae, *Conscience and Politics*, pp. 69–70.

34. See ibid., pp. 164–167.

35. See C. Braithwaite, "Legal Problems of Conscientious Objection to Various Forms of Compulsion under British Law" (1968) *Journal of the Friends Historical Society*, pp. 2–18, and *Conscientious Objection to Various Compulsions under British Law* (York: William Sessions, 1995).

36. Caroline E. Playne, *Britain Holds On*, p. 303.

37. See Fussell, *The Great War*, pp. 25–28.

38. E. Leed, *No Man's Land: Combat and Identity in World War I* (Cambridge: Cambridge University Press, 1979), p. 40.

39. Reminiscences of E. C. Powell, Imperial War Museum PP/MCR/37, 2–3.

40. B. Williams, *Raising and Training the New Armies* (London: Constable, 1918), p. 6.

41. Quoted in Graham, *Conscription and Conscience*, p. 89.

42. J. A. Hobson, *The Psychology of Jingoism* (London: Grant Richards, 1901), pp. 8–9.

43. Accounts of such attacks are given, for example, in Rae, *Conscience and Politics*, p. 189; Graham, *Conscription and Conscience*, p. 139.

44. See, for example, Rae's comments: *Conscience and Politics*, pp. 72–73.

45. Fussell, *The Great War*, p. 119. See also pp. 117–120.

46. *Evening News*, 29 September 1914.

47. See Fussell, *The Great War*, pp. 115–116. The original story described the bowmen of Agincourt coming to the aid of English soldiers, but people came to view these shining shapes as real angels.

48. The chairman of "a tribunal near London," quoted in Graham, *Conscription and Conscience*, p. 71.

49. Sir George Adam Smith, at his Inaugural Address as Moderator at the United Free Church Assembly of 1916, cited in Graham, *Conscription and Conscience*, p. 43.

50. A tribunal member at Worcester, quoted by Graham, *Conscription and Conscience*, p. 89.

51. Quoted in P. Chrisp, *Conscientious Objectors: 1916 to the Present Day* (London: Tressell Publications, 1988), p. 9. See also Graham, *Conscription and Conscience*, p. 71.

52. For example, see *The Tribunal*, 8 March 1916.

53. On degeneracy see, for example, W. Greenslade, *Degeneracy, Culture and the Novel, 1880–1940* (Cambridge: Cambridge University Press, 1994), especially chap. 1.

54. Cd. 2175.

55. M. J. Clarke, "Morbid Introspection," in W. F. Bynum, R. Porter, and M. Shepard, eds., *The Anatomy of Madness: Essays in the History of Psychiatry*, vol. III: *The Asylum and Its Psychiatry* (London: Tavistock, 1988), p. 72.

56. Graham, *Conscription and Conscience*, p. 71. See also R. L. Outhwaite 5 HC 80, col. 2435, 16 March 1916.

57. Snowden, *British Prussianism: The Scandal of the Tribunals* (Manchester: National Labour Press, 1916), p. 10.

58. For example, C. H. Norman notes this tendency in relation to tribunal members in F. Brockway, *The No Conscription Fellowship: A Souvenir of Its Work during the Years 1914–1919* (London: NCF, 1919), p. 25.

59. On decadency and homosexuality see, for example, E. Showalter, *Sexual Anarchy: Gender and Culture at the Fin de Siècle* (London: Virago, 1992), chap. 9. Greenslade, *Degeneracy*, describes decadence as a mutation of degeneration theory, p. 31.

60. See A. Sinfield, *The Wilde Century: Effeminacy, Oscar Wilde and the Queer Moment* (London: Cassell, 1994).

61. See Greenslade, *Degeneracy*, pp. 18–19.

62. Snowden, *British Prussianism*, p. 8.

63. September 1914. Also, for example, see an account of Nairn Tribunal. *The Tribunal*, 8 March 1916.

64. The offices of the National Council Against Conscription, the No Conscription Fellowship, and the Independent Labour Party were all raided by the police in 1916 and 1917, and anti-conscription leaflets, posters, and newspapers were confiscated. See PRO, HO 45/10801/307402. See also, P. Hoare, *Wilde's Last Stand: Decadence, Conspiracy and the First World War* (London: Duckworth, 1997), p. 26; D. Mitchel, *Women on the Warpath: The Story of the Women of the First World War* (London: Jonathan Cape, 1966), pp. 331–346.

65. PRO, KV1.

66. See, for example, Hoare, *Wilde's Last Stand*, p. 26.

67. One visitor to the center reported that "sacks of letters come and go, no doubt carrying instructions for those plans of bloodshed which may at some future time bring, according to our view, ruin, to England." *The Times*, 8 October 1917.

68. For the results of the inquiry into the death and the strikers' complaints see Major Terrell 5 HC 103, col. 1628–31, 28 February 1918. An intensification of attacks upon objectors in the press followed news of the strike.

69. See further L. Bibbings, "State Reaction to Conscientious Objection," in I. Loveland, *The Frontiers of Criminality* (London: Sweet and Maxwell, 1995), pp. 57–81.

70. "Contingency and Criminalisation," in Loveland, *Frontiers of Criminality*, p. 14.

71. H. W. Nevinson, "The Conscientious Objector" (1916) *Atlantic Review*, November, pp. 686–694, p. 690.

72. See, for example, Snowden, *British Prussianism*.

73. Ibid., p. 8.

74. H. E. Stanton diaries, vol. 1, p. 9 (unpublished manuscript). Harold Bing audiotape, 358, Reel 2 (transcript p. 7) (Oral History Recordings, Department of Social Records, Imperial War Museum).

75. Snowden, *British Prussianism*, p. 12.

76. Ibid., p. 8.

77. A military representative at Sheffield informed the applicant that there was only one way to get absolute exemption from the tribunal and that was death. Graham, *Conscription and Conscience*, p. 72. It is impossible to estimate just how widespread such harsh and unsympathetic treatment was in the tribunals because of the lack of full records—see n. 32 above.

78. PRO, CAB 37/147/35.

79. Quoted by Rae, *Conscience and Politics*, p. 160: Child's Notes for the Prime Minister on the History of Army Order X, Asquith Papers 127 (Bodleian Library, Oxford).

80. PRO, WO 32/2055/1714; *The Tribunal*, 12 July 1917; Graham, *Conscription and Conscience*, pp. 143–144.

81. The depth varies in the different accounts: PRO, WO 32/2054/1654; *Manchester Guardian*, 30 June 1917; Graham, *Conscription and Conscience*, pp. 140–143, who quotes the letter Brightmore smuggled out explaining his condition. See also the account of Mark Briggs' "duck-walk," which resulted in his requiring prolonged hospital treatment, in Graham, *Conscription and Conscience*, pp.128–129 and chap. IV generally.

82. There were a number of accounts of men being shipped to France. See, for example, Permanent Under Secretary for the War Office H. J. Tennant's statements, 5 HC 83, col. 523, 22 June 1916, 5 HC 83, col. 523, 26 June 1916; Graham, *Conscription and Conscience*, pp. 112–126, p. 135.

83. On 19 September 1916 a letter from the Army Council to all district commanders notes that there had been reports of "special treatment in the way of coercion" and warned them that in no circumstances was physical coercion to be used on COs. See J. I. Macpherson, Permanent Under Secretary, War Office 5 HC 96, col. 873, 23 July 1917.

84. For a discussion of this disenfranchisement see 99 HC 5, cols. 1135–1274, 20 November 1917.

85. For example, see Civil Service restrictions on employing COs: CAB 23/4/298 (18), 14 December 1917.

86. *The Tribunal*, 12 June 1919.

87. April 1916.

88. A. V. Dicey, "The Conscientious Objector" (1918) *Nineteenth Century*, February, pp. 357–373, p. 358, p. 360.

89. PRO, HO 45/10808/311118–4, 25.4.17. Druckers wrote a book about his prison experiences: *Handed Over* (London: Daniel, 1917).

90. See, for example, P. Hillyard, *Suspect Community: People's Experience of the Prevention of Terrorism Acts in Britain* (London: Pluto, 1993).

Chapter 10

The Popular Press and the Creation of Military Masculinities in Georgian Britain

Robert McGregor

INTRODUCTION

The impact of war on eighteenth-century British society was immense. For almost half of the century from 1700 to 1800, Great Britain was involved in warfare in Europe and farther afield. This involvement in warfare throughout the century exponentially increased the demand for men to serve in the army and navy during a conflict.[1] It also fundamentally affected the social construction of British masculinities in ways historians have traditionally overlooked. Britain's existence as a "masculine" nation seems taken for granted by many scholars; for example, Linda Colley, in her monograph *Britons: Forging the Nation*, remarks briefly upon the perception of Britain as an "essentially 'masculine' culture," but regrettably she does not elaborate as to differing standards within this culture.[2] For what was undeniably in many ways a society dominated by masculine influences in government, finance, and warfare—to quote Philip Corrigan and Derek Sayer, "the pervasive masculinity of 'the State,'"[3]—the nature of this oversight seems to be fundamental in nature. It would be foolish, however, to believe that this "masculine" culture was expressed in a consistently homogenous fashion throughout the century; for it was not. Michael Roper and John Tosh in particular emphasize masculinity in its "divergent, often competing, and above all, its changing forms,"[4] and this process of competition and change within masculine ideals can be discovered in eighteenth-century society. Frequent involvement in warfare created and reinforced a masculine ideology based upon ideals of heroism, honor, self-effacement, modesty, and jingoistic patriotism. But the values of this style of British military masculinity, continuously espoused by the popular press, were often challenged by other notions of masculinity and femininity, in particular, European notions.

There were internal challenges as well. The rise of middling- to upper-class "macaroni" culture based largely upon the importation of "European" luxuries following the Seven Years' War, reaching its height during the 1770s, provoked outraged response from the more vociferously patriotic areas of the British press. In particular, the threat of such macaroni values infiltrating the bastion of island defense, the officer corps of the navy and army, gave rise to a certain viciousness in the depictions of macaronis and also led to almost ridiculously high expectations of the British military. Those members of the masculine polity who somehow failed to live up to public expectations of military masculinity, in particular, those serving in the British armed forces in time of war, were heavily censured and depicted as being other than the dominant, martial type demanded by the public.

The role of the British press in engendering warfare was particularly important; in particular, it appears that the press at times led the charge against those other gender constructions that were seen as threatening to the fabric of British military masculinities. The rise of macaroni masculinity in the late 1760s and early 1770s was seen as symptomatic of a society thought to have become dangerously complacent about a peace hard won through war. There was resentment and concern expressed through the press that supposedly foreign influence should flourish in this way, at the expense of traditional masculinities. The relationship between masculine ideals and femininities is also important to this chapter, particularly in the ways the British developed negative images of European masculinities. French and Spanish gender constructions were seen as dangerous influences, or as George Mosse terms them, "countertypes" to the traditional image of British masculinity.[5] In particular, French forms of masculinity were derided and represented as feminine in the British press from early in the eighteenth century. The linkage of gender and class will also play a role in the discussion of masculinity in this context. Indeed, without a class framework to guide us, it is impossible to understand adequately the implications for British masculinities in the eighteenth century. Concepts of foppery and effeminacy, and their corresponding impact, were heavily associated with the burgeoning middle class and their consumption of luxury goods. In turn, these ideas were seen as continental influences; hardly British at all. Associated with the lower classes was the idea of a "Jack Tar" masculinity: the disdain of luxury, effeminacy, and foppery, and a rampant, almost jingoistic sense of nationalism. This form of lower-class masculinity was promoted as an exemplar for many in Britain to follow, particularly during the 1770s. George III and the royal family went to great lengths to associate themselves with this ideal at a time when the public profile of the King may have been less than popular.[6] The enlistment of Prince William Henry, the King's third son, in the navy during 1781 may have helped propagate ideals of military masculinity in a patriotic, lower-class context while symbolically demonstrating a rejection of the luxuries commonplace among the middle to upper classes at the time. This chapter will examine the relationship between masculinity and heroism; perceptions of cowardice and failure and the association of masculinity with developing British nationalism.

HEROISM AND MASCULINITY: JACK TAR IDEALS

In 1756 ships of the British East Indies squadron under Admiral Sir Charles Watson were engaged in battle against the Nawab of Bengal. This action was taken largely in support of the British East India Company, anxious to expand trading opportunities in South East Asia. Fort Baj-Baj, at Mayapore on the Hughli, remained to be taken, and the assembled soldiers and sailors determined to make camp until the morning, when an assault would be attempted. During the night one British seaman, named Strachan, fueled more with rum than thoughts of self-preservation, hurled himself into the fray and allegedly managed to capture the fort almost single-handedly. *The London Magazine* reported the story in 1773, seventeen years later:

Strachan, the hero of this adventurous action, was soon brought before the admiral, who, not withstanding the success that had attended it, thought it necessary to shew himself displeased with a measure in which the want of all military discipline so notoriously appeared. He therefore angrily inquired into the desperate step which he had taken. "Mr Strachan, what is this that you have been doing?" The fellow, after having made his bow, scratched his head, and with one hand twirling his hat upon the other, replied, "Why, to be sure, Sir, it was I who took the fort,—but I hope *there was no harm in it.*" ... Strachan, amazed to find himself blamed where he expected praise, had no sooner gone from the admiral's cabbin [*sic*] than he muttered these words"—"If I am flogged for this here action, I will never take another fort by myself as long as I live, by G-d!" Since these sheets ... he is become a pensioner to the chest at Chatham. At present he acts also as a sailor in one of the guard ships at Portsmouth; and he says that his highest ambition is to be made cook of one of his majesty's capital ships.[7]

Despite the dubious nature of such an anecdote, it was precisely the sort of masculine image middle- to upper-class Britons liked to believe about the men of their navy in the eighteenth century. Common sailors were represented as brave to a fault, aware of their position in society, and able to enjoy the benefits of (limited) social mobility via their meritorious conduct: as seen, the highest position Strachan aspired to was "to be made cook" of a ship of the line. That Strachan had blatantly disregarded the rules of gentlemanly warfare was obvious, but his conspicuous bravery won him a place in the public imagination: his masculinity had demonstrated a true "independence of state."[8] These qualities were standard markers for the British public to judge military masculinity, and the popular press was happy to refresh them. Indeed, that Strachan's story was published seventeen years after the actual event requires particular comment: At a time when the foppish macaronis seemed to be overrunning urban society, the recalling of such heroic, martial, masculine deeds was one way of contrasting the contemporary exemplars with those of the past.

The representation of the loyal British Tar, no matter how fictionalized, was an indication not only of increasing British nationalism but also of tensions in society. Jack Tar was seen by many to be a masculine exemplar for the nation to follow—an image to transcend class barriers in the eyes of the public at large, even if the reality was far different. Hence, the Jack Tar persona was used at given times within the upper ranks of society to enforce a militaristic, xeno-phobic national ideal against perceived threats from within and without the state. Indeed, high-ranking officers of the navy, such as Admiral Richard Kempenfelt, commented upon the perceptions of Jack Tar masculinity:

There is also a vulgar notion prevails amongst us, and that even with our gentry, that our seamen are braver than the French. Ridiculous to suppose courage dependent upon climate. The men who are best disciplined, of whatever country they are, will always fight the best.[9]

Kempenfelt, it must be admitted, was a sea officer in many ways ahead of his time, but the fact that he commented upon the existence of such a "vulgar no-tion ... even with *our gentry*" is worthy of note. Clearly, and despite Kempen-felt's realism, the elite belief in the lower classes as a bastion of Jack Tar masculinity was an important factor in national confidence regarding the navy. Strachan's actions in the previous anecdote exemplified much that was popu-larly perceived as masculine in Britain during a large part of the eighteenth century.[10] For Strachan was a representative of the navy: one of the quintes-sential expressions of British ideals. The navy, seen as the "wooden walls" of the nation and later, the key to expanding commercial opportunities overseas, was extremely popular with the press and public in many ways. It was seen as inherently safe to personal liberties, much safer than a standing army, which could be misused to the detriment of the people, as during the English civil war of the seventeenth century. In an era of growing nationalism and patriotism, celebration of the navy's victories was one way in which newfound "Britons" could identify with their country, and since the navy was perceived to be a tra-ditionally masculine service, the natural expansion of these masculine ideals into mainstream British society was virtually assured. The popularity of the Jack Tar myth, exemplified by Strachan, is one example of this.

MASCULINITY, COWARDICE, AND FAILURE

There was also a clear image of what was the very opposite of British naval masculinity, the defining other. In 1744, at the Battle of Toulon, Captain Richard Norris of HMS *Essex* demonstrated "other" failings to the letter. The *Essex* had been ordered to engage the enemy but showed no signs of doing so. Norris, according to several different sources, displayed his cowardice in al-most every conceivable way; when the ship's master struck up with a rousing song, celebrating British victories of the past, Norris told him to be quiet, saying: "It will be all over with us for presently, and we shall have no reason to sing." The first lieutenant pointed out that they could lend assistance to another British vessel that was sorely pressed. Norris apparently replied that they would not do so, for "if we do, we shall be sunk and tore to pieces." He allegedly later removed himself from the quarterdeck and hid under the hammocks in the starboard gangway.[11] Despite being the son of a senior admiral, Richard Norris was vilified for his inaction by the public and upon the strident demand of his junior officers tried before a court-martial , but he retired from service before any binding decision could be made on his fate. A mock trial of Norris "for perjury, fraud, and cowardice" was later published in a pamphlet designed to gain maximum exposure of the case.[12] It is significant because the failure of Norris, an officer, was more likely to be noticed by the press than any cowardice on the part of a common sailor. Failure on the lower deck was hardly deemed necessary to report, as it usually affected little; and, given the inequalities of eighteenth-century British society, it was important that caricatures like Strachan were seen to represent the lower-class ideal and to demonstrate that social mobility was possible through heroic service. Thus, the popular image of the hardy, masculine tar was rarely altered in the minds of the British public. By contrast, individual officers were genuinely expected to live up to public expectations and were exposed if they did not. Norris was an officer in command of a man-of-war, and aboard ship, he more than any other man was responsible for maintaining the fighting morale of his men by example. His failure also reinforced the problems of masculinity facing those higher on the social scale. His position in the navy was seen by many to have been achieved via his father, and it was rumored that Norris had not wanted to leave the domestic comforts of his wife and children to serve in the battle,[13] adding to his disgrace. His "counsel" in the mock trial made the point:

I am sorry to say, My Lord, that I have any Cause or Room to observe to this Court, that the greatest Part of our junior Officers both by Sea and Land are composed of such Butter-flies as these; and when they are put to the Test and Proof of War and Manhood, if they behave in a natural Sense, who can we blame more properly than these gross Silk-worms their Fathers?[14]

Norris's disgrace was therefore intimately connected with his father's honor and his own inherited privilege. The above quote also implies that Richard Norris had been well sheltered by his father's vast network of patronage. That he had failed the "Test and Proof of War and Manhood" was clear: He was seen to be totally unrepresentative of what was perceived as the British masculine type. In addition to this, the stigma of not wanting to leave his wife and children was seen as pure effeminacy: The place of the British man was not in the cocoon of the domestic sphere but, rather, in the public sphere, protecting home and hearth. Being dominated by a wife challenged the consolidated essence of eighteenth-century patriarchy and mocked the type of gentry masculinity Norris was expected to embody.[15]

A case similar to that of Richard Norris's was that of Rear-Admiral John Byng, an officer who commanded the British Mediterranean squadron against the French at the Battle of Minorca in 1756. Most of the nation was appalled that Byng, having an equal number of ships to the French, could possibly have been bested and that he failed to pursue the enemy, resulting in the capture of Minorca by the French. In the atmosphere of extreme patriotism engendered by the Seven Years' War, his behavior came to be despised, and Byng himself was sentenced to death following a court-martial that convicted him of failing to do his utmost in battle. One newspaper, *The Test*, made the following observation:

It is no Hardship upon the Gentlemen of the Navy, that the Law prescribes death for Cowardice, Disaffection, or neglect of Duty: It should prescribe it, and they who call for an Alternative, are not animated with a true heroic Fortitude and a Zeal for the Honour of their Country.[16]

The ideal of British masculinity did not tolerate failure easily. This was a rather harsh dictum by modern standards; however, it was obviously acceptable to many at the time. Although he did have his defenders, in an age of nascent nationalism Byng was largely seen as an influence to be rid of, one that could have dangerous consequences: "If our Admirals and Colonels are to refuse to fight where their duty calls them, this Nation is ruined; and it will be too late to call them to an account when the next shall run away from Plymouth, under Pretence of covering Portsmouth."[17]

Living up to the public ideal was difficult: Jack Tar masculinity often meant fighting to the bitter end. Arthur Gardiner, Byng's flag captain at the Battle of Minorca, redeemed his honor in February 1758 by chasing the French warship *Foudroyant*, which was more heavily armed than his own ship, the *Monmouth*. Gardiner lost his life during the action, but the *Foudroyant* was captured.[18] His honor, at the core of British masculinity, had been redeemed, and this was particularly noted by the press and other publications. Jonas Hanway, a philanthropist well known for his interest in naval affairs, noted in a pamphlet:

It is remarkable, that captain Gardiner who now engaged the *Foudroyant* in the *Monmouth* of 64 guns, and to which she struck (though not before he lost his life in the action,) commanded the *Ramellies* a 90 gun ship, when admiral Byng was on board two years before, and when the *Foudroyant* was considered by this admiral, as so formidable an object that he declined fighting the French; though the gallant admiral West had already begun the action.[19]

Personal honor in eighteenth-century Britain was very much a reflection of masculinity, and British military honor was a concept greatly cultivated by press and public throughout the century. The much-vaunted idea of the duel to reclaim one's honor, frequently expressed toward the end of the eighteenth century,[20] was only the most visible aspect of what was a complex social process. A recent article by Faramerz Dabhoiwala,[21] though concentrating on honor in terms of social reputation, neglects to make the connection between personal-familial honor and national honor, an interconnected ideal that is fundamental to any understanding of the British in the eighteenth century. John Byng's case, as mentioned previously, is a classic example. Byng's father had been awarded the title Viscount Torrington in recognition for his successes as a naval officer, in particular, for his part in brilliant victories at Malaga in 1704 and Cape Passaro in 1718. John Byng was seen by many to be the privileged inheritor of Torrington's honor, and great things were expected of him. His failure inspired great anger and resentment, as expressed by one naval officer, Captain Samuel Faulknor, in 1756:

No doubt but Mr Byng's behaviour on the late occasion off Mahon must anger and surprise you and every thinking man in the kingdom. Sad indeed; he's brought more disgrace on the British flag than ever his father the great Lord Torrington did honour to it.[22]

As Faulknor indicated, the disgrace was not restricted to John Byng alone; it affected his forebears, family, and most importantly in this case, his country. Extraordinary efforts were taken to portray Byng as atypical of the British military masculine exemplar. This was expressed in the most typical form of popular resentment: an effigy burning. *The Evening Post* of 26 August 1756 reported that an effigy of Byng was burnt by a mob on Tower Hill, "richly dressed in a blue and gold coat, buff waistcoat, trimmed & in full uniform." Masculine nationalism bred hysteria: Not far away, in Cheapside, a mob attacked an innocent man mistaken for Byng, who was said to have been walking with the "haughty" air the admiral was said to possess.[23] Clearly, Byng was being redefined and rejected as an early kind of macaroni: a beau, one used to luxurious living and elaborate French fashions.[24] Take, for example, the following ditty, published at the time:

> That Byng is an Admiral, all the World knows
>
> Of Great Taste in Building but Bashfull of Blows
>
> Polite in Behaviour and fond to Excess
>
> Can Boast much, can swear much, can fighting profess
>
> But when plac'd in the Van to the Rear can Retreat
>
> And without Rhime or Reason can write his Defeat. [sic][25]

The emphasis upon Byng's "taste in building" and "polite" behavior were thinly veiled references to continental stereotypes. Interestingly, Edward Thompson's previously mentioned play, *The Fair Quaker of Deal*, was performed in 1757, at the time of this controversy, and it portrayed not only the foppish Captain Mizen but also a true Jack Tar, Commodore Flip, who had been "all from Cook's Boy to a Commodore," and loathed luxury of any kind:

> I value myself for not being a Coxcomb, that is what you call a Gentleman Captain, which is a new Name for our Sea-Fops, who forsooth must wear white Linen, have Field-Beds, lie in Holland-Sheets, and load their Noddles with thirty ounces of Whore's Hair, which makes 'em hate the sight of an Enemy, for fear Bullets and Gun-powder shou'd spoil the Beau Wigg, and lac'd Jacket.[26]

Here, the public image of Byng as a "Sea-Fop" was being balanced with the characterization of an officer who embodied traditional militaristic, masculine virtues. But in the end, Byng's Jack Tar masculinity was redeemed through the absolute theater of execution.[27] At the last he refused to run: Augustus Hervey, a friend of the admiral, brought up the idea of escape; Byng flatly refused, however, saying he would rather die first than fly from death in such a manner.[28]

Yet, embodiment of conventional masculinity could ameliorate failure. Indeed, an officer such as Admiral Thomas Mathews could well have been the model for Thompson's Commodore Flip. Mathews' failure to beat the French and Spanish fleets at the Battle of Toulon in 1744 was equally as public, yet he did not suffer nearly as badly. This was because Mathews was identified as a true Jack Tar type: uneducated, uncomplicated, and demonstrably dependable. To Horace Mann, he once wrote, in thanks for some gifts: "I am much obliged to you for your kind present; the sweetmeats is good; so sayes sume of my gentlemen, is ye cheeses, but it's too good for me. I love nothing after ye French fashion [sic]."[29] This is a truly British masculine perspective if ever there was one.

Mathews was convicted on a technicality of failing to follow the sacred *Fighting Instructions:* His squadron closed to attack before forming a line of battle. Mathews' subordinate, Rear-Admiral Lestock, also escaped punishment, even though there was firm evidence that Lestock and his division ignored signals to engage the enemy. At the time, there was no death penalty for Mathews' error, however, and he was dismissed from the navy. Unlike Byng, he does not seem to have suffered any public backlash. He had fought in Torrington's victorious fleet at Cape Passaro in 1718, and as such he was entitled to a respectful place in society. His honor remained firmly intact, for unlike Byng, he had not "run away" from the enemy. Through their exploits, each had served to demonstrate the ideal of British military masculinity: Mathews' personification of this ideal probably saved much of his reputation, whereas Byng's exemplification of the reverse caused his stigmatization as other.

Hence, the vilification of cowardice on the part of Britain's military men was seen as consistent with a denial of other, European gender constructions. In the cases of Norris and Byng, tendencies toward femininity and fondness of luxury were emphasized by the popular press in attempts to identify them with continental masculinity and deny any influence upon the British masculine polity. The continuity of this process had profound implications for the British masculine self-image.

MASCULINITIES AND NATIONALISM

Britain's self-definition as a masculine nation was often made in relation to the victories that had occurred through war. A sense of national pride existed in the remembrance of historic events such as the Armada triumph in 1688, Blenheim in 1704, and much later, Trafalgar in 1805. There was a common thread running throughout many of these victories, and that was the seeming lack of military masculine virtues by the French. For example, Daniel DeFoe wrote in 1704:

Our Ancient English Histories have always spoken of the French with a great deal of contempt, and the English nation have been apt enough to have very mean Thoughts of them from Tradition, as an Effeminate Nation. This I am apt to believe, proceeds from the uninterrupted Victories which our ancestors have obtained over them.[30]

DeFoe explicitly connected what was seen as French effeminacy with their failure to prevail in warfare, and the story that the French enlisted female soldiers in the late eighteenth century was also a great source of amusement to the British.[31] The development of British nationalism was intimately connected with such notions; indeed, the comparisons between what was seen as British masculinity and French effeminacy were profusely distributed throughout society, especially in newspapers and journals.

Such contrasts were also reinforced by the proud perception that Britons had of themselves and their society. They remained stoutly proud of their Protestant Church and free constitution, believing them to be the envy of the world. Their independent and robust way of life was seen to be inherently superior to the oppressive Catholic regimes of Europe and their supposedly cringing populations.[32] Horace Walpole expressed this gendered patriotism best when ridiculing the character of Admiral Mathews to his correspondent in 1743: "I dare to say Mathews believes that God lives upon beef and pudding, loves prize-fighting and bull-baiting, and drinks fog to the health of Old England."[33]

This image of the masculine nation as God's elect was not merely literary. Throughout the century in many satirical cartoons, particularly those by James Gillray, the image of a stout John Bull tucking into a joint of roast beef, accompanied by a tankard of ale, with his equally well-fed family was contrasted to the imagined French ideal of a half-starved family living at the mercy of their overlords, eating little but garlic and snails, or worse (cats and frogs in particular were often pictured as staple French cuisine).[34] At the end of the century, faced with the challenge of the French Revolution, British freedoms were seen as the core of a superior masculine culture, one that created men who were stronger and more heroic than their continental neighbors:

> Thus Britons guard their ancient fame
>
> Assert their empire o'er the sea,
>
> And to the envying world proclaim,
>
> One nation still is brave and free—
>
> Resolv'd to conquer or to die,
>
> True to their KING, their LAWS, their LIBERTY.[35]

The final line here is the most important, for although this poem was written in 1798, at the height of the revolutionary wars, the substance of it was the idea of a pure libertarian tradition that had been sustained through the myth of the ancient constitution. The notion was that traditional British freedoms bred independent men; unfavorable comparisons with European countries were copious and obviously thought to be popular with the British public. For example, the middle-class-oriented *London Magazine* grandly presented the following anecdote to its readers in April 1773:

The Duke of Orleans, during his regency, interrogated a stranger as to the distinguishing characteristics of European nations. "I cannot better satisfy your Royal Highness (replied he) than by repeating the first question which is usually asked by the individuals of each, relative to a person on his first introduction to them. In Spain (added he) they enquire if he is a grandee, and of what rank?—In France, if he is known at court?— In Holland, what property he possesses?—In England, what sort of man he is?"[36]

This indicated that in England, unlike the European countries, masculinity stood for personal independence above all. The freedoms inherited by all Englishmen were universal, and in theory, if not practice, it transcended all social boundaries. Such perceptions, hardly capable of fulfillment for most, formed the basis of belief in a truly "British" way of life.

The British monarchy was well aware of the importance of subscribing to these ideals. George III sent his third son, Prince William Henry, into the navy to be trained as an officer,[37] and through the press he was quickly identified as a true Jack Tar type: disdaining luxury, engaging in the rough pursuits of life at sea, and showing true benevolence to "the people"[38] under his authority, partaking in their leisure expeditions ashore. Indeed, it seems this identification of royalty with the Jack Tar masculine type was a deliberate move on the part of the King: "I desire he may be received without the smallest marks of parade.... The young man goes as a sailor, and as such, I add again, no marks of distinction are to be shown unto him; they would destroy my whole plan."[39]

The success of the King's plan may be witnessed in press reports and memorials throughout the 1780s, as the young prince saw action and gained rank.

Importantly, he came to be seen as a national symbol of the masculinity that should have been embodied by all young men of his age:

Sir, While the community beholds with admiration, a son of their most gracious King, early devoting himself to the service of his country, and in the youthful season of his life, quitting the pleasures of a palace, to encounter the fatigues and perils incidental to every seaman; permit us, to offer our humble tribute of gratitude, as indulging, with the rest of our fellow-subjects, the pleasing hopes, that the British Flag will receive additional lustre from the heroic ardour of a Prince, the dawn of whose military genius promises a splendid meridian. At an age, when many princely and noble youths are just entering the walls of a college, Your Highness has fought and triumphed over the enemies of your country.[40]

It is particularly noteworthy that Prince William's enlistment in the navy came at a time when patriotic ideology throughout the nation was flagging badly. British involvement in the American revolutionary war was not only unpopular but also seen as unconstitutional by many throughout the nation, representing as it did an attempt to enforce a form of tyranny over a people who were thought to be entitled to the protections and liberties that ordinary Britons took for granted.

However, the fears regarding male foppishness appeared to have been justified following poor performances by the military during the American revolutionary war, and also after an engagement between the French and British fleets off Ushant, in 1778, after which both sides claimed a victory. In this context, the British press worked overtime to produce the impression that the French, with their foreign ways and effeminate masculinity, could hardly have bested the "wooden walls" of the nation:

On Sunday last a gallant young nobleman, who was on board the *Victory* during the late engagement between Admiral Keppel and the Brest fleet, dined at White's and there declared publicly, that the French fired four broadsides before the English discharged a single shot, that the French and the English Admirals were so close during the action that he often supposed that they would have grappled; and so well directed and continued were the fires of the *Victory*, that he saw the enemy drop in abundance; a circumstance which struck such terror to the survivors, that he clearly perceived, when the enemy was sheering off, they all had skulked under hatches.[41]

The definition of British military masculinity, therefore, was commonly made against the enemy other—in this favorite case, the French. Despite the fact that the British fleet had hardly won a "brilliant" victory on this occasion (in fact, the repercussions led to a bitter series of court-martials within the navy), the overall impression that British military masculinity had prevailed was gleefully conveyed through the press.

CONCLUSION

It cannot be denied that the British construction of military style martial masculinity was heavily influenced by the proliferation of macaroni, effeminate society in the 1770s. Even before this date, those military men who failed to fit the stereotypical mold of British fighting men were re-identified by the press and, consequently, the British public as being other than what was expected. The early-eighteenth-century depiction of the fop, or beau, had demonstrated the consequences of "deviant" masculinity.[42] Effeminacy and a general weakening of the British militaristic state were seen by many to be the inevitable consequences of exposure to foreign gender constructions: and in peacetime, the widespread growth of luxury items available on the British domestic market merely reinforced the perception that peace could have a damaging impact on the nation. Ironically, it was dominance and success in war that led to the importation of continental goods and ideas: As British naval power became dominant, the exchange of goods and tourists between the British Isles and the continent became almost commonplace.[43] The perceived importation of these ideas in such a context was viewed with contempt by some sections of the press, and although foppery and effeminacy as part of a masculine lifestyle were not altogether new to British society, their marginalization as a threat to the militaristic livelihood of the state was.

NOTES

1. John Brewer, *The Sinews of Power: War, Money, and the English State, 1688–1783* (London: Unwin Hyman, 1989).

2. Linda Colley, *Britons: Forging the Nation, 1707–1837* (London: Vintage, 1996), p. 265.

3. Philip Corrigan and Derek Sayer, *The Great Arch: English State Formation as Cultural Revolution* (Oxford: Blackwell's, 1985), p. 12.

4. Michael Roper and John Tosh, eds., *Manful Assertions: Masculinities in Britain since 1800* (London: Routledge, 1991), p. 1.

5. George Mosse, *The Image of Man: The Creation of Modern Masculinity* (New York: Oxford University Press, 1996), p. 50.

6. Linda Colley, "The Apotheosis of George III: Loyalty, Royalty and the British Nation, 1760–1820," *Past and Present* 102 (1984): 102.

7. *The London Magazine*, April 1773, pp. 192–193.

8. A. Mark Liddle, "State, Masculinities and Law: Some Comments on Gender and English State-Formation," *British Journal of Criminology* 36 (1996): 373.

9. Admiral Richard Kempenfelt to Captain Charles Middleton, 18 January 1780, *Letters of the English Seamen*, ed. E. Hallam Moorhouse (London: Chapman & Hall, 1910), p. 128.

10. Kathleen Wilson, "The Good, the Bad, and the Impotent: Imperialism and the Politics of Identity in Georgian England," in *The Consumption of Culture, 1600–1800: Image, Object, Text*, ed. Ann Bermingham and John Brewer (London: Routledge, 1995), emphasizes this process of "gendered definitions of citizenship and political subjectivity that valorized an aggressive masculinity as a touchstone of Englishness, while

devaluing and marginalizing 'effeminate' others both within and without the polity,"
p. 238.

11. Quoted in Ruddock Mackay, *Admiral Hawke* (Oxford: Clarendon Press, 1965), pp. 30–31. See also *An Appendix to the Minutes taken at a court-martial appointed to enquire into the conduct of Captain Richard Norris* (London, 1745), p. 25.

12. *The trial of the Hon R[ichar]d N[orri]s, Commander of one of His Majesty's Ships for Perjury, Fraud, and Cowardice* (London, 1745).

13. Ibid., pp. 7–8.

14. Ibid., 17–18.

15. Robert W. Connell, *Masculinities* (Sydney: Allen & Unwin, 1995), p. 190.

16. From *The Test*, 12 February 1757, quoted in *The London Chronicle*, 19–22 February 1757, p. 178.

17. *The London Chronicle*, 1–3 March 1757.

18. N.A.M. Rodger, *The Wooden World: An Anatomy of the Georgian Navy* (London: Fontana, 1988), p. 249.

19. Jonas Hanway, *The Seaman's faithful companion; being religious and moral advice to officers in the Royal Navy* (London, 1763), pp. 82–83.

20. Jonathan Clark, *English Society, 1688–1832: Ideology, Social Structure and Political Practice during the Ancien Regime* (Cambridge: Cambridge University Press, 1985), p. 114.

21. Faramerz Dabhoiwala, "The Construction of Honour, Reputation and Status in Late Seventeenth- and Early Eighteenth-Century England," *Transactions of the Royal Historical Society*, 6th ser., 6 (1996): 201–213.

22. Quoted in Rodger, *The Wooden World*, p. 248.

23. Dudley Pope, *At 12 Mr Byng Was Shot* (London: Secker & Warburg, 1962), p. 182.

24. Kathleen Wilson, *The Sense of the People: Politics, Culture, and Imperialism in England, 1715–1785* (Cambridge: Cambridge University Press, 1995), p. 189.

25. Reproduced in David Geiger, "To Encourage the Others," *British Heritage* 2,3 (1981): 52–53.

26. Edward Thompson, *The Fair Quaker of Deal*, p. 8.

27. For an interesting discussion on the various aspects of eighteenth-century execution, see Greg Dening, *Mr Bligh's Bad Language: Passion, Power, and Theatre on the Bounty* (Melbourne: Cambridge University Press, 1992), pp. 249–250.

28. David Erskine, ed., *Augustus Hervey's Journal* (London: William Kimber, 1960), p. 242.

29. Horace Mann to Horace Walpole, 26 March 1743, *The Yale edition of Horace Walpole's Correspondence*, ed. Wilmarth S. Lewis (New Haven: Yale University Press, 1954), vol. 18, p. 195.

30. Daniel DeFoe, *A Weekly Review of the Affairs of France*, 19 February 1704.

31. Davidoff and Hall, *Family Fortunes*, p. 19.

32. Colley, *Britons*, pp. 36–37.

33. Horace Walpole to Horace Mann, 16 October 1742, *The Yale edition of Horace Walpole's Correspondence*, ed. Wilmarth S. Lewis, vol. 18, p. 79.

34. The best examples can be found in Michael Duffy, ed., *The Englishman and the Foreigner* (Cambridge: Chadwyck-Healey, 1986).

35. From the *Anti-Jacobin*, 1 January 1798, quoted in E. P. Thompson, *The Making of the English Working Class* (Harmondsworth: Penguin, 1968), p. 86.

36. *The London Magazine*, April 1773, p. 164.

37. King George III to Sir Samuel Hood, 12 July 1778, *The Naval Miscellany*, ed. J. N. Laughton (London: Spotiswoode, 1902), vol. 1, pp. 225–226. The King mentioned that his son "neither wants resolution nor cheerfulness, which seem necessary ingredients for those who enter into that noble profession."

38. Common seamen were customarily referred to as "the people" in the eighteenth-century navy. Prince William's great benevolence is mentioned in *The Naval Atlantis; Or a display of the characters of such Flag Officers as were distinguished during the last war* (London, 1788), pp. 186–189.

39. King George III to Sir Samuel Hood, 11 June 1779, *The Naval Miscellany*, ed. J. N. Laughton, vol. 1, pp. 226–227.

40. *The London Magazine*, January 1781.

41. *The London Chronicle*, 4–6 August 1778.

42. Philip Carter, "Men about Town," p. 55.

43. John Gascoigne, *Joseph Banks and the English Enlightenment: Useful Knowledge and Polite Culture*, 61.

Chapter 11

The Militarization of Masculinity in the Former German Democratic Republic

Andrew Bickford

This chapter examines the relationship between militarization policies, gender, and the family in the former German Democratic Republic (GDR) and serves as an overview of the ideological and legal aspects of the militarization of masculinity in the GDR.[1] Militarization is understood as "the contradictory and tense social process in which civil society organizes itself for the production of violence."[2] My focus is primarily on the years 1978–1990 in the GDR and specifically on the lives of former *Nationale Volksarmee* (National People's Army, or NVA) soldiers and their families. I focus on these years in particular because of the introduction of *Wehrerziehung* (military education) in schools in 1978 and the passing of the *Wehrdienstgesetz* (Military Conscription Law) of 1982, the most draconian of all GDR conscription laws. Drawing on oral history interviews, archival research, and participant observation in a community of former soldiers and officers of the NVA, I examine the relationship between state ideals of male identity, as promulgated through military and paramilitary training, and the ways in which state programs for militarization and national identity articulated with the household, divisions of labor, and traditional forms of German identity.[3] I also examine how the GDR attempted to create legitimacy and reconstitute male identity after World War II by forging a symbolic link between men, the military, and the state predicated on "Peace" and "Defense."[4]

MALE IDENTITY, THE MILITARY, AND THE FAMILY IN THE FORMER GERMAN DEMOCRATIC REPUBLIC

In 1975 an East German mother wrote a letter to the women's journal *Für Dich*, enquiring whether it was safe and healthy to allow her son to play with toy soldiers and tanks. Dr. Ulrike Menke, a doctor of education, replied:

Even preschool children know that soldiers protect our Homeland. If the child is prevented from playing war through prohibitions or derogatory remarks, the child will find himself in a conflict situation. From these prohibitions and remarks, children in this age group can develop negative attitudes towards paramilitary training and their "duty of honor" in the National People's Army. The child must be made aware of the duties of the armed forces of our state—in the first line by the father and mother. Along with this it is also necessary to develop an age-appropriate "Friend/Enemy" viewpoint. (*Für Dich* 9/75)

This is a prime example of the relationship between male identity, militarization policies, and state ideals of the family in the former German Democratic Republic. During the 40-year history of the GDR, over a million men passed through the NVA and took part in compulsory military, paramilitary, and civil defense training. Mandatory military training and military service for men played a key role in transmitting the ideological and political aims of the Socialist Unity Party (SED), as well as the state-endorsed gender roles and identities SED deemed necessary for the maintenance of East German society.

Active military service in the NVA consisted of 18 months of mandatory service. In addition to the 18-month mandatory service, there also existed a 36-month enlistment as a non-commissioned officer (*Unteroffizier auf Zeit*), a 10- or 25-year enlistment as a career non-commissioned officer (*Berufsunteroffizier*), a 15-year enlistment as a warrant officer (*Fähnrich*), and a 25-year enlistment as a career officer (*Berufsoffizier*).[5] Whereas much has been written concerning the importance of "work" and "workers" in East German society,[6] as well as about the role of women in East German society,[7] men's experiences and the influence of militarization on East German identity and family life, both before and after unification, have been curiously overlooked despite the fact that the majority of men in the DDR were required to complete military and paramilitary service.[8]

The GDR viewed itself as the central "battleground" of the Cold War and the likely site of a war in Europe.[9] One of the founding tropes of the NVA and the cornerstone of the ideological preparation of youths for military service was "*Frieden*" (peace). Not only was the NVA portrayed and conceptualized as an "*Armee des Friedens*" (Army of Peace), but all members of the NVA view themselves as servants and guardians of peace. "*Wehrdienst im Sozialismus ist Friedensdienst*" (Military Service in Socialism is Service for Peace) was an oft-used slogan to promote this idea, and in 1986 at the XI Party Congress, the SED stated that the "meaning of being a Soldier in Socialism is to maintain Peace, and prevent weapons from speaking."[10] During interviews almost all informants stated that they believed this to be correct, and they were thoroughly convinced that they were in fact helping to maintain peace in Europe.[11] This was particularly evident among officers, who always stated that they served, not in an army of conquest, but in an army that defended socialism against aggression and conquest and therefore helped maintain peace in Europe. Many former officers stated in interviews that any offensive overtones in the NVA were merely responses to NATO militarization and aggressive actions. One officer claimed that although one could consider the GDR to have been a militarized state, there was no "war enticement" (*Kriegsbegeisterung*); rather, militarization was "peace enticement" (*Friedensbegeisterung*). "Defense" and "peace" were used as overarching master-tropes to promote militarization programs and the necessity of creating citizens willing and able to defend both the GDR and socialism. Women, whether as mothers, daughters, or girlfriends, and children were presented as in need of defense and worth dying for to defend; women were also portrayed as the "Hinterland" of male soldiers, a concept that created a symbolic link between the defense of the homeland and the defense of women.[12] By equating the GDR with women, both the country and women were made to seem threatened, in danger, and in need of defense by men. The contradictions inherent in these two sets of assumptions—men trained to commit acts of violence in the name of peace, and women conflated with the nation in such a way as to warrant violence on the part of these *"Soldaten des Friedens"* (Soldiers of Peace)—are emblematic of the confused and often contradictory logic of militarization in the GDR.[13]

MILITARIZATION AND GENDER: CREATING "SOCIALIST MILITARY PERSONALITIES"

Mandated by law, compulsory military training was designed to inculcate differing identity attributes according to gender. In 1969 a top-secret agreement among the *Ministerium f. Volksbildung* (Ministry of Education), the mass youth organizations, and the East German Red Cross, under the aegis of the SED, provided for the "unconditional preparation of all male students for military service"; the aim was to provide for "the unity of the political-moral, military- and military-technical, physical, and psychological abilities of students in preparation for military service." Despite rudimentary training in marksmanship and Atomic-Biological-Chemical (ABC) protection, girls and young women were expected to complete only courses in first aid and civil defense and to attain qualifications in the German Red Cross.[14] Although both male and female students received military education and to some degree participated in the same sorts of training, military education and training were always focused on males; eventually both men and women came to see military service as a "natural" part of a man's life-course and the fulfillment of their *"Ehrendienst"* (duty of honor). To refuse military service was to be a "dishonorable" man and to fall outside of civil society.[15] It was also the refusal to perform the very duty that defined one in a fundamental way as a "man." Although women were allowed to join the military in certain fields, a military career for a woman was viewed as something of an aberration, and this was looked upon as a positive development only in the late GDR.[16] As two former officers told me, "We didn't want our women to have the burden of military service, that was our burden. We thought you Americans were barbarians for having women in your army."[17]

Through a long-term process of militarization, the SED attempted to create the "New Socialist Man" and "New Socialist Woman," as well as "Socialist Military Personalities," in a concerted effort by the state-sponsored mass organizations, educational facilities, and military and paramilitary organizations.[18] Military socialization in the GDR was accomplished through a merger of schools, educational facilities, and mass organizations such as the *Ernst Thälmann Junge Pioniere* (Young Pioneers), the *Gesellschaft für Sport und Technik* (Society for Sports and Technology, or GST), and the *Freie Deutsche Jugend* (Free German Youth, or FDJ), as well as the NVA.

Militarization began at an early age. Children between the ages of 6 and 14 were expected to join the Young Pioneers. After the Young Pioneers, children were to move into the Free German Youth, where they would receive a more intense ideological training, and into the Society for Sports and Technology, where they would begin to learn the "military-technical" skills necessary for service in the NVA. In conjunction with the paramilitary organizations, military education in schools, or "*Wehrerziehung,*" was designed to develop a clear "picture of the enemy" (*Feindbild*) and further trust in the SED.[19]

To promote the militarization of children, close contacts were established between military units and kindergartens and schools, with soldiers making regular visits to classes. Soldiers and other military figures were to serve as role models for young children, especially boys, and "open house" days at military barracks were designed to familiarize children with military equipment, soldiers, and military life; they were also intended to inculcate an innate trust in the military.[20] Children were taught that members of the NVA were their guardians and protectors, and the official East German press stressed the close relationship between soldiers and children by constantly portraying them together. Children's books and preschool textbooks stressed the need to create close relationships between soldiers and children; a preschool book from 1983 featured a drawing of children visiting an NVA barracks and began, "Your child, like all children, is interested in the abilities of soldiers and military technology."[21] Beginning in 1969 children in the Young Pioneers were expected to take part in yearly "Pioneer Maneuvers," large-scale military exercises designed to further militarize youths, as well as allow them a chance to display their military knowledge and capabilities. The code names of these maneuvers, *Manouver Schneeflocke II* and *Freundschaft* ("Maneuver Snowflake II" and "Friendship"), were designed to mask their military nature. In 1969, 824,000 children participated in the "Snowflake II" war games;[22] these became annual events, with hundreds of thousands of children participating each year.[23] *Manouver Schneeflocke* was carried out in such a way that many children did not know that it was a form of military preparation; only during an interview did a few who had taken part in these maneuvers come to realize that the word *maneuver* was an indication of the military aspect of this exercise.[24]

Schools also operated along military lines, and as the "instruments of power of the ruling class,"[25] they were instrumental in the initial military socialization of children. As early as the first or second grades, before class children were required to stand in military formations organized around a student chosen as class leader. This student would take roll, march to the teacher, salute, and report, "Class X reports 200 Young Pioneers ready for action." The teacher would then address the students, "Young Pioneers, Be Prepared"!"—to which the students would reply in unison, "Always Prepared!"[26]

After the Young Pioneers, children and youths were pressured to join the FDJ, as well as the GST. The FDJ was responsible for the ideological training and indoctrination of youths, whereas the GST was the primary paramilitary organization in the GDR. The GST was mandated with the development of "*Verteidigungsbereitschaft*" (defense preparedness) in students and the preparation of all youths in various military and military-technical skills that would allow them to move quickly into the NVA; as such, the GST was known as the "*Schule des Soldaten von Morgen*" (School of the Soldiers of Tomorrow).[27] The GST also provided a constant reserve force that was to be made available in the event of war. The GST, however, did not function completely as desired or designed; interviews with people who took part in GST activities show that although they enjoyed the opportunities to scuba dive, parachute, or learn how to use radios, to a large degree most people took part in the GST to obtain their driver permits, which they could do much more quickly, and for free, through the GST.

Beginning in 1978 the GDR increased the pressure on boys to join the military; in this year, *Wehrerziehung*, or military education, became a required course in the ninth and tenth grades.[28] By introducing military education into schools, children were to be provided with a basic knowledge of civil defense, and their willingness to defend the country was to be developed.[29] The ultimate goal of *Wehrerziehung* was to combat pacifism, increase the willingness of men to fight, make individuals capable and fit to fight, and indoctrinate individuals with the ideological aims of the SED.[30] In addition, beginning in the seventh grade, boys were pressured by teachers and military recruiters to begin considering a career in the NVA. A clear picture has emerged of the attempts of the GDR government to intensify pressure on young men to join the military and choose the military as a career. Although teachers were to begin pressuring boys to consider a career in the military in the seventh grade, archival evidence and interviews show this often happened as early as the fifth grade.[31] In this way, children were enmeshed in a system of constant exposure to military themes; given the mandatory paramilitary, military, and reserve service for males, men were placed in a network of military obligations that extended well into their fifties. "Proper" citizenship was also based on military service; a pattern emerged in which "citizens" were coded as men conducting (or who had conducted) military service, whereas "girls" and "women" remained something outside of "true" citizenship and, in extreme cases, outside of "humanity."[32]

Military education in schools was conducted in subtle and not so subtle ways. A fourth-grade grammar text used border guards and watchdogs to teach subject-verb agreement, and a math textbook from the tenth grade used artillery-firing solutions to teach math equations. According to interviews with officers responsible for conscription, young men in high school were "tracked" for their eventual service in the NVA; for example, young men who were good at math were sent into the artillery service or became artillery officers, since they were able to do the math required to fire the howitzers and rockets. In the GDR, mathematics was considered a key component in the development and education of "socialist" individuals, and as such, math was considered an important means of "developing those personality traits that a citizen of our socialist state must posses."[33] Given that NVA soldiers hierarchically coded the various branches of the NVA according to prestige and "manliness," the "math nerds" of high school found themselves highly valued within the army because of the importance of artillery in modern combat. In this sense, "prestigious" masculinity in the NVA was fluid; physical size and strength were not necessarily the standards by which men were measured, rather more important was the ability to perform complicated tasks, operate certain types of weapons, and in the case of artillerymen, kill at a distance.

THE *WEHRDIENSTGESETZ* OF 1982

Furthering this process, the *Wehrdienstgesetz* of 1982, the final and most all-encompassing law in regard to the increased militarization of East German society, stated explicitly:

State organizations, as well as factories, leading industrial groups, concerns, installations, associations, societal organizations and groups are mandated with the preparation of all citizens for military service...preparation for military service is the main focus of education and pedagogy at comprehensive schools, installations for career training, trade schools, high schools, and universities.[34]

This law and the intense pressure applied to young high school men to join the military for longer periods of time, are demonstrated by the fact that at the end of 1982, the SED and NVA decreed that the number of young men choosing to become career officers was to be raised from the yearly average of 520 to 3,730.[35] The introduction of *Wehrerziehung* represented a quantitative leap in the militarization of East German society and the militarization of men in particular; in addition to further civil defense training at two-week summer camps, young men were given the chance to "volunteer" for light-weapons training with the NVA. In 1979, 20 percent of young men were to "volunteer" for this training, and by 1983 almost 100 percent of young men were to "volunteer."[36] *Wehrerziehung* was also to provide young men with an opportunity to engage in activities that validated male identity and their contribution to the state, a contribution that only they, as men, could make through mandatory military service or, rather, their "duty of honor."

The primary concern of militarization was the development and inculcation of the *"Sozialistische Persönlichkeit"* (socialist personality).[37] One essential component of this was the *"Freund-Feind Bild"* (friend-enemy viewpoint), in which East German children and youths (that is, primarily males) were to view the "enemy" with hatred while fully integrating themselves into the socialist community. Ultimately, the successful implementation of this "worldview" would result in "the creation of socialist-military warriors who are ready and able to follow every command of the Worker's and Peasant's State in an unhesitating manner, and who will fulfill all combat orders with their entire being."[38]

The concept of the *Sozialistische Persönlichkeit* was gradually subsumed under the rubric *"Sozialistische Wehrpersönlichkeit"* (socialist military personality).[39] The perfection of this ideal would be the development of soldiers who possessed the following attributes: "loyalty to socialist ideals, proletarian internationalism, socialist patriotism, solidarity, resilience in the face of adversity, courage, discipline, knowledge of how to achieve victory, loyalty to the party of the working class, willingness to sacrifice one's self, and hatred of the class enemy."[40] An additional goal of the early inculcation of these attributes was to offset and counter any form of pacifism. Thus, traits ascribed to the ideal socialist citizen were those associated with men, since women were prohibited from military service for the most part (only in 1984 did women begin to enter the officer corps, and only then as political officers). Ideals such as courage and self-sacrifice were the exclusive domain of men; women were expected to acquire other, more "feminine" traits that would complement militarized male identity. Seen from this angle, militarized masculinity requires a form of female identity that will support and sustain military service and indoctrination; in other words, the GDR needed to create a gender dynamic that both supported and induced compliance with military service in both men and women. In addition, this dynamic coded militarization was completely dependent upon heteronormative family forms and "traditional" forms of sexual interaction.[41]

ARMEE RUNDSCHAU: DREAMING OF SOLDIERS AND WIVES

An example of the complementary dynamic fostered by the state can be found in *Armee Rundschau* (Army Panorama). *Armee Rundschau* was one of the most widely circulated and read magazines in the GDR, with an average monthly readership of 1.5 million.[42] This magazine reads like a training guide for young men and focuses on how to be a good soldier, find and keep a girlfriend, and act like a "decent" man in a relationship and as a citizen of the GDR. In an interview with the former chief editor of *Armee Rundschau*, I was told that the main purpose of the magazine was to prepare boys and men for their military service and to prepare women to be good "wives and girlfriends."[43] Women were portrayed as passive, unsure of themselves, apolitical, and interested solely in establishing lasting relationships with men and becoming mothers.[44] Women were also portrayed as highly respectful and understanding of a man's decision to remain in the army, viewing it as more important than their own careers, and as willing to wait for the soldier despite the tremendous demands of military service.[45]

Armee Rundschau functioned as a means to maintain and enforce traditional patriarchal roles and expectations in men, reconstitute men's position of authority in society, and promote the idea that women also believed in traditional gender roles and values. It also functioned to assuage men's fears that military service would inhibit their chances of finding a girlfriend or wife, or of causing an already existing relationship to fail as a result of military service.[46]

NVA theorists viewed the family and heterosexual relationships as the "first line" of military socialization, for males were "to be positively influenced for military service by their parents, other relatives, wives, and girlfriends" to ensure that youths fulfilled their "duty of honor to the greatest degree possible."[47] Archival evidence also shows that the NVA instrumentalized the family, which was viewed as the most important "cell" of society and was seen as the primary site of indoctrination and militarization for East German society. Discussions of the family in NVA documents describe it as a site to be influenced and used for the maintenance of the military; no mention of love or affection is ever made in terms of soldiers and their families. Rather, such traits were to be developed in soldiers vis-à-vis their equipment and technology.[48] One can also trace the manner in which young boys were slotted into military service and careers, with girls and women encouraged to support them in their decision.

Letter exchanges between soldiers and women were printed in *Armee Rundschau*; these are always examples of relationships surviving the hardships of military service, and they always emphasize women's willingness to wait for their "soldiers" to return home.[49] The letters usually contained comments from women detailing the ways in which their partners have changed for the better as a result of military service. This opinion surfaced in a number of interviews with women concerning men after they have completed military service. Archival research shows that the militarization of women was of great concern to the East German military and government, and a number of documents show that the NVA considered it extremely important to direct effort and pressure toward women in order for them to support men to join and remain in the military.[50] The NVA and SED were of the opinion that men could be militarized only insofar as women were militarized and convinced to support men in the military. Women were expected, it seems, to understand the burden their men bore by having had to undergo some of the same training as men in the form of paramilitary training and civil defense training.

An example of the extent to which male identity and heterosexuality were bound to the military can be found in the following: I was told that of all the students in an informant's graduate class, only two of the men had not served in the military, both because of medical reasons. As a result, none of the women in the class would talk to them or date them, nor could the two men converse with the men in the class who had been in the military, since the NVA had its own very distinct jargon. The two men were marginalized because they had not served in the military and were thus not "real" men: Military service, it was commonly believed, was the only way to become a "man." Both men expressed a sincere desire to have been able to have served "for at least two months."[51] Following Connell, and Cornwall and Lindisfarne,[52] the vignette described above fits well with conceptions of "hegemonic masculinity." Hegemonic masculinity defines successful ways of being a "man," and in so doing, the term defines other masculine behavior as inadequate or inferior, leaving the "successful" way of being unreflected upon and uncriticized; it becomes the "natural" way of being a man. In the above example, the "real" men (for both the women and other men) are those who have served in the military. Although there was considerable resistance to military service in the GDR, it seems that the military was successful in shaping the normative ways of being a man; indeed, of being "good at being a man."[53]

In an interesting twist, a number of former soldiers told me they became better men and more successful in their relationships with women by having learned to sweep, mop, clean and generally keep a tidy house while in the army. Women also mentioned this as a very positive aspect of military service. This is noteworthy, given that East German women interviewed said they were generally not fond of conscripts or officers; it seems that military service was a necessary part of a man's curriculum vitae, but only if in the past. Although Shaw[54] may be correct in asserting that militarization and war preparation have become basic parts of economic and social structures in modern nation-states and are "first and foremost means of state power,"[55] one must also question just what kind of power this is and what the intended and unintended consequences of this power are. Militarization, it seems, is about producing not just "soldiers" who will fight but also partners who know how to iron and keep house.

HIERARCHY AND THE
ENTLASSUNGSKANDIDATBEWEGUNG

Within the NVA, and all militaries for that matter, branches of service are differentially valued: Some branches are considered more "tough" and manly; others are seen as effeminate, ineffective, and passive. Paratroopers and combat swimmers in the NVA were considered the toughest and most capable soldiers, whereas "normal" infantry soldiers surprisingly found themselves located toward the bottom of the scale, thought of as "stupid" and expendable. One can generalize a certain form of masculine identity from the outside, but once one looks within a military, it quickly becomes apparent that identities are multiple and contingent on a number of factors, such as one's job and the performance of that job.

An important means by which the NVA maintained discipline and unit hierarchy was the *"Entlassungskandidatbewegung"* ("Candidate for Release Program"), or EK for short.[56] Inductions into the NVA took place every six months; therefore, soldiers were organized into different service cohorts, or *"Diensthalbjahren."* Since basic military service lasted 18 months, there were always three different cohorts: *Erstes, Zweites, und Drittes Diensthalbjahr* (first, second, and third service cohort). Troops who had served longer periods of time would take advantage of the younger troops, making them polish their boots, clean the barracks, and perform those tasks that were the most unpleasant. Older troops would also force younger soldiers to take part in various rituals designed to mark them as belonging to their stage of service,[57] and they would compel them to somehow provide alcohol for these rituals (alcohol consumption in the barracks was strictly prohibited). The EK movement often resulted in brutal acts against the younger troops, such as forcing them to wear their gas masks and filling the breathing tube with cleaning powder, which the soldiers would then be forced to breath into their lungs.[58] In extreme cases, soldiers were forced to masturbate in public or lick urine out of older soldiers' helmets. One former soldier told me of an occurrence he witnessed: a soldier who had failed to complete a training mission successfully was forced by older soldiers"—"EKs"; younger soldiers were called variously *"Glatte"* or *"Spritzer"*[59]—to play *"Schnuffi."* He was made to don his gas mask, but without the filter; the EKs then placed the long filtration tube into a filled ashtray. When the soldier could no longer hold his breath, he had to inhale the contents of the ashtray.[60] Although the *EK-Bewegung* was an unofficial form of discipline within the NVA, officers and noncommissioned officers used it to keep the soldiers in line and increasingly came to depend on it and tolerate it. This was not prevalent in all NVA units, however; it seems to have been most widely practiced in larger units, such as *Mot-Schützen* (motorized infantry) companies and regiments, as well as those units in which a high degree of technical proficiency was not required. From the interviews it seems that the *EK-Bewegung* was most widely practiced in those units at the bottom of the "intelligence" hierarchy in the NVA; soldiers and officers agreed that it mostly took place in the "stupid" units—those units in which the soldiers were considered to be below average and who in wartime would have done most of the fighting.[61]

CONCLUSION

The vector of militarization and the family played a key role in shaping male identity in the German Democratic Republic. Although East Germany purported to have achieved complete gender equality, at least in regard to "work" and employment, and did have some success in destabilizing traditional forms of patriarchy and male domination in the household, the militarization of East German society valorized traditional gender roles and functions. Furthermore, the GDR promoted traditional forms of heterosexual behavior as necessary for the defense and perpetuation of the state; gender identity, sexuality, and defense formed a mutually supporting triad to uphold the state. Militarization also served to counter the "demasculinization" of East German society brought about by the political program of equality (*Gleichberechtigung*) designed to win women's support for the Socialist Unity Party after World War II. Through the discourse of "Defense" and "Peace," the SED was able to resurrect the military from the ashes of World War II; Germany's defeat in World War II brought about a crisis in masculinity in postwar Germany because men were blamed for the devastation of the war. By maintaining that the NVA worked solely for peaceful purposes and that "military service in socialism is service for peace," the SED was able to counter this trend and use the military to revalorize militarized male identity as a means of establishing greater control over the GDR.

NOTES

1. Research for this project was carried out from 1998 to 2000 and was funded by generous grants from Fulbright IIE, The Wenner-Gren Foundation for Anthropological Research, The Social Science Research Council Berlin Program for Advanced German and European Studies, a Woodrow Wilson Archival Research Grant, and a Rutgers University Special Research Award. Thanks to everyone at the SSRC Berlin Program Seminar and the Rutgers Center for Historical Analysis. In particular I would like to thank Uli Linke, Roger Lancaster, and Omer Bartov, who all provided valuable insights and comments on this chapter.

2. See John Gillis, ed., *The Militarization of the Western World* (New Brunswick: Rutgers University Press, 1989), p. 1.

3. John Borneman, *Belonging in the Two Berlins: Kin, State, Nation* (New York: Cambridge University Press, 1992); G. Kracht, "Der DDR-Mann: Eine rekonstruktive Annaherung an Mannsein und Mannlichkeit in der DDR-Gesellschaft," *Mitteilung aus der Kulturwissenschaftlichen Forschung 36: Differente Sexualitaten* (Heft 18, 1995): 130–142; I. Ostner, "Slow Motion: Women, Work, and the Family in Germany," in Jane Lewis, ed., *Women and Social Policies in Europe* (Hants: Edward Elgar, 1993).

4. See, for example, S. Jeffords, "The Remasculinization of Germany in the 1950s: Discussion," *Signs* 24, 1 (1998): 163–170; George Mosse, *Fallen Soldiers: Reshaping the Memory of the World Wars* (New York: Oxford University Press, 1990); and George Mosse, *The Image of Man: The Creation of Modern Masculinity* (New York: Oxford University Press, 1996).

5. See Holger Jens Karlson and Jörg Judersleben, "Die Soldatensprache der NVA: Eine Wortschatzbetrachtung," *Muttersprache* 2/94, pp. 143–164; Backerra 1992; Fischer 1995; Wenzke 1994.

6. See Borneman 1992; H. Buechler and J. M. Buechler, "Farm Managers and Social Identity in Sachsen Anhalt" (paper delivered at the American Anthropological Association 95th Annual Meeting, Washington, DC); Mary Fullbrook, *Anatomy of a Dictatorship: Inside the GDR, 1949–1989* (Oxford: Oxford University Press, 1995); and R. Woods, "The East German Contribution to German Identity," in M. Gerber and R. Woods, eds., *Studies in GDR Culture and Society 13: Understanding the Past—Managing the Future: Integration of the Five New Lander into the Federal Republic of Germany*, selected papers from the Eighteenth New Hampshire Symposium (Lanham, MD: University Press of America, 1994).

7. See Irene Dölling, "Gespaltenes Bewusstsein: Frauen und Mannerbilder in der DDR," in G. Helwig and H. M. Nickel, eds., *Frauen in Deutschland, 1945–1992* (Bonn: Bundeszentrale fur politische Bildung, 1993); E. Kolinsky, ed., *Women in Contemporary Germany: Life, Work, and Politics* (Providence: Berg, 1993); H. M. Nickel, "Women in the German Democratic Republic and in the New Federal States: Looking Backward and Forward (Five Theses)," in N. Funk and M. Mueller, eds., *Gender Politics and Post-communism: Reflections from Eastern Europe and the Former Soviet Union* (New York: Routledge, 1993); I. Ostner, "Slow Motion: Women, Work, and the Family in Germany," in Jane Lewis, ed., *Women and Social Policies in Europe* (Hants: Edward Elgar, 1993); D. Rosenberg, "Shock Therapy: GDR Women in Transition from a Socialist Welfare State to a Social Market Economy," *Signs* 17.

8. T. Beck, *Liebe zum Sozialismus-Hass auf dem Klassenfeind: Sozialistisches Wehrmotiv und Wehrerziehung in der DDR;* Luneburg 1983; E. Fischer, ed., *Ehemalige Berufssoldaten der NVA in der Bundesrepublik Deutschland, Report 1995* (Bonn: Karl-Theodor-Molinari Stiftung); R. Wenzke, "NVA-Inneres Gefuge: Das Leben in der Truppe" (unpublished manuscript, 1994).

9. Manfred Backerra, *NVA: Ein Ruckblick fur die Zukunft—Zeitzeugen berichten über ein Stuck deutscher Militärgeschichte* (Köln: Markus Verlag, 1992); T. Diedrich, H. Ehlert, and R. Wenzke, "Die bewaffneten Organe der DDR im System von Partei, Staat und Landesverteidigung. Ein Überblick," in *Im Dienste der Partei: Handbuch der bewaffneten Organe der DDR*, Herausgegeben *von Torsten Diedrich, Hans Ehlert und Rüdiger Wenzke* (Berlin: Christoph Links Verlag, 1998).

10. See Dietrich, Ehlert, and Wenzke 1998.

11. According to Dr. Dagmar Pietsch, a former NVA sociologist, men joined the NVA out of a strong personal conviction to help maintain peace. See Dagmar Pietsch, "Motivation des Wehrdienstes," in Wolfgang Wünsche, *Rührt Euch! Zur Geschichte der NVA* (Berlin: Edition Ost, 1998). Interviews with former NVA officers and soldiers contradict this official account; many former soldiers spoke of economic motivations, boredom, or pressure from family members as their reasons for joining the NVA. "Maintaining peace" was the official party line of the NVA; although some men may have joined for this reason, most came to accept it after the fact.

12. C. Eifler, "Zu Weiblichkeitsklischees in der NVA-Propaganda." *Offiziersbrief* 28 (1996 and 1999): 19–21. "Die Rede vom Frieden in der DDR." *Redemanuskript: Frauen und Männer im geteilten Deutschland,* 30, 9.99–2.10.99, Berlin.

13. An example of this can be found in a letter published in a 1987 issue of *Armee Rundschau*, a popular military magazine: Hinterland Katrin declared,

"I promise to remain a secure hinterland for my husband, because the strong and sure love between us will help us make it through the 18 months [of mandatory service]." In this sense, marriage, female gender roles, and space are conflated to create a unitary sign of weakness, a sign intended to shore up an active, traditional sign of male strength and defense.

14. Vereinbarung der MfVb, GST, FDJ, DRK, 30.5.1969; Diedrich, Ehlert, and Wenzke 1998, p. 651.

15. The only legal form of alternative service in the GDR was the so-called *Bausoldaten* (Construction Soldiers). *Bausoldaten* wore standard NVA uniforms, but they did not carry weapons. They were to provide support to the NVA through street construction and repair, logistical support, and the like. In a sense, they were more of a penal battalion; for volunteers for duty in the *Bausoldaten* discovered that their educational and career opportunities after enlistment were severely curtailed.

16. Only in the mid- and late 1980s did the NVA consider conscripting women; this was a result of demographic studies that showed that the military would not be able to meet its "manpower" requirements. Elaborate steps were taken to entice women to join the military, including promises of prized educational opportunities after military service. However, Erich Honecker, head of state of the GDR, decided to slash the overall size of the NVA in 1988–1989; consequently, a large number of women who had been promised military training and educational opportunities were told they were not needed and were no longer eligible for certain university slots.

17. FE, HP, PC: 1998.

18. T. Beck, *Liebe zum Sozialismus-Hass auf dem Klassenfeind: Sozialistisches Wehrmotiv und Wehrerziehung in der DDR* (Luneburg, 1983); Gunther Bohme and Wolfgang Spitzner, *Schutz des Sozialismus—Recht und Ehrenpflicht. Einheit* 5/1977; Fullbrook 1995; G. M. Meyer and S. Collmer, *Kolonisierung oder Integration? Bundeswehr und Deutsche Einheit: Eine Bestandsaufnahme* (Opladen: Westdeutscher Verlag, 1993).

19. See Diedrich, Ehlert, and Wenzke 1998.

20. Success was often measured by an absurd standard: A report concerning an open-house at a base stated in glowing terms that they had achieved immense success in exciting children about military service by serving them pea soup (*Erbsenpuree*) from field kitchens. A number of informants recalled being served pea soup at such outings; contrary to the report, all said they hated eating the soup and did it only because it was expected of them.

21. *Bald bin ich ein Schulkind: Ein Buch zur Vorbereitung der Kinder auf die Schule* (Berlin: Volk und Wissen Volkseigener Verlag Berlin, 1983).

22. Heinz Marks, *Gesellschaft für Sport und Technik: Vormilitärische Ausbildung in der DDR* (Köln: Markus Verlag, 1970).

23. See Udo Baron, *Die Wehrideologie der Nationalen Volksarmee der DDR* (Bochum: Unversitätsverlag Dr. N Brockmeyer, 1993).

24. Instead of being given rifles, children were issued sticks with red flags tied to the top. They were told that under no circumstances were they to lose their stick. The same type of order is given in basic training in militaries around the world regarding a rifle or other personal weapon. Awards and citations were given out for those who excelled in tactics, terrain navigation, and other skills. In addition, according to a number of informants, the Snowflake II war games were considered fun and exciting because the participants were able to miss school to "play."

25. Böhme and Spitzner 1977.

26. WR, PC: 1997.

27. Dietrich, Ehlert, and Wenzke 1998:51; Marks 1970:8.

28. B. Pröll, "Sozialistische Wehrerziehung in der DDR im Zeichen der Entspannung: Anachronismus oder unabdingbare Reaktion?" *IFSH-Diskussionsbeiträge* Heft 40, September 1985. Stefan Wolle, in *Die Heile Welt der Diktatur: Alltag und Herrschaft in der DDR, 1971–1989* (Berlin: Ch. Links Verlag, 1998).

29. Wolle 1998, p. 258.

30. Baron 1993, p. 53.

31. DY30/IV/2.2039/201.

32. From SAPMO DY6/4856 *Nationalrat der Nationalen Front der DDR Informationsbericht* 15.08.78: "There are still divided opinions concerning the introduction of military education. The point has been raised that the young people are being ideologically prepared for their service in the NVA; it is also being asked how the education for the girls will be structured." The word "*Menschen*" (people, humans) is used to indicate young men being prepared for military service; it is not used to include the education of girls (*Mädchen*). This raises the question, are young boys *Menschen* because they will serve in the military and they are therefore human, whereas girls, because they are not allowed to perform military service as men do, remain something less than human? By implication it seems that the only way to become a proper citizen, and therefore human, is to serve in the military. The original passage from the report, written 14.08.1978:

> "Zur Einfuhrung des Wehrunterrichts gibt es nach wie vor geteilte Meinungen. Zum Teil wird hervorgehoben, dass die jungen Menschen durch den Wehrunterricht rechtzeitig besonders ideologisch auf ihren Wehrdienst in der NVA vorbereitet werden, dabei wird auch gefragt, wie sich der Unterricht fur die Madchen gestalten wird."

33. See Gerhart Neuner et al., *Allgemeinbildung—Lehrplanwerk—Unterricht* (Berlin, 1972), as quoted in Sterling Fishman and Lothar Martin, *Estranged Twins: Education and Society in the Two Germanys* (London: Praeger, 1987). For an official overview of GDR education policy in the early 1980s, see *Das Bildungswesen der Deutschen Demokratischen Republik* (Berlin: Volk und Wissen Volkseigener Betrieb, 1983).

34. *Wehrdienstgesetz* 1982, p. 6. Once again, "citizens" are only those who conduct military service, in other words, men.

35. SAPMO DY 30/IV/2/2039/201 Gewinnung des militärischen Berufsnachwuchses, Ministerium f. Volksbildung/Hauptabteilung Oberschulen. Stefan Wolle, in *Die Heile Welt der Diktatur: Alltag und Herrschaft in der DDR, 1971–1989* (Berlin: Ch. Links Verlag, 1998), reports a similar figure from the same archival source.

36. See Ulrich Mählert and Gerd-Rüdiger Stephan, *Blaue Hemden, Rote Fahnen: Die Geschichte der Freien Deutschen Jugend* (Opladen: Leske and Budrich, 1996).

37. Maria Elisabeth Müller, *Zwischen Ritual und Alltag: Der Traum einer sozialistischen Persönlickeit* (Berlin: Campus Verlag, 1997).

38. Baron 1992, p. 53.

39. D. Bald, *Die Nationale Volksarmee: Beiträge zur Selbstverstandnis und Geschichte des deutschen Militärs von 1945–1990* (Baden Baden, 1992); P. Jungermann, *Die Wehrideologie der SED und das Leitbild der Nationalen Volksarmee vom sozialistischen deutschen* Soldaten (Stuttgart: Degerloch, 1973); G. Merkl and W. Wunsche, *Die Nationale Volksarmee der DDR-Legitimation und Auftrag: Alte und Neue Legenden kritisch hinterfragt* (Berlin: Forschungs und Diskussionskreis DDR Geschichte, 1996).

40. Ideological training in the NVA and paramilitary groups was often referred to as *Rotlichtbestrahlung*, or "red radiation." The implication is that ideological training was designed to "mutate" recruits into "socialist personalities," presumably against their will. "Red radiation" indicates that ideological training was not simply accepted; indeed, there was considerable resistance to this type of training. See Beck 1982 and Karlson and Judersleben 1994.

41. Sexuality was a difficult topic to discuss with former officers. Although they would sometimes brag and boast about women, to move the discussions away from such banter proved difficult. They would become embarrassed and uneasy unless the discussion remained at a somewhat humorous level. When asked about homosexuality in the NVA, officers routinely drew a blank; the majority claimed there was no homosexuality in the military; a few, including the former minister of defense, claimed that homosexual acts between soldiers occurred so infrequently that they demanded little attention. However, interviews and archival evidence show that the NVA was very concerned about homosexuality and either transferred soldiers suspected of having homosexual relationships to different units or dismissed them from the military.

42. UG, PC: 1999.

43. Ibid.

44. Eifler 1996, p. 20.

45. Ibid.

46. Thomas Spanier, "In Erinnerung an meine Dienstzeit: 18 Monate als Wehrpflichtiger in der NVA," in M. Backerra, ed., *NVA: Ein Ruckblick für die Zukunft— Zeitzeugen berichten über ein Stück deutscher Militärgeschichte* (Köln: Markus Verlag, 1992).

47. Pröll 1985, p. 58.

48. Militärarchiv Freiburg AZN P2979, *Soziologische Untersuchungen, Dezember 1980, Politische Hauptverwaltung, Abteilung Information.* The NVA's view of technology is somewhat contradictory, but it is nonetheless entwined with notions of manhood. During the Kosovo war I interviewed a number of former officers concerning their views of the war, the ethics of it, should Germany be involved, and so on. One of the defining features of these interviews was the officers' desire to discuss NATO weaponry and technology: They were both fascinated and appalled. When describing the use of depleted uranium rounds by the U.S. Air Force, one officer said, "Our country is once again

engaged in nuclear war. What you are doing is inhumane—we knew about these weapons, but only now have I seen their effects—they're like small mushroom clouds" (FF, PC: 1999). Another officer said it was simply an example of what they had thought all along: "Technology is an example of American cowardice [amerikanische Feige]; you use high-tech weapons to accomplish what we would have simply used men for"(HB, PC: 1999). In this context, high-tech weaponry, usually coded as hyper-masculine and as a defining point of militarized masculinity, is turned upside down and made into an example of cowardice; only cowards use technology to accomplish what "real men" use physical bodies to do, even if this means certain death for those involved.

According to Shaw (1991) and Luckham (1984), "Armament Culture," or the fetishism of weapons and the reduction of human relationships in a military context to a relationship between weapons and targets, is a defining feature of modern militaries. In this instance, it seems that NVA officers had a contradictory view of technology and perhaps did not completely accept the "love of technology" that the military espoused, even if it meant sacrificing soldiers. This is somewhat paradoxical: High-tech weapons are designed to injure and kill large numbers of the enemy while sparing one's own soldiers' lives. They kill indiscriminately, but they are said to save the lives of attacking soldiers. Are the views of the NVA soldiers more humane because they eschew high-tech weapons and consider them examples of cowardice, even though their view is perhaps a modern view of trench warfare tactics?

49. Whereas women's letters contained passages about willing to remain at home, waiting for the soldier to return, men's letters contained poems concerning the stress of being on the "front line of peace." Men's poems celebrated soldiers as heroes and often utilized a fictive female voice to speak of "waiting for my hero." In this way letters and poems helped create a wartime atmosphere by establishing an artificial war front/home front dichotomy.

50. See DY30/901 SED Abteilung Sicherheitsfragen Information 03.85 and DVW1/55631 Protokoll der Sitzung des Kollegiums des Ministerium f. nationale Verteidigung 30.09.1983. In a report from 1985 to the Ministry of the Interior from the deputy minister of the interior in Suhl, the necessity of targeting women was made explicit: "Immer starker arbeiten die Gruppen des DFD mit den Muttern, Frauen, Braeuten und Freundinnen der Bewerber, aber auch mit allen anderen Frauen, um sie von der Notwendigkeit der Ergreifung militarischer Berufe zu uberzeugen, sie mit dem Leben an der Seite eines Offiziers, Fähnrich oder Unteroffiziers vertraut zu machen und sie zu gewinnen, für die Bestarkung der Bewerber und die Festigung ihres Wehrmotivs [The working groups of the German Women's Association are working with increasing intensity with the mothers, wives, brides, and girlfriends of the (military) applicants, but also with all women, to convince them of the necessity (for men) to take up military careers, to educate women about life at the side of an officer, warrant officer, or non-commissioned officer, and to win them over to strengthen the resolve of the applicants]." From DY30/901.

51. WR, PC: 1997.

52. See R. W. Connell, Masculinities (Berkeley: University of California Press, 1995); A. Cornwall and N. Lindisfarne, Dislocating Masculinity: Comparative Ethnographies (New York: Routledge, 1994).

53. See Michael Herfeld, *The Poetics of Manhood: Contest and Identity in a Cretan Village* (Princeton: Princeton University Press, 1985).

54. See Martin Shaw, *Post-military Society* (Philadelphia: Temple University Press, 1991), p. 30.

55. Ibid., p. 30.

56. R. Gehler, "EK, EK, EK—bald bist du nicht mehr da!" *Soldatenkultur in der Nationalen Volksarmee* (Schriftenreihe des Museums der Stadt Hagenow, 1998); and R. Gehler and D. Keil, *Die andere Realität: Alltagserfuahrnung Wehrdienstleistender in den Kasernen der DDR* (Ludwig-Uhland Institut f. Empirische Kulturwissenschaften der Uni. Tübingen/Inst. F. Eur. Ethnologie der Humboldt-Universität zu Berlin, 1992).

57. These rituals run from the comic to the grotesque: *Schildkröte* (Turtle), in which helmets were tied to a conscripts knees and elbows so that he would glide over the floor; *Heimfahrt* (Journey Home), in which conscripts were forced to fashion palm trees from whatever was available on base and then run around soldiers from a higher age cohort to simulate the passing of trees before a train window; *Musikbox,* in which a recruit was placed inside a locker, coins were pushed through the ventilation slits, and he was forced to sing; and the *AriTest* (Artillery Test), in which anal intercourse was simulated using a soldier's elbow and shoe polish. An additional ritual, which drew on Nazi imagery, was *Kristallnach:* Soldiers of all age cohorts would consume a large amount of alcohol and throw the empty bottles out the barracks windows. Soldiers from the first age cohort were then responsible for sweeping up the shards of glass before the officers reported for duty.

58. Spanier 1992. There is some doubt as to the veracity of this form of hazing; officers claimed it was a myth, but conscripts claimed it actually occurred, and there is some indication from disciplinary reports that such forms of hazing did occur.

59. The sexual connotation, according to informants, was intentional and meant to denote the youth of the new conscripts vis-à-vis the conscripts in other age cohorts. *Spritzer* was meant to designate someone who could not control himself sexually and was thus a "young" man.

60. HR, PC: 1999.

61. It seems, however, that these men were not so stupid; in a number of secret surveys conducted by NVA sociologists during the 1980s, a recurring theme emerged in combat units: "Wir sind das Himmelfahrtskommando der ersten Stunde [We are the suicide squad of the first hour]" was the general consensus of combat troops concerning their role in any confrontation with NATO and gave explicit recognition of the primary role of the NVA in war. The NVA was expected to be completely destroyed within the first three to five days of any major conflict with NATO, and so it was intended merely to block NATO forces while Soviet reserve forces moved to the front. The term "Himmelfahrtskommando" was used in concentration camps to designate those who were to dispose of bodies; the use of this term by NVA soldiers needs further consideration and attention (O. Bartov, PC: 2000).

Chapter 12

Militarism and Masculinity as Keys to the "Jewish Question" in Germany

Gregory A. Caplan

INTRODUCTION

At first glance, the concept "military masculinity" does not seem to have anything to do with German-Jewish history. Although historians often assert that only religion distinguished Jewish from non-Jewish Germans by the beginning of the twentieth century, German Jews did not subscribe to their compatriots' conceptions of manliness until the nineteenth century had almost come to a close. Early modern Jewish communities looked upon war making and the values of the soldier as gentile phenomena. Religious sources portrayed military figures as "wicked sons" who had dissociated themselves from the Jewish community to become part of gentile European society. Nevertheless, all participants on the debate on overemancipation stipulated that military service would be an obligation of Jews as citizens of German states. German citizens of the Jewish faith never called this duty into question, yet the German cult of masculinity, which emerged from the gymnastics movement in the Napoleonic era, had little impact on the Jewish community of the nineteenth century. Instead, a secularized version of the physically passive, yet intellectually accomplished student of the Torah retained its power as a masculine ideal among German Jews. Their commitment to reason, refinement, and intellectual achievement precluded the recognition of heroic masculinity, militarism, and other romantic indulgences as consistent with, much less part and parcel of, Jewish identity. However individual German-Jewish men conceived of themselves, physical prowess and bravery belonged to the catalogue of German, not Jewish, masculine attributes in the popular imagination of Jewish and non-Jewish Germans alike.

After the wars of unification led to the creation of the German Empire in 1871, Prussian militarism, military masculinity, and German nationalism became ever more intertwined. Despite the efforts of Jewish reformers to leave behind the legacies of early modern ghetto life, moral degeneracy, unsuitability for military service, nervousness, and sickliness—all traits associated at the time with women—remained staple fare in German representations of Jews. The first collective expression of assertive masculinity by Jews *qua* Jews did not come until 1886, when a handful of German-Jewish students established their own student fraternity in Breslau. Their project, which would not come to fruition until the outbreak of war, was nothing less than the completion of the otherwise successful acculturation of Jews into the German bourgeoisie.

DIVERGENT MASCULINITIES IN THE ERA OF EMANCIPATION

Jewish principles and Christian stereotypes cast Jewish men as the foil for romantic imagery of male bravery, valor, and heroism well into the nineteenth century. In traditional Jewish culture, rabbinic authorities rejected the valorization of war making, dueling, and romantic love as *goyim naches*, or games of the gentiles.[1] Barred from military service and dependent on Christian territorial rulers for physical protection from an often-hostile majority, religious leaders made virtue of necessity by seeing "power in submission."[2] In contrast to the male ideal embodied in the valiant knight of Christian Europe, rabbinical writings prescribed an "alternative paradigm" of masculinity, which emphasized humility, restraint, and self-abnegation.[3] The traditional Jew "was expected to be able to control his anger, not to be provoked; his feelings of inner dignity were sustained by a belief in his own spiritual superiority which a ruffian and a 'Goy' can in no way touch." Jewish men were therefore to follow the pious example of the rabbis, devoting themselves to Torah study while their wives earned a living in the profane world of the gentiles.[4] Only rabbis and teachers could hope to achieve this ideal of the purely religious life, but Talmudic texts, folk songs, and memoirs from the period still encouraged Jewish girls to desire gentle, studious husbands. Glueckel of Hameln, a seventeenth-century Jewish wife, mother, and businesswoman, described her husband, whom she believed to be the model companion, as meek, sickly, and long-suffering. "He was the perfect pattern of a pious Jew," she wrote, "as were his father and brothers."[5]

The Cult of Masculinity

The image of the physically fit and "manly" German, meanwhile, first emerged at the end of the eighteenth century. Worried by a seeming lack of strength and vitality in the nobility and educated bourgeoisie, educators and medical specialists, among them gymnastics pioneer Johann Friedrich Guts-Muths, warned that "our distinguished men could soon turn completely into distinguished women."[6] Their lamentations of the effeminacy of upper-class men combined a belief in the interdependence of mind and body with a conception of male beauty based upon classical Greek models. This new masculine ideal set such traits as strength, willpower, determination, bravery, and a readiness to resort to violence against the allegedly feminine characteristics of weakness, humility, dependency, compliancy, and emotionalism.[7]

In response to the military collapse of Prussia in 1806, a vocal, largely Protestant minority of early German nationalists insisted that this "heroic masculinity" be cultivated as a vital element in the revival of Teutonic grandeur. Heroic masculinity incorporated the conviction that a healthy mind required a physically fit body into the language of romantic nationalism. After the liberation of central Europe and the restoration of the *ancien regime*, associations devoted to the cultivation of physical vigor, strength, and readiness to use violence among German men attracted the suspicion of anti-revolutionary governments. Jahn nevertheless continued to pursue the political unification of the German nation by preaching the primacy of manliness within the gymnastics movement. In advocating the transformation of German boys into German men, he coined the German term *Turnen* as a nationally authentic substitute for the Latin word "gymnastic." In his writings and in the programs of the hundreds of *Turnvereine* that he and his followers established in the German states, physical exercise was celebrated as the guarantor of healthy and beautiful bodies, disciplined and moral individuals, and a loyal nation of patriotic Germans. This masculinist ideology held that material luxuries and apathy had resulted in a dearth of natural power and health in the population. The resulting symptoms of a feminized society, which included physical weakness, sickliness, cowardice, passivity, dependence on others, and uncontrolled tempers, could be countered only by a masculine elite of the German nation. The *Turnen* believed themselves to represent just this elite.[8]

Secularizing Jewish Masculinity

This conception of masculinity did not concern Jewish reformers in the first half of the eighteenth century. David Sorkin has coined the term "ideologists of emancipation" to signify the first teachers, rabbis, journalists, and scholars to propagate German enlightenment values within a newly emerging Jewish institutional landscape. Having broadened their own intellectual vistas through secular study, the ideologists of emancipation believed that the Jewish community should model its program for renewal on their own experiences. They sought to reconcile the Jewish faith with a commitment to reason and secular learning and proclaimed that a regeneration of Jewish life along these lines would facilitate the smooth integration of Jews into an open and tolerant German society. Their "ideology of emancipation" also prescribed the adoption of the German language and standards of decorum and civility; the participation of Jews in agriculture and handicrafts to foster an occupational profile similar to that of the non-Jewish population, and the profession of loyalty to King and the Fatherland.[9]

By placing the concept of *Bildung* at the center of their ideology, these reformers secularized the passive masculine ideal of rabbinical Judaism. *Bildung,*
which referred to the education and cultivation of the individual in the spirit of
rational enlightenment thought, accommodated both the universalist humanism necessary for the integration of Jews into German society and a gendered
implementation that preserved a patriarchal social order based on a male monopoly of education. In traditional Jewish and enlightened German culture,
only males studied subject matter deemed critical to intellectual development
and the fulfillment of public duties. Moreover, the "soft," domesticated masculinity of the urban German bourgeoisie approximated the standards of rabbinic Jewish culture. Both models of masculinity placed priority on the role of
the father within the family, and neither attached value to physical prowess,
heroism, or bravery. Finally, Jewish modernizers claimed that the religious reforms they were introducing would transform Judaism from an irrational,
hence effeminate, faith into a rational, and thus masculine, confession.[10]

A Citizen Army or an Army of Subjects?

Although heroic masculinity as such did not interest Jewish modernizers, all
participants in the debate over emancipation agreed that Jews could stake no
claim to citizenship unless they contributed as soldiers to the defense of the
state. This consensus held that military service demonstrated loyalty to the
state and fulfilled the duty of all who could justifiably claim its protection. Pro-
ponents of emancipation saw legal exclusions as the only obstacles to Jewish
military service. Their opponents disagreed, contending that the command-
ment to observe the Sabbath, and their small stature would prevent Jews from
fulfilling the duties of a soldier. Indeed, some rabbis worried that Jewish soldiers would fail to observe religious laws, and possibly leave the faith, during
their time in the military. Nevertheless, as early as 1787 Jewish reformers in
Berlin petitioned the Prussian king for the right to serve.[11]

In their belief that military service conferred upon soldiers the rights of the
citizen, Jewish reformers stood virtually alone among the subjects of the Prussian monarchy. Whereas no one questioned the connection between Jewish
emancipation and military service, other estates in Prussia remained exempt
from such an obligation. Townspeople and merchants did not have to become
soldiers to enjoy the protection of the Prussian state. Peasants were also reluctant to send their sons to the army, "not only because they would thereby lose
vitally important labor, but also because they feared the coarsening influence of
the military."[12]

Two related discourses did not, therefore, overlap in the generations preceding the mid-century revolutions. On the one hand, bourgeois nationalists associated heroic and military masculinity with German national identity. In the
political climate of the *Vormärz* era, however, they did not yet tie masculinity
to military service per se. On the other hand, participants in the emancipation

debate recognized the connection between military service and citizenship, but neither side showed the slightest interest in the manly German identity advocated by Jahn.

THE JEW AS CITIZEN-SOLDIER

Prussia first allowed Jews to fight in its armies in 1812 as a consequence of the Edict of Emancipation. Grateful for the chance to prove themselves worthy of the citizenship that the king had granted them, hundreds of Jewish men responded eagerly to the royal call to arms. Pamphlet literature published by Jewish university students called on the "youth of the Jewish nation" to rally to the defense of the Fatherland. Such exhortations spoke of the fulfillment of duty and the growing self-confidence and patriotism of Jews, as well as the desire to refute anti-Semitic stereotypes that Jews could not make good soldiers. Given the largely rural and traditional makeup of the Jewish communities in the German states at the time, these voices cannot be viewed as representative. Nevertheless, within the first year of the war against Napoleon, Jews in every province of the monarchy had volunteered for service. In the province of Mecklenburg, 1.2 percent of the Jewish community volunteered to fight the French, whereas only 0.4 percent of the general population took to the field.[13]

The Disputed Legacy of the Napoleonic Wars

Enlightened Jewish public figures insisted that the Jewish contribution to the war effort had made irreversible the emancipation of the community as a whole. Dependent on the German states of the old regime for the benefits to be gained from emancipation, they also highlighted the "sacred duty" of Jews to show their gratitude for the "royal favor" granted them in the Edict of Emancipation. In doing so, however, they eschewed the romantic imagery of military heroism, bravery, and the allure of the German Volk family in their discussions of the Wars of Liberation. Although references to the "sweet death" afforded those who fell on the battlefield did echo the romantic nationalism of Ernst Moritz Arndt, Jahn, and others, the rhetoric of German-Jewish reformers differed significantly from that of non-Jewish Germans. Whereas Arndt's call to arms evoked a collective German will, that of the Jewish community spoke of providing "evidence of loyalty" to their rulers and compatriots. Arndt urged individual Germans to sacrifice themselves to an organic community greater than the sum of its individual members; Jews wanted to prove their equality as a group in relation to other subjects of the crown. In defense of the "tolerant and outward-looking spirit of the German people," the prominent Jewish writer Saul Ascher argued that respect for the law formed the foundation of the modern state and that the Jews had proven their commitment to that law beyond doubt with the impressive number of Jewish volunteers at war.[14]

Regardless of the force of this logic, the repressive climate of the restoration era prevailed. All Jewish civil servants in Prussia were forced to leave their posts in June 1816. One year later, the state restricted military service to Prussian citizens and declared that the Edict of Emancipation would not apply to provinces annexed after the defeat of Napoleon. The majority of the Jewish population in Prussia was thereby deprived of both citizenship and the right to serve. With few exceptions, similar conditions prevailed in the other German states as well.[15]

Not until the 1840s did a liberal coalition gain momentum in the debate over Jewish military service. Instead of insisting upon the moral regeneration of Jews in return for emancipation, as had previous generations of Jewish reformers, Gabriel Riesser and his fellow liberals turned the issue into a legal question grounded in principles of individualism and natural rights. A Jewish lawyer who had been denied a university position because of his religion, Riesser insisted that there be no conditions set upon Jewish legal equality other than the fulfillment of the duties of the citizen.

Succumbing to these liberal pressures, Prussia reinstituted general conscription in 1845 in such a way as to require all Jews to serve and make them eligible for promotions to non-commissioned officers. Prussian officials also had their own motives in reinstating this obligation. Some policymakers believed that removing Jews from their families and placing them in a military setting would result in their conversion to Christianity. Above and beyond the missionary function, however, they also believed that military service would improve the poor physical condition of Jews, intensify their patriotism, and develop a theretofore lacking sense of honor. Prussia and other German states deemed Jews to be less physically fit for military service than the rest of the population. In 1845 an internal War Ministry paper on Jews in the Prussian military explained this alleged physical inferiority with reference to "hereditary nervousness."[16]

Notwithstanding these official concerns, Jewish soldiers contributed with distinction to the military campaigns that culminated in the political unification of Germany in January 1871. More than one thousand Jewish soldiers fought on the side of Prussia against Austria in 1866. The novelist Theodor Fontane lauded their accomplishments in his chronicle, *The German War of 1866:* "It was as if they had vowed to themselves to put an end to the old notion of their aversion to and incompetence at war." Approximately six thousand Jewish soldiers fought in the Franco-Prussian war of 1870–1871, yet Prussia made no provision for Jewish field chaplains, and Bavaria remained the only state to grant them the possibility to serve as officers.[17]

THE JEW AS EFFEMINATE OTHER

The circumstances surrounding German unification altered the relationship between the military and Prussian society in a fundamentally illiberal fashion.

Bismarck's co-optation of the national liberals in the 1860s and 1870s brought the goals of the gymnastic and student movements into harmony with those of the Prussian military. Following the wars of unification, teachers and professors instilled in their students pride in the glorious Prussian military tradition that had made this rise to German greatness possible. On holidays marking the an-niversaries of historic battles and the emperor's birthday, military parades drew enormous crowds, thereby reinforcing the centrality of the military in German national culture. Although potential recruits had used every available excuse to avoid military service in the first half of the century, German patriots of the im-perial period "praised universal military service as the foundation of political liberty and training in blind discipline as the finest school of character." Beyond their narrow military function, then, officers came to understand their mission as the preparation of recruits for civilian life as German men.

The increasing importance of the reserve officer's role in the Prussian mili-tary also contributed to what Gerhard Ritter has dubbed the "militarization of the German middle class." In the aftermath of the Franco-Prussian war, mili-tary reforms compelled the regular officer corps to work more closely with re-serve officers. Prussian officers responded to this potential threat to their status by screening the social background of candidates very carefully, consistently denying the applications of Jews, supposed leftists, peasants, artisans, and work-ers. The preeminence of the Prussian military in German society, meanwhile, moved those bourgeois Germans with aspirations to a higher social status to seek a reserve commission. Even as Bismarck's diplomacy reassured foreign ob-servers that they had nothing to fear from the young German Empire, middle-class Germans thus emulated the heroes whose aggressive military campaigns had created that empire.[18]

This valorization of military masculinity only intensified the sense of dishonor among German Jews, who had virtually no chance to pursue military careers. Jewish leaders campaigned aggressively but without success to open the reserve officer corps in the Prussian army to unbaptized Jews. A number of Jewish men did receive commissions as reserve officers in the fifteen years following German unification, but only one did so after 1880, and none of the men advanced to ac-tive duty in the officers' corps before the outbreak of war in 1914. Denying that the issue involved constitutionally protected rights, government officials simply deferred to the judgment of the officer corps, which claimed to judge each appli-cation based upon individual merit rather than religious affiliation.[19]

In public discussions of Jewish military service, meanwhile, anti-Semites did not mince words. A pamphlet entitled *Israel in the Army*, which appeared first in 1889 and then in at least a dozen more editions, incorporated every conceiv-able stereotype of the Jewish body to support the argument that Jews could never be German men:

They lack bodily strength and active temperament.... Their entire skeleton is defective; the breast is not broad and is arched, shoulders not straight and flat, neck and head not upright....It is an annually recurring affair that the Jews offer a much smaller contingent of usable military recruits than the rest of the population, and they make up a highly disproportionate fraction of those who can't complete marches and maneuvers....Such physical inferiority is rarely the foundation of warrior-like bravery.[20]

Marginal anti-Semites were by no means the only observers to make these connections, nor were all these observers German.

Asserting Jewish Virility

In October 1886, twelve Jewish students in Breslau published a manifesto announcing the establishment of *Viadrina*, the first exclusively Jewish student fraternity in Germany. Implicit in the manifesto was an acknowledgment that Jewish reformers had hitherto failed to propagate the masculinity borne of the nineteenth-century German national experience. The students built their project upon the Greek ideal of physical training as the "most powerful impulse toward forming body and mind." They cited *Turnvater* Jahn as a source of their inspiration and expressed their regret that the Jewish community had yet to benefit from his teaching. Furthermore, they insisted on the importance of an aggressive masculinity as a means of undermining the discourse of Jewish femininity:

We have to fight with all our energy against the odium of cowardice and weakness, which is cast on us. We want to show that every member of our association is equal to every Christian fellow-student in any physical exercise....Physical strength and agility will increase self-confidence and self-respect, and in [the] future nobody will be ashamed of being a Jew.[21]

By the turn of the century, nine Jewish fraternities subscribing to the same agenda were united in a national association called *Kartell-Convent der Verbindungen deutscher Studenten jüdischen Glaubens* (KC). Reflecting on his first semester in Munich in 1900, Friedrich Solon remarked that the KC-affiliated fraternity Licaria had provided him with an "education into manhood [*Erziehung "zum Mann"*]."[22]

The militancy of these Jewish students had implications that extended beyond campus life. Having grown up in patriotic German-Jewish middle-class families of the young German Empire, they had not experienced the struggle for emancipation; some of their fathers had even fought in the wars of unification. Their parents' commitment to rationalism, humanism, and German culture outweighed whatever loose connection they had felt to Jewish religious traditions. Having acculturated as completely as their parents would have thought possible, the young German patriots of *Viadrina* ventured one step further than previous generations of German Jews. They sought as Jews to demonstrate publicly their embrace of "the Teutonic ideals of virile virtues."[23]

The KC enjoyed no monopoly on organized Jewish student activity. A variety of Zionist student organizations soon adapted the KC project into a Jewish national framework. In doing so, they employed the rituals and symbols of masculinity that were the trademarks of all German fraternities. Foremost among these practices were military obedience and dueling. Bearing the insignia and colors of their fraternities, Jewish students sang German songs, fenced, and "gave satisfaction" in duels. Indeed, many members of Jewish fraternities conceived of themselves as belonging to a military academy.[24]

One hundred years after the ideologues of emancipation began to advocate German-Jewish acculturation, Jewish student fraternities thus supplemented the German-Jewish subculture with a self-consciously Jewish military masculinity. Although their colors, dress, and activities resembled those of all German fraternities, the fight against anti-Semitism and for a self-confident German Jewry constituted elements of a collective identity that set Jewish students apart from their non-Jewish peers. Determined to stand up for themselves as had no previous generation of German Jews, they cultivated what Solon referred to as "a sort of zeal for war [*Kriegsbegeisterung*], a high sense of honor, and a complete readiness to sacrifice, to intervene against the anti-Semitic enemy wherever and as often as possible."[25] In this sense, anti-Semitism and military masculinity constituted an essential element in the construction of both Zionist and German liberal Jewish identity.

Toward a Muscle Jewry

Members of Jewish-national fraternities found inspiration in the writings of Zionist leaders Theodor Herzl and Max Nordau. Herzl had himself been expelled from a fraternity during his student days in Vienna. Because he was Jewish, his peers at the university had deemed him devoid of honor. The father of political Zionism was therefore preoccupied with developing in Jewry the honor and bravery that German culture associated with masculinity. In his 1895 play, *The New Ghetto,* the lead character, Samuel, dies in the closing scene from a wound sustained in a duel. In the last line of the original manuscript, Samuel exclaims, "Jews, my brothers—they will only let you live if you know how to die." Only by providing a "previously emasculated Central European Jewry with an honorable and manly posture" did Herzl believe the goal of regeneration in a Jewish state could be achieved.[26]

Nordau, meanwhile, approached the problem of Jewish masculinity as both a Zionist and a physician. European Jewry, he believed, had lost its physical and spiritual vitality as a result of two thousand years of exile. Echoing the words of *Turnvater* Jahn, Nordau wrote that only gymnastics and the cultivation of "deep-chested, taut-limbed, steely-eyed men" would foster in Jews the confidence, sense of duty, and discipline necessary for their regeneration. His writings and speeches moved Zionists to make gymnastics and the creation of a "muscle Jewry" (*Muskeljudentum*) a primary pillar in the early movement. A monthly newsletter, the *Jüdische Turnzeitung,* extolled the virtues of a modern version of Jewish manliness that celebrated the military heroism of the

Maccabees and Bar Kochba, figures viewed with ambivalence in the rabbinic Jewish culture. In addition to articulating for the first time a desire to foster a new brand of German-Jewish masculinity, the Jewish student movement produced many future leaders for both Zionist and German liberal Jewry.[27]

Before the First World War, though, the cultivation of military masculinity became a priority for no more than a small minority of German-Jewish men. These initiatives faced skepticism within the Jewish community. To the extent that German Jews accepted the contention that the "normal balance between the body and mind is absent from the Jew," they generally felt that Jewish youth should enter German sports and gymnastic clubs.[28] The impression of Jewish exclusivity that specifically Jewish clubs might foster would, some feared, provoke the resentment of their non-Jewish compatriots. Moreover, some observers considered it somehow un-Jewish to adopt the German rituals of manliness. As a Jewish intellectual, a pacifist, and a member of the SPD, Philipp Loewenfeld felt that the antics of Jewish student fraternities in Munich at the turn of the century were all the more ridiculous for being practiced by Jewish men. "When I got some insight into their spirit and activities," he later recalled, "I quickly convinced myself that they were an exact copy of the drinking and fighting...traditions of the 'Christian' fraternities, except all the more ridiculous because for being Jewish."[29] Partly because of such reservations, the membership numbers of Jewish fraternities and gymnastics associations remained small in relation to the size of the community as a whole. By 1914, at a time when more than 500,000 Jews lived in Germany, only 1,325 students were united in the largest Jewish student association, the KC. Their agenda nevertheless represented a potential rejoinder to a growing consensus on Jewish physical inferiority.[30]

Walther Rathenau, the son of a wealthy Jewish industrialist and an accomplished writer in his own right, published a notorious attack on Eastern European Jews in 1897 that betrayed how intimately linked were the discourse of Jewish physical inferiority, German-Jewish disillusionment with their incomplete integration, and hostility toward Jewish immigrants. A German patriot enthralled by Prussian militarism, Rathenau wanted to reject his father's materialism and pursue a career as an officer in the Prussian army. After the officers' corps denied him this goal, he joined the family business after all. He then unleashed his German nationalism and military masculinity in an article provocatively titled "Hear, O Israel!" in reference to a prayer recited daily by observant Jews. In the essay, Rathenau demanded that Jewish immigrants regenerate themselves and conform to the standards of the German nation:

You must ensure that, amid a race that is bred to strict military discipline, you do not make yourself a laughing-stock by your slovenly, shambling appearance. Once you have recognized your ill-constructed build, your high shoulders, your clumsy feet, the soft roundness of your forms, as signs of physical decay, you will have to spend a couple of generations working on your external rebirth.

For Rathenau, as for so many of his fellow German Jews, Eastern European Jews symbolized the conditions in which their own ancestors had found themselves at the dawn of the age of emancipation in the early nineteenth century. Believing himself to be a product of the "external rebirth" of an emancipated German Jewry, he lambasted his non-German co-religionists for all of the alleged deviations from the masculine ideal for which anti-Semites ridiculed their phantom image of "the Jew." This expression of rage served as an outlet for Rathenau's disappointment with being forced, in spite of his best efforts at conforming to the military masculine ideal, into the physically passive, materialist role of his father and forefathers. As his frustrated military ambitions suggest, Jews lived in a German Empire that granted Jews equality in word but not deed.[31]

Defending Jewish Honor, Acknowledging German-Jewish Inferiority

It was not only in Germany that liberal Jews were anxious to counter the spread of anti-Semitism in the 1890s. The question of Jewish suitability for military service figured prominently elsewhere as well. An influx of Jewish refugees from czarist Russia was strengthening popular anti-Semitism in the United States at the time. American-Jewish leader Simon Wolf consequently felt compelled to publish a comprehensive account of Jewish participation in the Union Army during the Civil War in 1895. In France, meanwhile, anthropologists and other social scientists did not share the Germans' fascination with Jews as an object of racial study, but the anti-Semitic violence that accompanied the national trauma of the Dreyfus Affair exceeded even the worst excesses of contemporary German anti-Semites. Three years after Alfred Dreyfus was arrested in 1894, Maurice Bloch documented "the military virtues of Jews" in a journal of Jewish studies.[32]

Although they shared an interest in demonstrating Jewish military accomplishments with U.S. and French Jews, German Jews departed from their foreign co-religionists insofar as they conceded that the men in their community were still plagued by physical and psychological inferiorities that hampered their ability to serve in the military. On behalf of an interfaith group devoted to the refutation of anti-Semitic propaganda, liberal German-Jewish leader Paul Nathan published a brochure entitled *Jews as Soldiers* in 1896. After compiling all the available material on Jewish soldiers in the Wars of Unification and surveying the evidence of Jewish military service in several other countries, Nathan issued a critical disclaimer:

It is correct that the slavery in which the Jews were kept for centuries and centuries diminished their physical constitution.... One cannot deny that Jews even began to doubt their own soldiers' fulfillment of duty.... Fatalistically it was said: We are not born for it; a past that was forced upon us has made us unsuitable for it.[33]

Reviewing Nathan's work, Ernst Schaeffer quoted this passage and seconded it. In other states, he claimed, Jewish physical inferiority had already been remedied, but for Germany, "it cannot be determined if the physical utility [of Jewish men] is gradually increasing. In order reliably to [do so], precisely military recruitment is needed, so it is in the interest of Jewry itself eagerly to fulfill the duty of the soldier."[34] Schaeffer closed his article with an exhortation to the Jewish community to discharge its obligation to itself and the German state by taking full advantage of the military as a "school of masculinity."[35]

To be sure, the realities of German-Jewish life often contradicted notions of Jewish physical inferiority. Thousands of Jewish soldiers absolved a single year of military service in Wilhelmine Germany. Jewish men joined and participated in the activities of *Turnvereine* and veterans' associations. On occasion, they even held the chairmanships of these groups. Furthermore, research on Jewish everyday life in the imperial period has revealed what one historian calls "a kind of assertive masculinity, an earthy 'don't shove me around' attitude" on the part of cattle dealers in rural Jewish communities.[36]

Stereotypes of the physically passive and intellectually inclined Jewish man nonetheless dominated discussions of Jewish masculinity at universities, in the Zionist movement, and among urban Jews more generally. In the cities of fin-de-siècle central Europe, both Jewish and non-Jewish social scientists, to say nothing of anti-Semitic agitators, ignored these isolated cases and instead gave scientific validation to perceptions of male Jewish effeminacy and physical inferiority. The treatment of Jews in and by the German militaries only strengthened these stereotypes, which underlay the agenda of the young Jewish men who established the first institutions dedicated to the cultivation of an explicitly Jewish military masculinity.

The First World War transformed their struggle for a robust, heroic Jewry from an agenda supported by a tiny minority into a daily necessity for tens of thousands of German-Jewish soldiers. For more than a century, male Jewish leaders had devoted themselves to the refined masculine ideal of enlightened German culture and resisted the influence of romanticism. The war, however, intensified the influence of neo-romantic currents already at work within the prewar German-Jewish community. Between 1914 and 1918 more than one third of the male Jewish population donned a military uniform, and the exigencies of war forced the Prussian army to abandon its unwritten policy of excluding Jews from its officers' corps. Some 2,000 Jewish soldiers became officers, and 80,000 Jewish soldiers served on the front lines. Ever conscious of stereotypes of the effeminate Jew, many of these men believed the trenches to be the crucible in which a new German-Jewish man would be produced. Throughout the Weimar era and into the Third Reich, Jewish veterans of the First World War propagated military masculinity within the German-Jewish community in the hope of bridging the chasm that continued to separate Jews from their non-Jewish compatriots. In interwar Germany, however, Nazi anti-Semitism prevailed over the values of militarism.

NOTES

1. I am speaking here of a common Jewish culture based on a set of teachings, rituals, and social practices that united Ashkenaz communities. For a social historical analysis of early modern Jewish communities, see Jacob Katz, *Tradition and Crisis: Jewish Society at the End of the Middle Ages* (New York: New York University Press, 1993). For approaches that emphasize the heterogeneity of Jewish life in early modern Europe, see Pierre Birnbaum and Ira Katznelson, eds., *Paths of Emancipation: Jews, States, and Citizenship* (Princeton: Princeton University Press, 1995).

2. Jacob Neusner, "The Virtues of the Inner Life in Formative Judaism," *Tikkun* 1 (1986): 81.

3. Daniel Boyarin, *Unheroic Conduct: The Rise of Heterosexuality and the Invention of the Jewish Man* (Berkeley: University of California Press, 1997), chap. 1; Barbara Breitman, "Lifting up the Shadow of Anti-Semitism: Jewish Masculinity in a New Light," in Harry Brod, ed., *A Mensch among Men: Explorations in Jewish Masculinity* (Freedom, CA: The Crossing Press, 1989), p. 106. On the image of the knight in early modern Europe, see Peter Burke, *Popular Culture in Early Modern Europe* (New York: Harper Torchbooks, 1978), pp. 149–50; 157–158.

4. Martin S. Bergman, "Moses and the Evolution of Freud's Jewish Identity," *Israel Annals of Psychiatry and Related Disciplines* 14 (March 1976): 12; cited in Daniel Boyarin, "Goyim Naches: The Manliness of the Mentsch," in Bryan Cheyette and Laura Marcus, eds., *Modernity, Culture, and "the Jew"* (Stanford: Stanford University Press, 1998), p. 64.

5. *The Memoirs of Glueckel of Hameln* (New York: Schocken, 1977), p. 34.

6. Quote from Johann Christoph Friedrich GutsMuths, *Gymnastik für die Jugend. Enthaltend eine praktische Anweisung zu Leibesübungen. Ein Beytrag zur nöthigsten Verbesserung der körperlichen Erziehung* (Schnepfenthal, 1793), p. 17; cited in Ute Frevert, "Das Militär als Schule der Männlichkeit," in Ute Frevert, ed., *Militär und Gesellschaft im 19. und 20. Jahrhundert* (Stuttgart: Klett-Cotta, 1997), p. 150.

7. George L. Mosse, *Image of Man: The Creation of Modern Masculinity* (New York: Oxford University Press), pp. 29–34. See also idem., *Nationalism and Sexuality: Middle Class Morality and Sexual Norms in Modern Europe*, 2nd ed. (Madison: University of Wisconsin Press, 1988); and Thomas Kühne, "Männergeschichte als Geschlechtergeschichte," in Thomas Kühne, ed., *Männergeschichte-Geschlechtergeschichte: Männlichkeit im Wandel der Moderne* (Frankfurt/New York: Campus Verlag, 1996), pp. 7–30.

8. Frevert, "Das Militär als Schule," p. 150; Daniel A. McMillan, "'die höchste und heiligste Pflicht ... ' Das Männlichkeitsideal der deutschen Turnbewegung, 1811–1871," in Kühne, ed., *Männergeschichte-Geschlechtergeschichte*, pp. 88–90.

9. David Sorkin, *The Transformation of German Jewry, 1780–1840* (New York: Oxford University Press, 1987), pp. 79–99.

10. Susannah Heschel, "Sind Juden Männer? Können Frauen jüdisch sein? Die gesellschaftliche Definition des männlichen/weiblichen Körpers," in Sander Gilman et al., eds., *"Der schejne Jid" Das Bild des "jüdischen Körpers" in Mythos und Ritual*

(Wien: Picus Verlag, 1998), p. 91. On genteel conceptions of bourgeois masculinity in the nineteenth-century, see Anne Charlott-Trepp, *Sanfte Männlichkeit und selbstständige Weiblichkeit*, and John Tosh, *A Man's Place: Masculinity and the Middle-Class Home in Victorian England* (New Haven: Yale University Press, 1999).

11. Horst Fischer, *Judentum, Staat und Heer in Preussen im frühen 19. Jahrhundert: Zur Geschichte der staatlichen Judenpolitik* (Tübingen: J.C.B. Mohr, 1968), p. 10; Johann David Michaelis, "Arguments against Dohm," in Jehuda Reinharz and Paul R. Mendes-Flohr, eds., *The Jew in the Modern World: A Documentary History* (New York: Oxford University Press, 1980), p. 38; Leon Poliakov, *The History of Anti-Semitism, vol. 3: From Voltaire to Wagner* (New York: Vanguard Press, 1975), p. 177. Felix Theilhaber, "Militärdienst der Juden," *Jüdisches Lexikon* (Berlin, 1927), vol. 4, p. 182.

12. Ute Frevert, "Das jakobinische Modell: Allgemeine Wehrpflicht und Nationsbildung in Preussen-Deutschland," in Ute Frevert, ed., *Militär und Gesellschaft im 19. und 20. Jahrhundert* (Stuttgart: Klett-Cotta, 1997), p. 22.

13. Fischer, *Judentum*, p. 52; Erik Lindner, *Patriotismus deutscher Juden von der napoleonischen Ära bis zum Kaiserreich: zwischen korporativem Loyalismus und individueller deutsch-jüdischer Identität* (Frankfurt a. M.: Peter Lang, 1997), p. 58.

14. Stefi Jersch-Wenzel, "Legal Status and Emancipation," in Michael A. Meyer, ed., *German-Jewish History*, p. 34; Lindner, *Patriotismus*, p. 200.

15. Fischer, *Judentum*, pp. 56, 69; Jersch-Wenzel, "Legal Status," pp. 28–30.

16. Fischer, *Judentum*, pp. 47–51; 79–84; 98–100; 113, n. 38; 131, n. 110; 148–149; 161; 174–176.

17. Theodor Fontane, *Der deutsche Krieg von 1866, Bd. 1, Der Feldzug in Böhmen und Mähren* (Berlin, 1870), p. 413, cited in Ernst Schaeffer, "Die Juden als Soldaten," *Nathanael* 13 (1897): 99; Lindner, *Patriotismus*, p. 311; Felix Theilhaber, "Militärdienst der Juden," pp. 183–184.

18. Frevert, "Das Militär als Schule," pp. 162–163; Gerhard Ritter, *The Sword and the Scepter: The Problem of Militarism in Germany* (Coral Gables: University of Miami Press, 1970), Vol. II, p. 99. On the militarization of masculinity within the gymnastics movement in the wake of German unification, see Svenja Goltermann, *Körper der Nation: Habitusformierung und die Politik des Turnens, 1860–1890* (Göttingen: Vandenhoeck & Ruprecht, 1998), pp. 290–325. For a comparative analysis of such public military rituals, see Jakob Vogel, *Nationen im Gleichschritt: der Kult der "Nation im Waffen" in Deutschland und Frankreich, 1871–1914* (Göttingen: Vandenhoek & Ruprecht, 1997).

19. Werner T. Angress, "Prussia's Army and the Jewish Reserve Officer Controversy before World War I," *LBIYB* 17 (1972): 20, 29, 40.

20. H. Naudh, "Israel im Heere," *Die Deutsche Wacht: Monatsschrift für nationale Entwicklung* 1 (1879): 12–14.

21. "Ein Wort an unsere Glaubensgenossen," trans. in Adolph Asch and Johanna Phillipson, "Self-Defence at the Turn of the Century: The Emergence of the K.C.," *Leo Baeck Institute Yearbook*, 1958, p. 124. Paul Posener, a former member of the fraternity, offers a much more critical perspective on the history of Viadrina in his memoir, *The Young Maccabees*, which is held in the Leo Baeck Institute Archive in New York.

22. Monika Richarz, ed., *Jüdisches Leben in Deutschland*, (Stuttgart: Deutsche Verlags-Anstalt, 1979), vol. 2, p. 436.

23. Asch and Phillipson, "Self-Defence," pp. 131–132; Posener, "The Young Maccabees," pp. 57–58.

24. Moshe Zimmerman, "Jewish Nationalism and Zionism in German-Jewish Students' Organisations," *Leo Baeck Institute Yearbook* 27 (1982): 132–133. On dueling in fraternity life more generally, see Ute Frevert, *Men of Honor: A Social and Cultural History of the Duel* (Cambridge: Polity Press, 1995), chap. 5.

25. Richharz, ed., *Jüdisches Leben*, vol. 2, p. 436.

26. Cited in Matti Bunzl, "Theodor Herzl's Zionism as Gendered Discourse," in Ritchie Robertson and Edward Timms, eds., *Theodor Herzl and the Origins of Zionism* (Edinburgh: Edinburgh University Press, 1997), p. 80.

27. Max Nordau, "Muskeljudentum," in *Jüdische Turnzeitung* (June 1900): 10–11; cited in Michael Berkowitz, *Zionist Culture and West European Jewry before the First World War* (Cambridge: Cambridge University Press, 1993), p. 107; Boyarin, *Unheroic Conduct*, pp. 273–274. For a classic Zionist analysis of Jewish physical inferiority, see Balduin Groller, "Die körperliche Minderwertigkeit der Juden," *Die Welt*, May 1901, pp. 3–5.

28. Eli Samgar, "Jüdische Turnerschaft," *Die Welt*, December 9, 1898, pp. 8–10; cited in Geoge Eisen, "Zionism, Nationalism and the Emergence of the Jüdische Turnerschaft," *Leo Baeck Institute Yearbook* 28 (1983): 247.

29. Richharz, ed., *Jüdisches Leben*, vol. 2, p. 316.

30. Thomas Schindler, "'Was Schandfleck war, ward unser Ehrenzeichen....' Die jüdischen Studentenverbindungen und ihr Beitrag zur Entwicklung eines neuen Selbstbewusstseins deutscher Juden," in Brandt and Stickler, eds., *"Der Burschen Herrlichkeit,"* p. 343.

31. Walter Rathenau, published under the pseudonym W. Hartenau, "Höre Israel!" *Die Zukunft* 18 (March 16, 1897): 458; see also Ritchie Robertson, "Historicizing Weininger: The Nineteenth-Century German Image of the Feminized Jew," in Cheyette and Marcus, eds., *Modernity*, pp. 30–33; Ernst Schulin, "Walther Rathenau und sein Integrationsversuch als 'Deutscher jüdischen Stammes,'" in Walter Grab, ed., *Jüdische Integration und Identität in Deutschland und Österreich, 1848–1918* (Tel Aviv: Universität Tel Aviv, Institut für Deutsche Geschichte, 1984), pp. 13–38.

32. Simon Wolf, *The American Jew as Patriot, Soldier, and Citizen* (Philadelphia, 1895); Maurice Bloch, "Les vertus militaires des Juifs," *Revue des études juives* 34 (1897): 18–53. For an in-depth comparison of German and French anti-Semitism, see Shulamit Volkov, "Kontinuität und Diskontinuität im deutschen Antisemitismus, 1878–1945," *Vierteljahrsheft fur Zeitgeschichte* 33 (1985): 221–243.

33. Paul Nathan, *Die Juden als Soldaten* (Berlin, 1896), cited in Schaeffer, "Die Juden als Soldaten," pp. 104–105.

34. Ibid.

35. I take this term from the title of Ute Frevert's article, "Das Militär als Schule der Männlichkeit." See n. 8 above.

36. Marion Kaplan, e-mail to author, October 31, 2000. Her study, *Jewish Daily Life in Germany,* was published by the Leo Baeck Institute in New York in 2002. On Jews in the associational life of Imperial Germany, see Utz Jeggle, *Judendörfer in Württemberg* (Tübingen, 1969), pp. 249–252; Richarz, ed., *Jüdisches Leben,* vol. 2, pp. 167–168, 181, 193, 215.

Chapter 13

The Military and Masculinities in Israeli Society

Uta Klein

INTRODUCTION

In Israeli society members of the Israeli Defense Forces (IDF) are not seen just as soldiers. In newspapers and in TV people talk about *our children* and—in spite of the conscription of women—more often about *our sons*. When soldiers get killed as a result of military confrontations, their names and pictures appear in the newspapers the next day. Details of where they lived and their parents are included.

When in 1997 seventy-three young soldiers, members of the Israeli Air Force, died on their way to Lebanon after two helicopters transporting them collided, newspaper articles, television programs, and speeches of politicians in the following days and weeks named the dead young men "the best of our boys" and "the best of our country's youth."

In Israel the motivation for military service and for combat units has been extremely high. Military service is seen as part of the transition to the male adult world and as a right of the individual to express affiliation to society. Military service defines who is "in" and who is "out" with respect to the collective and the informal system.

It is worth exploring why military and masculinity in Israeli society are deeply interconnected and why a defense orientation is an inherent part of masculinity in a state where women have been conscripted since the foundation of the state.[1] In spite of the conscription of Jewish Israeli women, gender images, gender symbols, and gender relations have not changed. The defender is male. The memorials for fallen soldiers, which can be found in each kibbutz and each town, are called Yad le'banim, which means house or place of the sons.

CHILDHOOD, ADOLESCENCE, AND THE
MILITARY IN ISRAEL

For Israeli Jewish males, military service is an inherent part of maturation, a rite of passage to male adulthood. "Military service is internalized by members of the Israeli Jewish collective as essential to a boy's right to belong to this group and, more specifically, to the inner circle of adult males. A rite of passage is related to and spoken of in fatalistic, quasi-religious terms, as an inevitable, inescapable, pseudo-biological phase of male maturation."[2]

REASONS FOR GENDER DIFFERENCE

Military service in Israel is compulsory. As a result of agreements between the religious parties and the ruling party Jewish men and women are conscripted on unequal terms. The Defense Service Law (1949) specifies which persons are automatically exempted from service: married women, pregnant women, mothers, and women who declare that religious reasons prevent them from serving.

The law does not exempt men for reasons of religion, conscience, or marital status. Yet in praxis Jewish religious men who are actually studying in a *Yeschiwa* are exempted. Among the Arab population, only Druse men are obliged to serve. Bedouin men can volunteer, and Muslims are excluded.[3] The length of service is different too; according to the law, men have to serve for three years, women for two years.

The percentage of the female population to be drafted, together with the number who complete their whole length of service tends to be disputed. However, the figures we do have suggest that about 90 percent of the men are drafted, versus 60 percent of the women. In a recent paper Stuart A. Cohen states that 80 percent of the male recruits complete their statutory length of service. In comparison, only 15 percent of female conscripts complete twenty-four months. What is called "universal" conscription is selective rather than universal as far as the female population is concerned. Furthermore, only men are regularly called to reserve duty up to the age of 50 or 52 years.

As a result of the prohibition of combat roles for women, in Israel, as in other armed forces around the world, men are identified as the protectors and women as the protected.[4]

HISTORICAL TRAITS

Historical traits of gender images help us to understand current elements of gender in a given cultural context. Analysis of the history of Zionist masculinity helps us to understand the overstress in current Israeli military attitudes and thinking.[5]

Zionism developed at the end of the last century as a reaction to pogroms in southern Russia and the eruption of modern anti-Semitism in central Europe. Viewing the history of the Jewish people as one of continuous persecution, the Zionist movement aimed to renew the national life of the Jewish people in Palestine.

The Zionists perceived the Diaspora Jew as passive and effeminate. The Zionist ideal of manliness was constructed as an antithesis of the Diaspora Jew. Physical strength and readiness to defend honor by means of fighting were the desired characteristics of the "new Jew." We must not forget that the Zionist movement emerged as a latecomer among European nationalist movements. Because assimilated Jews had adopted traits of courage held up as ideals in the Gentile world, the Zionist movement utilized symbols that were familiar to other nationalist movements: patriotic songs, glorification of the heroes of the past, and military education. The ideal of manliness was very much the same as that of other nationalist movements. Zionism envisaged a nation like all other nations, and on the level of reform of the Jewish psyche its men were to be like all other men.[6] Nevertheless, a particularly potent drive stemmed from its rejection and contempt for the Diaspora. The complete transformation of the Jewish people could take place only in Palestine; the colonization of Palestine has been a remasculinization-process.[7]

The Zionist ethos of masculine ideals of physical force and strength underwent an intensification because of the *Shoah*, the Holocaust, and is since engraved in Jewish Israeli society. It is part of the mythological *Sabra*, the prototype of the Israel-born new Jew, that the native Israeli is a person who is soft inside but thorny on the outside. The Jewish-Arab conflict and existence in a continuous state of conflict has enhanced this ethos. The state of Israel was "born" in a war (1948–1949), which ended with armistice agreements and with the recognition that the conflict between Arabs and the Israelis was deep and complex. The Holocaust syndrome and political geography conditioned a sense of isolation. Israel regarded its neighbors as enemies, an attitude that has, so far, changed only with respect to Egypt and Jordan. In its fifty years of existence Israel has experienced six wars, each of which has strengthened the drive to excel in the military realm.[8]

Strength is of tremendous importance to Israelis and their identity. Any signs of weakness are regarded as threats to identity. Culture, especially myths and rituals, perpetuate the construction of the defense-oriented man.

How do children get into contact with these rules of life? One example is the structure of holiday celebrations in kindergarten. According to Mirta Furmann, messages are transmitted by teachers and kindergarten teachers emphasizing heroism and active self-defense.[9] The basis for cohesion of the Jewish Israeli collective is the warrior figure, whose major trait is being Jewish and masculine. Folk tales present historical figures like Bar Kokhba or Judah Maccabee in the expectation that they will serve as models of identification.

Furmann observed that children are confused about history and presence and draw a connection between historical figures and their own brother or father participating in wars and reserve duty: "The stories of exemplary personalities forge the emotional foundation for constructing attitudes and behavior, such as the belief in the necessity of military service and the inevitability of war."[10]

As an example, consider the following quotation from a textbook and the response sheet used in first grade to talk about Independence Day. First, the children had been asked to read the following text:

Who is a hero?

On Independence Day the children went to see the parade of the Israeli Defense Forces. They stood on the sidewalk and they saw battalions of soldiers marching and singing. In the sky airplanes fly fast, and large tanks crawl by slowly. Ronen said: "When I grow up I will be a pilot. I will fly in a plane way up high. Only a pilot is a hero." Avner said: "And when I grow up I will be a sailor. I will be the captain of a huge ship. The ship will guard our country's shores. Only a sailor is a hero!" Uri said: "And I will be a simple soldier. A simple soldier is also a hero. He guards the State of Israel day and night! Who is right?"[11]

The children were then asked to fill in the blanks of the following text:

Ronen wants to be a _____. Avner wants to be a _____. Uri wants to be a _____. (...) I am _____ years old. In another _____ years I will be a soldier.[12]

Thus military socialization in Israel begins not with the influence of the defense forces on conscripts but, rather, with the inculcation of kindergarten and school-age children. In school, Israeli Jewish youths prepare themselves to join the military forces. Members of the IDF hold lectures to give information and impressions of life in the Israeli Army. Some youths volunteer for special units or undergo preinduction courses. Almost every Jewish Israeli pupil takes part in the yearly Yom Hakheilot, a one-day seminar held in cooperation with the schools and the army.

This Yom Hakheilot shows that military service for males is a *bodily* experience. Boys and girls are separated. Films showing soldiers in action and exciting military life are shown to the boys. The young men are told that physical exercise is essential in preparing for military service. Girls, however, do not see films about women in action. Physical performance is scarcely ever mentioned. The main emphasis of lectures and talks for girls lies in emotional questions involving military service like separation from parents.[13]

Male and female youths have very different reasons for joining the army, and participation means something very different for their self-perception. Research shows that when asked for their motivation to serve in the IDF, males assign higher importance to normative reasons ("to be like everyone") and value roles, which can be recognized from outside: "to be a fighter" and "to do something prestigious" are reasons given for preferring a certain IDF job, which show a clear gender difference. Female youths instead show a more intrinsic motivation ("meeting new people," "doing something interesting"); public recognition doesn't seem to play a big role.[14]

Parents play an important role in this context. They support their sons' maturation process and their fulfillment of the military task, seeing it as a necessary, justified sacrifice. Rela Mazali sees in this phenomenon the upholding of what "is arguably the most fundamental social contract in Israeli Jewish society."[15] By this, so her argument goes, soldier sons in Israel are performing the task of resocializing their parents to the collectivity. Even when the son is still a small child, it is the parents' assumption that he will become a soldier, possibly a member of a combat unit. Tamar Katriel describes a talk with a father in his mid-thirties, a paratrooper, during one of the common Saturday picnic meetings of parents and their soldier children. The man told her he got the creeps thinking of the possibility that his son, when he became a soldier, should find himself in some of the situations in which he had found himself during his own days as a young soldier. He added that the thought of his son's military service sometimes kept him awake at night. When she asked him when his son was going into the service, he replied that the boy was only 8 years old.[16]

MILITARY SERVICE AND THE CONSTRUCTION OF MASCULINITY

Usually society and armies see the soldier as an embodiment of traditional male sex role attitudes and behavior. Army service can thus be described as a rite of passage to male adulthood, where the socializing process aims to teach toughness and masculinity and to eliminate what is regarded to be effeminate. That the military in general is a male institution proves Kimmel's argument that masculinity is largely a "homosocial enactment," that it's other men who judge masculinity.[17]

Although in Israel (Jewish) women are conscripted, military service must be understood as a rite of passage to *male* adulthood. On the one hand, this is a result of the expectation of society. Society still expects a young man—if he is not orthodox—to be ready to fulfill his obligation to serve. On the other hand, it is a result of a gendered institution. Conscription on unequal terms, different length of service, and combat restriction (until January 2000) block the career of women in the forces. Among the officers, the percentage of women in the rank of major general in 1995 was 0 percent, brigadier 0 percent, brigadier general 0.8 percent, colonel 2.2 percent, lieutenant colonel 10.3 percent, and major 22.5 percent.

In a ranking that David and Mady Wechsler Segal and Bradford Booth used to compare the integration of women and homosexuals in a cross-national survey, Israel was listed with 8.3 as the mean rank for women (in a scale with 1 serving as the most integrated and 18 serving as the least integrated).[18] The United States, Norway, Canada, and Great Britain had a better mean rank.[19]

Even if figures have changed, women in the IDF are still overrepresented in service and administrative positions.[20] Whereas 50 percent of female soldiers were appointed for office work, today a Chen-commander talks of 20 percent of all female soldiers.[21] This percentage is now disputed, however, since the terminology has changed: A secretary is no longer called a secretary, though the work remains more or less the same.[22] The other most popular areas for women concern education, welfare, and communications.

It seems that from the point of view of the defense forces, women are not as necessary as men. Stuart A. Cohen states that only 15 percent of female conscripts complete their statutory length of service.[23] In comparison, 80 percent of the male recruits do.

A further element of conscription policy is to be seen in a gender context: Men are taken regardless of education, whereas women must have eight years of formal education. On the one hand, this means that the average qualification of female soldiers is higher, but on the other hand, this practice "reinforces the social handicap of those women."[24] Ten years ago, according to Reuven Gal,[25] low level of education or intelligence was the second largest category of women exempted from military service.

Military service is a bodily experience, a physical exercise. Pictures in newspapers and official brochures show male soldiers mostly appearing in groups, always moving, sweating, exhausted, the eyes directed on a distant point. Female soldiers are shown more often alone or in twos; they smile, they are more static.

Eyal Ben-Ari observes that masculinity is never achieved once and for all, but must constantly be proven: "emotional control, conquering of fear, and performance are not givens but must constantly be struggled for."[26] Even the style of walking can have masculine characteristics. As one young man, an Israeli soldier, reflects:

The hikes got longer, with heavier loads to carry. For every hike we usually got some reward. You hike for the strap of your rifle, for the paratroopers' insignia, for your cap. Gradually you learn to love those night marches, and you get to know yourself really well. Your odor, the sound of your footsteps.... You admire the performance of your squad leader—he walks while you run and you still cannot catch up with him. Gradually you discover that he knows *how* to walk—and you learn this too.... After fourteen months of training together, I was able to identify my buddies from a distance by their way of walking.[27]

Although motivation to join combat units seems to be decreasing, it remains high compared with that in other countries. To be a fighter means, first of all, to control feelings of fear. The confession "'I'm afraid' is an admission all Israeli soldiers learned to deny during their instruction," writes Yaron Ezrachi.[28] Interesting in this context is the Hebrew verb *lehitgaber*. It means "to overcome," "to get over," and is based on the same root as *gever*, "man." *Gibor*, "the hero," is derived from *gever*. Nevertheless, an erosion of the myth of the hero has become apparent.

This is the case among the Sabras, the Israel-born men and women. Motivation is stronger among immigrants, especially among Russian immigrants.

IMPACT OF MILITARY SERVICE ON THE
PUBLIC SPHERE

The centrality of the military and of security in society leads to a symbolic and a practical marginalization of women because they are regarded as incapable of defending the country and taking part in security discourse. Jewish Israeli men gain from their military service by accumulating social capital, by establishing contacts for their professional careers (networking), and by achieving material and symbolic benefits. Men accumulate what Pierre Bourdieu calls social and symbolic capital, which grants them advantages in civilian life.[29] In contrast, the capital Jewish women accumulate is not valued very highly in the civilian labor market.

Service in the higher echelons of the army is a pathway toward positions of importance and influence in public life. Until a few years ago the IDF served as a stepping stone for most of the senior officers who pursued a civilian career. In high-tech industry the links between defense forces and civilian employers remain very strong. A manager says about Israeli companies: "Israeli entrepreneurs have technological experience and prefer teams that have already worked together in the army or the defense industry."[30] In other fields, military experience is even a condition for getting a job: Israel's national airline, El-Al, for example, until recently used to recruit its pilots exclusively from the military. Until a court decision in 1995, the defense forces excluded women from pilot training, so only men were chosen by EL-AL. Research exploring the mechanisms used to recruit and select job applicants in Israeli firms shows that a third to a half of companies considered individuals' army records when selecting managers, professionals, technicians, clerical staff, and craftsmen, and a third did so when hiring operatives and laborers. The firms consider "army service as a means of screening out unreliable individuals and identifying potentially high achievers."[31]

Men convert their military rank into analogous ranks within political parties. The political sphere is dominated by men who in the last ten or fifteen years retired as generals while in their forties and transferred into the political realm. Ehud Barak, the last Israeli prime minister, had been chief of general staff and as prime minister surrounded himself exclusively with retired military men. Ariel Sharon, the current prime minister, can be identified only through his military career and his controversial decisions as defense minister.

A military background is regarded as a necessary precondition for public office. Thus, the percentage of women in the Knesset since the establishment of the Israeli state never exceeded 10 percent until it reached just 12 percent in the current parliament. Besides the exclusion of women in the orthodox religious parties, the predominance of military experience in society as a whole is responsible for that low percentage. For it is predominantly men who gain the military rank that in civilian life can be parlayed into analogous positions of political power.

CONCLUSION

Although the Israeli Army is still perceived as the main mechanism for building a *national* identity,[32] in particular it has become the basis of a *male* self-image and a source for *male* social mobility in society.[33]

The military turns out to be the main agent of society in shaping gender roles, constructing masculinity, and thus it serves as the main source of gender inequality in society. In spite of the participation of women in the military, Israeli experience shows that ideologies of manhood and the dominant position of the military in society are deeply intertwined.

Research shows that messages related to military roles are transmitted through rituals even in kindergarten and that by the time Israeli youth reach the army, they "have internalized the knowledge, the motivation and the demands associated with soldiering."

Nevertheless, we can observe an increasing public discourse relating to the centrality of the military and on Zahal itself. One example is the discussion about sexual harassment in the army. What had been denied in the past seems now to have become an issue of public debate. Since the introduction of the 1998 Sexual Harassment Prevention Law, the highest number of complaints filed has been in the Ministry of Defense. When the former general and then minister of transport Yitzhak Mordechai was recently investigated on suspicion of sexual assault against an employee in his ministry, several women charged that Mordechai had harassed them as well during his army tenure.[34] In some circles, there is much confusion and alarm about a decline in willingness to serve (although motivation in general is still high). The New Profile movement, which works for the acceptance of conscientious objection in Israel, may well be marginal, but at the same time it shows that there are young people refusing to carry out the obligation of military service. In my perspective a gender-democratic society can develop only with a volunteer force selecting people according to ability regardless of gender. To recruit women is not enough to change gender roles.

NOTES

1. In China women are also conscripted, but less than 10 percent of each age group is called, so this statistic is negligible.

2. Rela Mazali, "Soldiers Born—Military Service as Initiation Rite in Israel," (unpublished manuscript, September 1993).

3. That means my remarks about masculinity apply to the Jewish Israeli collective. On the one hand, the IDF creates a common bond between Jewish Israelis who come from different ethnic backgrounds; on the other hand, it might be worth exploring how the exclusion of most Arab males leads to the creation of what Connell calls marginalized and subordinated masculinities along national ethnic lines. See Uta Klein, "Nationale, ethnische und religiöse Konfliktachsen in der israelischen Gesellschaft," in Armin Nassehi (Hg.), *Nation, Ethnie, Minderheit. Beiträge zur Aktualität ethnischer Konflikte* (Köln [u.a.], 1997).

4. Judith Hicks Stiehm, "The Protected, the Protector, the Defender," *Women's Studies International Forum* 5, 3/4 (1982): 367–376.

5. See Uta Klein, "'Our Best Boys'—The Gendered Nature of Civil-Military Relations in Israel," *Men and Masculinities* 2, 1 (July 1999): 47–65.

6. The link between the construction of heterosexuality and masculinty is shown in *Unheroic Conduct* by Daniel Boyarin. See Daniel Boyarin, *Unheroic Conduct: The Rise of Heterosexuality and the Invention of the Jewish Man* (Berkeley [u.a.], 1997).

7. The political Zionist approach was not the only one. Ahad Ha-Am advocated a spiritual Zionism, which rejected the emphasis on physical strength. According to his interpretation of Jewish history, the secret of the survival of the Jewish people was the respect of spiritual power and not to be impressed by physical strength. Instead of lauding the fighters of Jewish history, he praised Rabbi Yohanan ben Zakkai, who—as legend tells—fled from Jerusalem under siege hidden in a coffin and established the rabbinical center *Yavneh*. The "true Jew" in his view was not ashamed of physical weakness. Nevertheless, political Zionism represented by Herzl became the mainstream of the Zionist movement. The colonizing process of Palestine can be understood as a masculinization process. Even the transformation of language, the transformation of *Jiddish*—as a female connoting "mother tongue"—to Hebrew, can be read as part of the transformation process. See Uta Klein, *Militar und Geschlect in Israel* (Frankfurt a. M., 2001); Amia Lieblich, *Transition to Adulthood during Military Service: The Israeli Case* (Albany, NY, 1989).

8. (If we count the War of Attrition, then we speak of seven wars.) Every war, of course, was experienced in a different way. The most traumatic one was the Yom Kippur War (1973). The Lebanon war (1982) was a watershed, for it provoked the criticism of a huge part of the population and led to the rise of a strong peace movement. The second Gulf War (1991) was the first local war that Israel didn't join actively—the impact of this enforced passivity on male identity will be addressed later in the chapter.

9. Mirta Furmann, "Army and War: Collective Narratives of Early Childhood in Cotemporary Israel," in Edna Lomsky-Feder and Eyal Ben-Ari, eds., *The Military and Militarism in Israeli Society* (Albany, NY, 1999).

10. Ibid., p. 149.

11. Ibid., p. 155.

12. Ibid., p. 155f.

13. In the proposal for the curriculum the activities for boys are all aimed at a fighter role. The proposal contains physical training exercises and several lectures about the fighting units. See Pakal Gius, *Pakal Gius. Tachnit ha'chana le Zahal* [Preparation plan for Zahal], ed. Ministry of Defense, Center of Chief Education and Youth Officer Headquarter Zahals (Jerusalem: Hebr, 1998).

14. Ofra Mayseless and Reuven Gal, *Gender Differences in Decision-Making concerning Military Service in Israel*, Israeli Institute for Military Studies (Zikhron Ya'akov, 1993), pp. 9 and 13.

15. Rela Klein Mazali, "Parenting Troops: The Summons to Acquiescence," in *The Women and War Reader*, ed. Lois Ann Lorentzen and Jennifer Turpin (New York: [u.a.] 1998), S., pp. 272–288.

16. Tamar Katriel, *Communal Webs: Communication and Culture in Contemporary Israel* (New York, 1991), p. 80.

17. Michael Kimmel, *Manhood in America: A Cultural History* (New York: 1996), p. 7.

18. David R. Segal, Mady Wechsler-Segal, and Bradford Booth, "Gender and Sexual Orientation Diversity in Modern Military Forces: Cross-National Patterns," *Beyond Zero Tolerance: Discrimination in Military Culture*, ed. Mary Fainsod Katzenstein and Judith Reppy (Lanham, MD: [u.a.] 1999).

19. The study was done before the bill for opening all jobs passed in the parliament.

20. Klein, 2001.

21. "Fighting the Wrong War?" *Jerusalem Report* 20 (December 1999). Women who serve in the defense forces are administratively controlled by *Chen*, an abbreviation of *cheil nashim*, which means "Women's Corps." In Hebrew the abbreviation means "charm."

22. See Klein, 2001, for a detailed discussion and numbers of gender segregation in the IDF.

23. Stuart A. Cohen, "Towards a New Portrait of the (New) Israeli Soldier," *Israel Affairs* 3, 3/4 (1997): 93.

24. See Martin Van Creveld, "Conscription Warfare: The Israeli Experience," in *Die Wehrpflicht. Entstehung, Erscheinungsformen und politisch-militärische Wirkung*, ed. Roland G. Foerster (München, 1994), pp. 228–239, n. 3.

25. Reuven Gal, *A Portrait of the Israeli Soldier* (New York: [u.a.] 1986).

26. Eyal Ben-Ari, "Tests of Soldierhood, Trials of Manhood: Military Service and Male Ideals in Israel" (manuscript, 1997).

27. Lieblich, 1989, p. 5.

28. Yaron Ezrachi, *Gewalt und Gewissen. Israels langer Weg in die Moderne* (Berlin: IWN, Israeli Women's Network, 1998). *Progress in the Status of Women in Israel since the 1995 Beijing Conference* (June 2000), p. 138.

29. Pierre Bourdieu, "Ökonomisches Kapital, kulturelles Kapital, soziales Kapital," *Soziale Ungleichheiten, Soziale Welt*, Hg. Reinhard Kreckel, Sonderband 2. (Göttingen, 1983), S., pp. 183–198.

30. Dafna N. Izraeli, "Gendering Military Service in the Israeli Defence Forces," *Israel Social Science Research* 12, 1 (1997): 129–166.

31. Benjamin W. Wolkinson, "Recruitment and Selection of Workers in Israel: The Question of Disparate Impact," *Ethnic and Racial Studies* 17, no. 2, pp. 260–268, p. 271.

32. I should add that because most Palestinian citizens of Israel are excluded from military service; here the military becomes an ethnic border marker.

33. Klein, 1999.

34. See Israeli Women's Network (IWN), "Progress in the Status of Women in Israel since the 1995 Beijing Conference" (June 2000).

Chapter 14

Concluding Thoughts: Looking to the Future

Paul R. Higate

INTRODUCTION

The term "military masculinity" has been used by contributors in this volume in a wide range of ways that have, nonetheless, tended to center on both the genesis and the sustaining of military masculine identity. Here the archetypal warrior figure tends to be constructed in opposition to a range of others, marginal masculinities, femininities, and civilians.

The developing concept of military masculinity has provided us with empirically informed ways of thinking about the actions of individual military men and groups of military men. The corollary of these discussions opens the way for more speculative comments around the ways in which military gendered culture might develop in the future. It is this last point—the future of the military—to which this brief chapter is addressed. To what extent are developments in the British military likely to dilute the hypermasculine elements of gendered culture within this most traditional of institutions? Will the spillover elements of military masculinity decline, and will the sharp dichotomy between men and women in the military workplace become more loosely defined, giving way to a softening of masculine performance and greater acceptance of female service personnel?

THE FUTURE MILITARY: TWO SCENARIOS

Given recent and current trends, what might we expect military culture to look like in 2020? In what ways might an increasing proportion of female and gay service personnel, in addition to changes in military missions, in particular, affect gendered military culture?

A hypothetical all-volunteer British armed forces of the year 2020 could take the form of a culturally homogeneous single service organization. It might differ from the armed forces of today by virtue of representative levels of gender, sexual orientation, and ethnic minority integration across all military occupations. Service people in this future organization would be held in high public esteem and would enhance, rather than degrade,[1] the local civilian communities in which they worked and lived. To these ends, there would be no sign of "camp-following" sex workers sustained by servicemen[2] nor evidence of violence in drinking establishments within garrison towns—phenomena normally arising from a spilling over of the combat masculine warrior ethic. Indeed, future service personnel would be perceived as well-remunerated professional "technocratic warriors" carrying out risky and challenging work on behalf of the state.

In the second scenario, we note little difference to the British armed forces seen today. The three services would retain their discrete identities, together with the continued underrepresentation of women, gay personnel, and ethnic minorities. Women would still be banned from the combat arms. Although public opinion of the armed forces generally would remain high,[3] service personnel would continue to be involved in occasional high-profile violent incidents in and around garrison towns and would be implicated in the disproportionate incidences of domestic violence in military communities and sexual harassment in the military workplace; the ambivalent label of squaddie would remain.

Both hypothetical organizations would be smaller in size when compared to today's tri-service armed forces, and they would be configured to respond rapidly to global hotspots, routine peacekeeping operations (PKOs), and assisting the civil powers in anti-terrorism, drug enforcement, and illegal immigration.[4] Missions would mainly be "Euro-national" in composition. Considerable advances in technology would come to supplant individual troop differences in physical and mental capability, and there would be a far greater reliance on quickly mobilized reserve forces.

Which of these two ideal typical organizations is most likely to arise, and how might we understand potential changes to gendered culture? Before discussing the two possible futures for the British armed forces, I will consider some contextual comments focused on the current organization.

LOCATING THE CONTEMPORARY MILITARY

It has been argued that the military is a microcosm of society.[5] Framing the military in this way provides us with the key point of departure when envisioning how the organization might transform, for we cannot ignore future economic, political, and social change across the host society and beyond, into the global context. Though there have been considerable changes to the military in respect to the integration of women, the formal acceptance of homosexuals, and the transforming nature of missions, what does this mean on the ground in terms of military gendered culture; in particular, what is its significance in the context of the extremes of hypermasculinity that spill over into civilian environments? Does the equal opportunities rhetoric translate into quantifiable progress for previously marginalized groups within the military context? If the armed forces have truly become postmodern as some have suggested, then we might expect to see the celebration of diversity—rather than its begrudging acceptance—as it is asserted to represent a key dimension of the postmodern condition. Put like this, and located at the polar extreme of diversity, it has been suggested that a postmodern military might mean no military at all because *uniformity* remains the key philosophy on which military culture turns.[6] Further, a brief look at the host society provides evidence that the advances much vaunted by a range of individuals and groups concerning women's progress in both paid employment and the private sphere may have been largely illusory.[7] In these terms, and given that the military reflects many aspects of its host society, the equal opportunities discourse and its alleged outcomes both outside and within the military requires close scrutiny.

RECENT AND FUTURE TRENDS

Current and future political climates at the national level are likely to significantly affect the gendered characteristics of military cultures, with a continuum ranging from traditional (conservative) through "detraditional" (liberal) signposting the extent to which equal opportunities are prioritized.[8] In particular, issues around the integration of women across all military roles and the *cultural* acceptance of homosexual service people may well be crucial when considering the ways in which military masculine culture could evolve. Yet, currently, dominant forms of public discourse limit the extent to which women and homosexuals are accepted as potentially able to effectively enter the male bastion of combat and the military more generally for reasons explored by Kovitz (Chapter 1) and other contributors to this volume. At the time of writing it is expected that the ban on integration of women into the combat arms of the British armed forces will be retained. Units tasked with closing with the "enemy"—for example, the infantry, the Royal Marines, the Royal Air Force Regiment, and the Royal Armoured Corps—will remain men-only enclaves.[9] Although this decision may yet be overturned through human rights legislation, it is a sign of the extent to which the armed forces, in conjunction with civilian consultants, believe that combat effectiveness may be undermined through the inclusion of women. Justifications for the continued ban of women from combat[10] include the perception that women would have a "negative impact on unit cohesion." It is my intention not to explore these complex and much-debated issues here, but to stress that both formal attitudes (rhetoric) *and* informal attitudes (the lived experience of military gendered culture) continue to be characterized by a relatively stable constellation of military masculine cultures within the British armed forces.

The armed forces, though likely to decline in size, will be buttressed by an increasing number of reservists and civilians. The presence of these citizen-soldiers and civilians could be accompanied by the importation of less hypermasculine values, particularly within the context of the acceptance of homosexuals and women in the workplace, a process that has evolved more fully in civilian life.[11] Further, the development of an occupational attitude to military service has received considerable attention over the years, though the extent to which this influences gendered culture has been neglected. Might there be a correlation between occupational attitude to military service and positive perceptions of the drive for equal opportunities? The alignment between military and civilian workplaces in terms of values and beliefs could be considered as further eroding the more traditional views of gendered culture within the organization, since this somewhat sheltered environment is exposed to more enlightened influences. For example, if physical brutality were to be considered an accepted and previously unquestioned component of military masculine ideology, then changes to basic army training through which recruits are more empowered (rendering them less likely to physical and mental assault from instructors) also represents a further important development.[12] Career structures in the armed forces have also changed dramatically over the last twenty years with shorter engagements becoming the norm.[13] It seems likely that this trend will continue, and that more flexible working conditions will further align the organization with developments in civilian labor markets and in so doing have the potential to give relatively greater opportunities to women who wish to take career breaks to raise families.[14]

Tendencies running in the other direction—toward divergence from civilian society—are less prevalent, but worthy of mention with regard to their potential impact on the armed forces' gendered cultures. The paradox of commentary around the ascendancy of the so-called New Man, identifiable through his ability to empathize with others and perform gender in a more feminized way, could be of significance, as these ways of "doing masculinity" are argued to be gaining both legitimacy and popularity.[15] Given that the military is a microcosm of wider society, we might expect these considerably less hypermasculine values to slowly pervade the armed forces through current and future recruits, whose views and attitudes help to shape military cultures. Yet the term "New Man" is often taken for granted. One way in which to make sense of the term is suggested by Hondagneu-Sotelo and Messner: "[W]hen analysed within a structure of power, the gender displays of the New Man might best be seen as strategies to reconstruct hegemonic masculinity by projecting aggression, domination and misogyny onto subordinate groups of men."[16]

In any case, debates around New Men may be less than relevant to the changing constitution and culture of the armed forces because notions of convergence between civilian and military environment tend to ignores the extent of *self-selection* among young male enlistees, particularly those destined for the combat arms. I have argued elsewhere that these individuals are likely to import hypermasculine values as a result of their earlier experiences of growing up in deprived areas where frequent exposure to and the use of physical aggression, for example, may represent a component of the motivation to enlist.[17] The degree to which recruits self-select is unlikely to change, so long as these masculine subcultures persist and the combat masculine warrior (cmw) ethic is linked to the armed forces in the minds of the wider public and potential recruits.

MAINSTREAMING GENDER: CRITICAL MASS

Women continue to be a thorny issue in debates around gender integration in many institutions, not least the armed forces, with men remaining invisible and unchallenged in their privileged positions. In relation to a review of the literature examining the the Canadian military, Donna Winslow and Justin Dunn highlight the domain of combat, although women have been allowed to enter the combat arms since 1989, they still face many barriers that are rooted in the negative attitudes of their male peers who still believe that combat is a male domain.[18]

Canada might be considered to have one of the more enlightened armed forces with regard to equal opportunities, and although recent integration trials have not gone as far as some would prefer, it has nevertheless been argued that a base has been established for further progress.[19] Through time it is expected that full integration, including the combat arms, may occur within the Canadian military forces; however, what might that mean for the gendered cultures? Is the presence of more women, particularly at the heart of the male bastion of face-to-face combat, likely to affect the nature of the cmw ethic? Assumptions of this sort may rely on naturalist discourses of sex and gender, and they implicitly view femininity in a somewhat homogeneous way.[20]

The influence of increased proportions of women in the military is yet to be assessed conclusively, although some have suggested that it may bring positive benefits,[21] particularly within the context of specific missions such as peacekeeping.[22] In addition, accessibility to local civilian communities who have suffered at the hands of militarized men might be improved by greater inclusion of civilian and serving military women. Here, masculinized gender ideologies can be challenged, and less aggressive responses to volatile situations implemented. There are parallels between developments in the military and the British construction industry with respect to equal opportunities. Both spheres might be considered masculinized, traditional, hierarchical, and resistant to change. Clara Greed's work on the British construction industry resonates with the parallel situation in the military and is worthy of a brief mention. She states that

critical mass...is one of the most frequently used terms in the [construction] industry when discussing equal opportunities...[it] is highly optimistic and over-simplistic if used as a predictive social concept *without acknowledging the immense cultural and structural obstacles present.*[23]

The approach currently taken by the MoD is to stress the opening up of posts. Women may well be accepted, but will they be accepted as equals?[24] How would we know if the negative aspects of military masculine culture—in particular those that serve to marginalize women—had been neutralized? What exactly do equal opportunities look like? Might not the influx of women into certain military jobs result in the perceived feminization and decline in status of particular specialties where women come to be concentrated?[25] The fuller integration of women into the armed forces has necessarily to take place within a framework of formalized and wide-ranging equal opportunities. If the military is to more fully integrate women, a number of issues will have to be addressed:

- The granting of maternity leave and career progress
- Dual service marriages
- The availability of child care and single-parent households
- The posting of women away from families
- Overall family support policies in times of increasing pressure on resources.[26]

FUTURE MISSIONS

Changes to British military doctrine invoke the possibility that "pure fighting functions will become of secondary importance" and that the military's tasks after 2000 will be to "protect, help and save."[27] These changing doctrines seem to suggest that although a need for combat will remain, its significance and centrality may decline. Given that the cmw ethic is derived from the military's unique purpose of conducting face-to-face violence, questions might be raised about future military masculine cultures.[28] Will this result in a parallel decline in the spillover features of the cmw ethic implicated in violence in military and civilian communities, in military homes, and in the military workplace?

It has been argued that a future military located within rapidly changing situations, tasked with multirole missions, and able to cope with the scrutiny of the media will need to rely increasingly on the role of the soldier-scholar and the soldier-statesman to augment those involved with fighting in war.[29] These two roles are strongly gendered, and it is not clear how women might be easily assimilated into them. In terms of the first, the soldier-scholar, it is expected that technological and political conditions represent the central issues with which personnel would have to deal. Once again, these realms continue to be dominated by men (and no doubt these gendered processes are intensified within the context of the armed forces), and there would need to be considerable thought given to the ways in which they can be opened up to women, not just at the level of accessibility, but in a cultural sense. In terms of the second, the soldier-statesman, there may be more acceptance of female service personnel from the perspective of commanders because of their handling of "delicate missions"[30] requiring diplomacy and sensitivity. With these points in mind, a consensus has emerged that the recent U.S. forces work in Somalia was achieved effectively and with little disruption to local communities—events typically associated with hypermasculine excess—because of the U.S. forces' mixed-gender units, since "female soldiers display compassion found less frequently amongst men."[31] In the British case, the parachute regiment might not be the best suited for these duties, so focused are they on the "sharper end of warfighting."[32] Other changes signaled in the UK Armed Forces Strategic Defence Review (SDR) include their greater role in counterterrorism, operations that women have historically excelled in.[33]

MILITARY MASCULINE IDENTITY: THE THREE SERVICES

At the heart of the 1998 SDR is the desire to increase substantially the "co-ordination of the three services."[34] This was the rationalization for suggesting that a single service organization could come to replace the three branches of the armed forces we see today. The tendency toward what some might see as unification has already occurred in a number of areas, including joint operations between the Royal Air Force (RAF) and the Royal Navy (RN) in respect of the Harrier aircraft force, and given the pressure on resources, joint operations seem likely to increase.[35]

One of a number of anchor points for gendered identity in the armed forces is the individual service and nature/status of task, as Frank Barrett has demonstrated within the context of the U.S. Navy.[36] If the Canadian experiment of service unification is mirrored,[37] the dissolution of individual organizational identity tends to be resisted at every turn, not least by those who take pride in their distinct service and occupation. Given the historical impetus and saturation of the three services' selfhood with distinct histories, in the shape of past and more recent conflicts, it is difficult to envisage an identity derived from an amalgam of the services: soldier, sailor, or air "man." In the absence of individual service identity, however, occupation might come to play a more central role. In this case, we might take our lead from developments at that time in the civilian labor market in assessing the centrality of military masculine identity. The disembedding of specific service identity from military trade or branch could open up possibilities for more gender-neutral occupational identities as the historical weight of individual armed service tradition is lifted, although earlier comments around the perceived feminization of occupations should not be underestimated.

TECHNOLOGY AND GENDER

Morris Janowitz suggested that changes in technology influence both organizational behavior and the characteristics of combat within the military.[38]
Given that overall, technological developments have tended to erode the significance of physical strength and aggression, we might expect women to be more
accepted in the role of "closing with the enemy." However, it is the embodied
elements of their combat effectiveness that have constantly been questioned.[39]
It is claimed that this "blurring" of the "cyborg" soldier's gender is likely to
intensify as technology develops.[40] As Chris Hables-Gray states: "It seems the
female soldier's identity is beginning to collapse into the archetype soldier persona creating a basically male vaguely female mechanical image,"[41] though I
would argue that this view exaggerates developments and is unrealistic about
future possibilities. A vision of the future in these somewhat idealized postmodern terms could take technological transformations to their end point; here
combatant women would come to be considered as wholly interchangeable
with male soldiers. However, another derivative of the argument that women
simply "are not up to" the physical exigencies of ground-based combat in respect to closing with the enemy, concerns conflicts between opposing forces
that are broadly similar in respect to their technological capabilities. In these
circumstances, the human equation remains; for example, what capacity do the
troops have in terms of physical strength—how fast can ammunition be
"man"-handled?[42] More significantly, and within the context of the scenario
introduced at the start of the chapter, I would argue that technological developments themselves will continue to be masculinized, and women's role within
them considered somewhat peripheral. To take computer systems as one important example of vital current and future military technology:

They are "masculine," in the full ideological sense of that word which includes, inte-
grally, soldiering, and violence. There is nothing far-fetched in the suggestion that much
AI [artificial intelligence] research reflects a social relationship: "intelligent" behavior
means the instrumental power Western "man" has developed to an unprecedented extent under capitalism and which he has always wielded over woman.[43]

The gendering of science and war as masculine looks unlikely to change in
the near or distant future. Indeed, could an example of the pinnacle of technological advance, the missile defense system proposed by George W. Bush, ever
have been called the *daughter* of star wars? We are dealing with society-wide
discourses that tend to close off the technological arena from women both
structurally and culturally.

SEXUAL ORIENTATION AND MILITARY MASCULINE
CULTURE: CURRENT AND FUTURE TRENDS

Mark Simpson and Steven Zeeland illuminate the homoerotic and homosexual rather than the straightforwardly heterosexual elements of life in the

armed forces in the case of the British and U.S. militaries.[44] Further, anecdotal evidence suggests that a "significant proportion" of the more senior of the female officers in the British Army are homosexual,[45] although this label tells us little of their explicit view and attitude toward the organization and how it might evolve, raising interesting questions about gay identities in the armed forces. David Morgan's autobiographical writing of British National Service includes reflection on an effeminate colleague who was presumed by some to be homosexual. He was described as a popular man whose camp and comical performances were celebrated rather than condemned.[46] The notion that there exists a uniform culture of (hetero)sexuality in the British and other militaries functions at the level of rhetoric rather than reality.

The inscription of heterosexuality into all aspects of culture ranging from language through leisure activities is deeply bound up with the cmw ethic. What of the future scenario outlined above in which sexuality, like gender, is no longer an issue within the military environment? Might not the already present inconsistencies flagged above give way to greater toleration in the future as civilian society becomes more disposed to subvert sexuality and as these less-dichotomized ways of conceptualizing sexuality permeate the military mindset? The MoD's equal opportunities statement represents the formal face of the organization and explicitly links "sexual orientation" with "tolerance." Although future catalysts for change may be rooted in both formal policy and human rights legislation, it is difficult to envisage the ways in which advances toward equality at the level of culture can be satisfactorily achieved. Given the maliciousness that had characterized the identification and removal of homosexuals from the armed forces in the very recent past, future enlightened developments look unlikely.[47]

NATIONALITY AND MILITARY MASCULINE CULTURE

Military masculinities are embedded into discourses of nationalism.[48] Constructions of Englishness or Britishness, invoking past victories and resonating with the imperial and colonial trajectories of the United Kingdom, have remained tenacious for both the military and its host society. "Our boys" belong to us and not "the (foreign) other," and military service identity is constructed around this sharp dichotomy. The experience of being deployed overseas frequently amplifies this distinction, and expressions of nationality are refracted through military masculinity. In addition, we might note the ways in which social class structures these performances, with the more junior ranks embarking on high-profile drinking binges as a way in which to rowdily celebrate their nationality and mark themselves out from the local "foreigners."[49] The squaddies' reputation of celebrating the masculinized ritual of high alcohol consumption is unlikely to disappear within the context of either a home posting or farther afield, since particular elements of civilian society continue to reinforce "lad culture."[50]

Concern continues to be raised around the links between the presence of troops and the impact on the local sex industry. Are these patterns of exploitation—and legitimation by commanders[51]—likely to continue? Overseas deployments will almost certainly increase within the context of "reinforced international commitments,"[52] as it will with the formation of the European Rapid Reaction Force (RRF), dubbed by some as the Euroarmy. These developments are suggestive of an increase in overseas operations, albeit in less permanent bases than was evident during the Cold War. It is the more harmful spillover aspects of the cmw ethic that seem to flourish while servicemen are abroad. Given the new, more mobile roles of the armed forces, deployments overseas look set to continue, with a number of service personnel exporting the worst kind of colonial and misogynist attitudes to cultures considered inferior to their own.

CONCLUSION

Institutions are highly effective at many things, including the ability to dehumanize, and their potential for destruction can take on an immanent and somewhat autonomous logic. In *Modernity and the Holocaust*, Zygmunt Bauman[53] argues that it was the authorized, routinized, and dehumanized characteristics of the Nazi genocide, rather than the inherent evil of all individuals involved, that should concern us most. The currency of contemporary and no doubt future terms such as "friendly fire," "collateral damage," and "smart weaponry" has a particular resonance within the context of the following: "[T]he civilizing process is ... a process of divesting the use and deployment of violence from moral calculus, and of emancipating the desiderata of rationality from interference of ethical norms or moral inhibitions."[54]

In these terms, it is the impersonal, bureaucratic, and hierarchical aspects of an institution capable of "ultra rationality"—for example, of indiscriminate and, for those involved in the operations, relatively risk-free "carpet bombing" from 50,000 feet during the conflict in Kosovo[55]—that reinforce the fear Bauman articulates.

Might not the military aspire to be *more humane* than the society from which it comes in respect to the spillover elements of military masculinity, rather than somewhat resignedly declare its microcosmic characteristics, replete with masculine excess? After all, its ability to socialize individuals into roles that are pursued with dedication, commitment, and, above all, self-discipline suggests powerful structural influences that could be used to challenge rather than collude with the darker aspects of masculinity. In terms of the broader context, Bob Connell reminds us that the category "men" is not monolithic:

Almost all soldiers are men, but most men are not soldiers; though most killers are men, most men never kill or even commit assault; though an appalling number of men do rape, most men do not. It is a fact of great importance, both theoretically and practically, that there are many non-violent men in the world.[56]

Connell's observation is important, though it could be taken further to include the category 'soldier'; is there any potential here to mobilize and give legitimacy to the less hypermasculine elements that undoubtedly constitute this group?

If it is the case that the term "military masculinity" represents progress in critically deconstructing the practice of men and the ideologies of men located within particular institutions, then considerable work remains to be done in the case of the military as the experience of women in the military and the spillover aspects of military masculinity demonstrate.

If the present is able to offer a guide to the future—an increasingly difficult proposition given the detraditionalization of many institutions, not least the armed forces—then future gendered military cultures look set to retain many of the hypermasculine features we note today. The prevalence of domestic violence within military communities,[57] sexual harassment within the military workplace,[58] and the ongoing violence in and around military establishments[59] continue, seemingly unabated, despite the oft-repeated message that the military has, and is, changing.[60] Even if the gendered composition is transformed significantly, in the ways described in the first scenario at the head of the chapter, I remain pessimistic that the impact the organization confers symbolically and materially across society will follow suit, not least because militaries continue to relish their traditional status replete with the "naturalized" actions of military men.

NOTES

1. I am highlighting one aspect of the impact of military establishments on local communities. For example, another view might be that military communities, in particular the militia, may play an important role in the development of civic society. For details of how this might look in the Canadian context, see Terry Willetts, *Canada's Militia: A Heritage at Risk* (Colorado: Westview Press, 1990),

2. See Cynthia Enloe, *Maneuvers* (California: UCLA Press, 2000).

3. Christopher Dandeker, "The United Kingdom: The Overstretched Military," in Charles *Moskos*, John Allen Williams and David R. Segal, eds., *The Postmodern Military* (London: Oxford University Press), pp. 38–40.

4. Christopher Dandeker, *Facing Uncertainty, Flexible Forces for the Twenty-first Century* (Sweden: National Defence College, 1999), pp. 1–94.

5. Martha Chamallas, "The New Gender Panic: Reflections on Sex Scandals and the Military," *Minnesota Law Review* 83, 2 (1998): 307. For example, in drawing connections between the host society and military operations, it has been argued that a domestic context of relatively greater equality between men and women translates into higher levels of state pacifism within the context of foreign policy behavior. See Mary Caprioli,

"Gendered Conflict," *Journal of Peace Research* 37, 1 (2000): 53–68. Donna Winslow points up the unevenness of the military-civilian interface. Drawing on the work of Charles Moskos, she states that the plural military is "both convergent and divergent with civilian society as it simultaneously displays organizational trends that are civilianised and traditional" Donna Winslow & Jason Dunn, "Women in the Canadian Forces," in Gerhard Kummel, (ed) *The Challenging Continuity of Change and the Military: Female Soldiers—Conflict Resolution—South America*, (Strausberg: Sozial Wissenschaftliches Institut der Bundeswehr, 2001), p. 19.

6. Bradford Booth, Meyer Kestenbaum, and David R. Segal, "Are Post-Cold War Militaries Postmodern?" *Armed Forces & Society* 27, 3: 319–342.

7. Office of National Statistics.

8. Dandeker, *Facing Uncertainty*, p. 64.

9. Matthew Hickley, "Girls Stay Banned," *The Daily Mail*, July 7, 2001, p. 17. A number of commentators conflate the feminization of the military with its decline; for example, see Martin Van Crefeld, "The Great Illusion: Women in the Military," *Journal of Peace Studies* 29, 2 (2000): 429–442. See Judith Hicks Stiehm, "*It's Our Military Too: Women and the Military*" (Philadelphia: Temple University Press, 1996), who hopes to "encourage...women to accept and exercise [the] responsibility of joining the military'" (preface, first page).

10. Where does combat take place? Is there any longer a discernible front line from which women might be excluded? According to Rosemarie Skaine, "The repeal of the exclusionary rule on women in combat aircraft occurred because in the modern battle where mobility and long-range standoff weapons have made even rear-echelon lethal, the argument that women should not be exposed to danger no longer has any meaning." See Rosemarie Skaine, *Women at War: Gender Issues of Americans in Combat* (North Carolina: McFarland & Company, 1999), p. 202.

11. Dandeker, *Facing Uncertainty*, p. 31.

12. Ibid., p. 36. Similar developments "towards less authoritarian models...more compatible with feminine perspectives" are noted in the U.S. military by Skaine (*Women in Combat*, p. 138).

13. Dandeker, *Facing Uncertainty*, p. 40.

14. It is interesting to note that neither of the equal opportunities statements issued by the Ministry of Defence or a similarly masculine institution—the civilian police—tackle issues linked to childbirth or childcare. See *A Policy for Personnel* (London: Her Majesty's Stationery Office, 1998) and Carol Martin, "The Impact of Equal Opportunities Policies on the Day-to Day Experiences of Women Police Constables," *British Journal of Criminology* 36, 4 (1996): 510–528.

15. BBC Website, "UK Seeking Millennium Man," *http://news6.thdo.bbc.co.uk/hi/english/uk/newsid-83000/83178.htm*.

16. Pierrette Hondagneu-Sotelo and Michel A. Messner, "Gender Displays and Men's Power," in Harry Brod and Michael Kaufman, eds., *Theorizing Masculinities* (London: Sage), p. 215.

17. Paul Higate, "Traditional Gendered Identities: National Service and the All Volunteer Force," in the *Journal of Comparative Social Research*, 20 (2002), 229–235.

18. Donna Winslow and Jason Dunn, "Women in the Canadian Forces," p. 50.

19. Ibid., p. 50.

20. The complexities of the debate around the extent to which women will *necessarily* import traditional feminine values are outside the scope of this chapter. It has been suggested, however, that a not insignificant percentage of women enlistees do *not* embody traditional feminine values. Again, the point of self-selection is important here, and to survive in the cut and thrust of the military environment the necessity to develop "masculine values" may be pressing. (Personal communications with former recruiter-officer of commissioned army personnel at Sandhurst.) Further evidence for the values encouraged from high-achieving female service personnel comes from the U.S. context. Said one West Point graduate: "Women who are in military training to be an officer are not the girl next door or your mother or your sister. They were among the top athletes in college. Military women are just like men who become airborne—he is not your average guy—he's in the top five percent." Quoted in Skaine, *Women at War*, p. 74.

21. In terms of the civilian police force, an institution resonating with a similar culture to that of the military, Martin makes the following point: "The increasing presence of women in police stations both as officers and as civilian staff was thought to have had a noticeable impact on the language and behaviour of male officers." See Martin, "The Impact of Equal Opportunities," p. 523.

22. See Louise Olsson, Jullyette Ukabiala, Ylva I. Blondle, Leonard Kapungu, and Peter Wallensteen, *Mainstreaming a Gender Perspective in Multidimensional Peacekeeping Operations* (Sweden: Uppsala University, Department of Peace and Conflict Resarch, 1999), pp. 1–24.

23. Clara Greed, "Women in the Construction Professions: Achieving Critical Mass," *Gender, Work and Organization* 7, 3 (2000): 183.

24. In discussing Canadian women's experience of the combat arms and drawing on the work of Davis and Thomas, Donna Winslow and Jason Dunn state: "[F]or these women, the mental and physical demands of the work were not the real challenge of entering a traditionally male occupation. The real challenge was enduring the systematic rejection and bias against them that was evident in both covert and overt attempts to get them out of the combat arms." Winslow and Dunn, "Women in the Canadian Forces," p. 48.

25. See Rosemary Pringle, *Secretaries Talk: Sexuality, Power and Work* (London: Verso, 1989), on the thoroughgoing feminization of a previously male-dominated profession.

26. Winslow and Dunn, "Women in the Canadian Forces," p. 50.

27. Dandeker, *Facing Uncertainty*, p. 60.

28. This point is hotly debated, and discussion is polarized between those who consider that a "world without war," whereas utopian, "is by no means wholly lacking in realism" (see Booth, Kestebaum, and Segal, "Are Post-Cold War Militaries Postmodern?" p. 338). Others, particularly serving military personnel, remain adamant that troops should be trained for combat and should be involved in closing with the enemy and face-to-face fighting. The low-intensity guerrilla conflict in Kosovo is a case in point, since traditional forms of combat represented the daily currency of fighting

between the various factions. It has been argued by Drake that wars are here to stay and that they are likely to be characterized by a "new global political division between cosmopolitan, universalist multicultural values...and particularist identity." See Mike Drake, "They Made a Desert and Called It Peace," in *Sociological Research Online* 4, 2 (1999): 5, *http://www.socresonline.org.uk/socresonline/4/2/drake.html*. In these terms we might expect the relevance of traditional fighting to continue—invoking fear about "allies in body-bags" as a result of the mooted ground war in Kosovo in 1999—and the need of "more muscular" interventions in the future. The thesis that armed forces will no longer require the capacity for traditional combat operations may be somewhat premature.

29. Dandeker, *Facing Uncertainty,* p. 36.

30. Serving RAF officer Squadron Leader E. G. Jones states: "There is a tendency for armies to spend more time dealing with civilians in crisis, as with the peacekeeping forces in Yugoslavia and Northern Ireland or the Kurdish refugee aid in Iraq. Different skills are involved in dealing with these delicate situations, and they are skills which women possess as much as, and sometimes more than men." Squadron Leader E. G. Jones, "Women in Combat—Historical Quirk or the Future Cutting Edge?" *Royal United Services Institute for Defence Studies,* August 1993, p. 40.

31. Dandeker, *Facing Uncertainty,* p. 56.

32. Ibid., p. 63.

33. See Sarah Ford, *One Up* (London: HarperCollins, 1997); Sharon MacDonald, Pat Holden, and Shirley Ardener, eds., *Images of Women in Peace and War* (Madison: University of Wisconsin Press).

34. Government Report, *The Strategic Defence Review* (London: The Stationery Office, July 1998), p. 2.

35. Dandeker, *Facing Uncertainty,* p. 28.

36. Frank Barrett, "The Organizational Construction of Hegemonic Masculinity–the Case of the US Navy," *Gender, Work and Organization* 3, 3 (1996): 129–142.

37. On the Canadian experience of military unification, Christopher Dandeker states, "The UK does not wish to repeat the problems of the Canadian effort to merge the services." Dandeker, *Facing Uncertainty,* p. 34.

38. Winslow and Dunn, "Canadian Women in Combat."

39. See Carol Cohn, "'How Can She Claim Equal Rights When She Doesn't Have to Do as Many Push-Ups as I Do?'" *Men and Masculinities* 3, 2 (2000): 131–151.

40. Chris Hables-Gray, *Postmodern War: The New Politics of Conflict* (London: Routledge, 1997), p. 247.

41. Ibid., p. 175.

42. This is the personal view of a serving individual working within the Ministry of Defence. Debate around the issue of physical strength is extensive, although few if any commentators have taken a longer-term view of the situation. Personal communication with military commanders on the question of women in combat almost always invokes "the here and now." The women under their command are thus discussed in terms of their "tendencies" to be less physically able than their male colleagues, a point not easily disregarded. As Chris Shilling has argued, however, socialization along gender lines

produces physical capital oriented to different ends. See Chris Shilling, "Educating the Body: Physical Capital and the Production of Social Inequalities," *Sociology* 25, 4 (1991): 653–672. With only the smallest of imaginative leaps, it is possible to conceive of a different future vis-à-vis the axis of opposition along physical lines between men and women. In this way, gender-neutral socialization of the body (if such a thing were possible) would help to minimize the gendered differences in embodied "raw material" that is developed through military training.

43. Hables-Gray, *Postmodern War*, p. 246.

44. Mark Simpson and Steven Zeeland, *The Queen Is Dead* (London: Arcadia Books, 2001).

45. Personal communication with serving British Army officer.

46. David Morgan, "'It Will Make a Man of You': Notes on National Service, Masculinity and Autobiography," *Studies in Sexual Politics* 17 (Manchester: University of Manchester Department of Sociology, 1987).

47. See Edmund Hall, *We Can't Even March Straight* (London: Vintage, 1995), and Peter Tatchell, *We Don't Want to March Straight* (London: Listen Up!, 1995).

48. Martin Shaw, *Post-military Society* (Cambridge: Polity Press, 1991), p. 110; and Graham Dawson, *Soldier Heroes* (London: Routledge, 1994), p. 235.

49. John Hockey, *Squaddies: Portrait of a Subculture* (Exeter: Exeter University Press, 1986), pp. 112–122.

50. See BBC Website, "Health: Lad Culture Blamed for Suicides," in http://news.bbc.co.uk/hi/english/health/newsid_475000/475253.stm.

51. A story recently relayed to me captures this point. A representative of an NGO had asked a military commander deployed to the former Yugoslavia what he thought about the appearance of sex workers in close proximity to the base. The commander had replied by saying that indeed "it was a problem...because we can't always ensure our guys use condoms." Once again, the welfare of the exploited camp follower is seen as secondary to that of the soldier whose "natural sex drive" simply must have an "outlet." For further discussion see Cynthia Enloe, *Does Khaki Become You? The Militarisation of Women's Lives* (London: Pluto Press, 1983), and Enloe, *Maneuvers*, pp. 49–107.

52. *Strategic Defence Review*, pp. 2–4.

53. Zygmunt Bauman, *Modernity and the Holocaust* (Cambridge: Polity Press, 1989).

54. Ibid., p. 28.

55. Drake, "They Made It a Desert," p. 8.

56. Bob Connell, "Arms and the Man" (paper for UNESCO meeting on Male Roles and Masculinities in the Perspective of a Culture of Peace, Oslo, September 1997), p. 2.

57. "[H]igher rates of aggression...[of spousal abuse]...in the severe physical aggression category" were found within the U.S. Army, and a similar situation was found within the U.S. Marine Corps. Stephen J. Brannen and Elwood R. Hamlin II, "Understanding Spouse Abuse in Military Families," in James A. Martin, Leora N. Rosen, and Linette R. Sparacino, eds., *The Military Family: A Practice Guide for Human Service Providers* (Westport, CT: Praeger, 2000), p. 170. Deborah Harrison (this volume) found evidence to suggest relatively higher incidences of domestic abuse within the Canadian

military forces. The situation in the British armed forces is unclear, but anecdotal evidence is suggestive of parallels with other militaries.

58. Literature focusing on sexual harassment in the military workplace is extensive, although within the "total institution" context of the ship—a forum in which we have been ensured that every effort has been made to ensure equal opportunities for female service personnel—a number of serious cases of harassment and bullying have been noted. See Hearn and Parkin, *Gender, Sexuality*, p. 59.

59. Okinawa has been the scene of a further (at this stage, alleged) rape of a Japanese citizen by U.S. Staff Sergeant Timothy Woodland, who is stationed at Kadena Air Base on the island. At the time of writing the case is going to court. See http://news.bbc.co.uk/hi/english/w...pacific/newsid_1455000/1455096.stm for updates.

60. These issues raise potentially difficult questions linked to gauging change. The equal opportunities discourse undoubtedly brings with it raised awareness and possibly an increase in reporting rates of sexual harassment and domestic violence. For example, recently one victim of domestic violence in the military setting was described as "coming to think of the abusive behaviour as normal, and taking on a lot of guilt" (Hearn and Parkin, *Gender, Sexuality*, p. 59). Over time these views of self-blame will, we hope, diminish as alternative discourses highlighting the responsibilities of the perpetrator gain currency. However, in my own experience of recently interviewing forty military personnel from across the ranks and services, I was interested to hear more enlightened views about previously marginalized groups such as women and homosexuals than had been the case during my eight years of service in the Royal Air Force between 1983 and 1991.

Selected Bibliography

Arkin, William and Dobrofsky, Lynn, R. "Military Socialization and Masculinity." *Journal of Social Issues* 34 (1978): 151–168.

Armor, David J. "Race and Gender in the U.S. Military." *Armed Forces & Society* 23(1), 1996: 7–27.

Backerra, Manfred. *NVA: Ein Ruckblick fur die Zukunft Zeitzeugen berichten über ein Stuck deutscher Militärgeschichte.* Köln: Markus Verlag, 1992.

Badinter, E. *On Masculine Identity.* New York: Columbia University Press, 1995.

Bald, D. *Die Nationale Volksarmee: Beiträge zur Selbstverstandnis und Geschichte des deutschen Militärs von 1945–1990.* Baden Baden: Nomos Verlagsgesellscha, 1992; 1995.

Ballinger, Adam. *The Quiet Soldier: On Selection with 21 SAS.* London: Orion, 1992.

Barnett, Anthony. *Iron Britannia.* London: Allison & Busby, 1982.

Baron, Udo. *Die Wehrideologie der Nationalen Volksarmee der DDR.* Bochum: Unversitätsverlag Dr. N. Brockmeyer, 1993.

Barrett, Frank J. "The Organisational Construction of Hegemonic Masculinity: The Case of the US Navy." *Gender, Work and Organisation* 3 (1996): 129–142.

Beevor, A. *Inside the British Army.* London: Corgi Books, 1991.

Bere, Regan de. S. *Military Identities: Men, Families and Occupational Change.* Unpublished Ph.D. thesis, University of Plymouth, 1999.

Berkowitz, Michael. *Zionist Culture and West European Jewry before the First World War.* Cambridge: Cambridge University Press, 1993.

Billière, Peter de la. *Looking for Trouble: SAS to Gulf Command: The Autobiography.* London: HarperCollins, 1994.

Bird Francke, Linda. *Ground Zero: The Gender Wars in the Military.* New York: Simon & Schuster, 1997.

Birnbaum, Pierre and Katznelson, Ira, eds. *Paths of Emancipation: Jews, States, and Citizenship.* Princeton: Princeton University Press, 1995.

Blake, Joseph A. "The Organization as Instrument of Violence: The Military Case." *Sociological Quarterly* 11 (1970): 331–350.

Bonvillain, Nancy. *Women and Men: Cultural Constructs of Gender.* Englewood Cliffs: Prentice-Hall, 1995.

Bourke, Joanna. *Dismembering the Male: Men's Bodies, Britain and the Great War.* Chicago: University of Chicago Press, 1996.

Breitman, Barbara. "Lifting up the Shadow of Anti-Semitism: Jewish Masculinity in a New Light." In Harry Brod, ed., *A Mensch among Men: Explorations in Jewish Masculinity.* Freedom, CA: The Crossing Press, 1989.

Brittain, Vera. *Lady into Woman: A History of Women from Victoria to Elizabeth II.* London: Dakers, 1953.

Brittain, Victoria. *The Gulf between Us.* London: Virago, 1991.

Brittan, Arthur. *Masculinity and Power.* Oxford: Basil Blackwell, 1989.

Brod, Harry. *The Making of Masculinities.* London: Allen & Unwin, 1987.

Burke, Peter. *Popular Culture in Early Modern Europe.* New York: Harper Torchbooks, 1978.

Burrell, G. and Hearn, J. "The Sexuality of Organisations." In J. Hearn, ed., *Sexuality of Organisations.* London: Sage Publications, 1989.

Butler, Judith. "Gender Trouble: Feminist Theory and Psychoanalytic Discourses." In Linda Nicholson, ed., *Feminism/Postmodernism.* London: Routledge, 1990.

Chandler, J., Bryant, L. and Bunyard, T. "Notes and Issues: Women in Military Occupations." *Work, Employment and Society* 9(1), 1995: 123–135.

Churchill, Winston. *The Second World War. Volume I: The Gathering Storm.* London: Reprint Society, 1950.

Clegg, S. and Hardy, C., eds. *Studying Organisation: Theory and Method.* London: Sage, 1999.

Cockburn, Alexander and Cohen, Andrew. "The Unnecessary War." In V. Brittain, *The Gulf between Us.* London: Virago, 1991.

Collier, Richard. *Masculinities, Crime and Criminology: Men, Heterosexuality and the Criminal(ised) Other.* London: Sage, 1998.

Collison, M. "In Search of the Highlife: Drugs, Crime, Masculinities and Consumption." *British Journal of Criminology* 36(3), 1996: 428–444.

Connell, R. W. *Gender and Power.* Cambridge: Polity Press, 1987.

Connel, R. W. *Masculinities.* Cambridge: Polity Press, 1995.

Connell, R. W. "Masculinity, Violence and War." In Michael Kimmel and Michael Messner, eds., *Men's Lives.* 3rd ed. Boston: Allyn & Bacon, 1995.

Contamine, Phillipe. *War in the Middle Ages.* Oxford: Basil Blackwell, 1984.

Cornwall, A. and Lindisfarne, N. *Dislocating Masculinity: Comparative Ethnographies.* New York: Routledge, 1994.

Coulter, Jim, Miller, Susan and Walker, Martin. *State of Siege.* London: Canary Press, 1984.

Craib, I. "Masculinity and Male Dominance." *The Sociological Review* 34 (1987): 721–743.

Crossley, Nick. "Merleau-Ponty, the Elusive Body and Carnal Sociology." *Body and Society* 1 (1995): 43–63.

Dandeker, C. *Surveillance, Power and Modernity.* 1st ed. Cambridge: Polity Press, 1990.

Dandeker, C. "New Times for the Military: Some Sociological Remarks on the Changing Role and Structure of the Armed Forces of the Advanced Societies." *British Journal of Sociology* 45(4), 1994: 637–654.

Dandeker, Christopher and Segal, Mady Wechsler. "Gender Integration in the Armed Forces: Recent Policy Developments in the United Kingdom." *Armed Forces & Society* 23(1), 1994: 29–47.

Dixon, N. *On the Psychology of Military Incompetence.* London: Jonathan Cape, 1976.

Dölling, Irene. "Gespaltenes Bewusstsein: Frauen und Mannerbilder in der DDR." In G. Helwig and H.M. Nickel, eds. *Frauen in Deutschland, 1945–1992.* Bonn: Bundeszentrale fur politische Bildung, 1993.

Duncombe, J. and Marsden, D. "Love and Intimacy: The Gender Division of Emotion and 'Emotion Work.'" *Sociology* 27(2), 1993: 221–241.

Duncombe, J. and Marsden, D. "'Stepford Wives' and 'Hollow Men'? Doing Emotion Work, Doing Gender and 'Authenticity' in Intimate Relationships." in G. Bendelow and S.J. Williams, eds., *Emotions in Social Life.* London: Routledge, 1998.

Edley, N. and Wetherall, M. "Jockeying for Position: The Construction of Masculine Identities." *Discourse and Society* 8(2), 1997: 203–218.

Edmonds, M. *Armed Forces and Society.* Leicester: Leicester University Press, 1988.

Ehrenreich, Barbara. *Blood Rites: Origins and History of the Passions of War.* New York: Metropolitan Books, Henry Holt and Co., 1997.

Elias, N. *The Established and the Outsiders* 1st ed. London: Sage Publications, 1994.

Enloe, C. *Does Khaki Become You? The Militarisation of Women's Lives.* London: Pluto Press, 1983.

Enloe, C. "Beyond 'Rambo': Women and the Varieties of Militarized Masculinity." In Eva Isaksson, ed., *Women and the Military System.* New York: St. Martin's Press, 1988.

Ferrill, Arthur. *The Origins of War.* London: Thames & Hudson, 1985.

Fischer, E., ed. *Ehemalige Berufssoldaten der NVA in der Bundesrepublik Deutschland.* Bonn: Karl-Theodor-Molinari Stiftung Report, 1995.

Ford, Sarah. *One Up: A Woman in Action with the SAS.* London: HarperCollins, 1997.

Foucault, M. *The Birth of the Clinic.* London: Tavistock, 1976.

Foucault, M. *Discipline and Punish.* Harmondsworth: Penguin, 1977.

Foucault, M. *Madness and Civilisation.* London: Tavistock. 1987.

Freeman, Mike. *The Empire Strikes Back: Why We Need a New Anti-war Movement.* London: Junius Publications, 1993.

Gal, Reuven. *A Portrait of the Israeli Soldier.* New York: Greenwood Press, 1987.

Gelber, Marilyn G. *Gender and Society in the New Guinea Highlands.* Boulder, CO: Westview Press, 1986.

George, Jackie and Ottaway, Susan. *She Who Dared: Covert Operations in Northern Ireland with the SAS.* London: Leo Cooper, 1999.

Geraghty, Tony. *Who Dares Wins.* Glasgow: Fontana/Collins, 1980.

Giddens, A. *The Constitution of Society.* Cambridge: Polity Press, 1984.

Gill, Lesley. "Creating Citizens, Making Men: The Military and Masculinity in Bolivia." *Cultural Anthropology* 12(4), 1997: 527–550.

Gillis, John, ed. *The Militarization of the Western World.* New Brunswick, NJ: Rutgers University Press, 1989.

Gilmore, David. *Manhood in the Making.* New Haven: Yale University Press, 1990.

Goffman, E. *Asylums: Essays on the Social Situation of Mental Patients and Other Inmates.* Harmondsworth: Pelican, 1968.

Goldman, N. and Stites, R. "Great Britain and the World Wars." In L. Goldman, ed., *Female Soldiers—Combatants or Non-combatants? Historical and Contemporary Perspectives.* Westport, CT: Greenwood Press, 1982.

Goode, E. "The Place of Force in Human Society." *American Sociological Review* 37 (1972): 507–518.

Gough, I. and Edwards, G. "The Beer Talking: Four Lads, a Carry out and the Reproduction of Masculinities." *The Sociological Review* 46(3), 1998: 409–435.

Graef, R. *Talking Blues: The Police in Their Own Words.* London: Fontana, 1990.

Gramsci, A. *Selections from the Prison Notebooks.* 1st ed. Edited by Q. Hoare and G. Norwell-Smith. London: Lawrence and Wishart, 1971.

Graves, Charles. *The Home Guard of Britain.* London: Hutchinson & Co., 1943.

Gray, Chris Hables. *Postmodern War: The New Politics of Conflict.* London: Routledge, 1997.

Groot, Gerard de. "Whose Finger on the Trigger? Mixed Anti-aircraft Batteries and the Female Combat Taboo." *War in History* 4(4), 1997: 434–453.

Hacker, Sally L. "Military Institutions and the Labor Process: Non-economic Sources of Technological Change, Women's Subordination, and the Organization of Work." *Technology and Culture* 28(4), 1987: 743–775.

Harries-Jenkins, Gwyn. "Role Images, Military Attitudes, and the Enlisted Culture in Great Britain." In D. R. Segal and H. W. Sinaiko, eds., *Life in the Rank and File*, pp. 254–271. Washington, DC: Pergamon-Brassey's, 1986.

Harris, Ian M. *Messages Men Hear.* London: Taylor & Francis, 1995.

Hearn, J. "A Critique of the Concept of Masculinity/Masculinities." In M. Mac an Ghaill, ed., *Understanding Masculinities.* Buckingham: Open University Press. 1996.

Hearn, J. and Collinson, D. *Men as Managers, Managers as Men: Critical Perspectives on Men, Masculinities and Managements.* London: Sage, 1996.

Hearn, J. and Parkin, W. *Sex at Work: The Power and Paradox of Organisational Sexuality.* 1st ed. New York: St Martin's Press, 1987.

Hicklin, Aaron. *Boy Soldiers.* Edinburgh: Mainstream Publishing, 1995.

Higate, P. "The Body Resists: Everyday Clerking and Unmilitary Practice." In S. Nettleton and J. Watson, eds., *The Body in Everyday Life.* London: Routledge, 1998.

Higate, P. "Ex-servicemen on the Road: Travel and Homelessness." *The Sociological Review* 48(3), 2000: 331–348.

Hillyard, Paddy and Percy-Smith, Janie. *The Coercive State.* London: Fontana, 1988.

Hochschild, A. *The Managed Heart: Commercialization of Human Feeling.* Berkeley: University of California Press, 1983.

Hockey, J. "Putting down Smoke: Emotion and Engagement in Participant Observation." In K. Carter and S. Delamont, eds., *Qualitative Research: The Emotional Dimension.* Aldershot: Avebury, 1996 .

Hockey, J. *Squaddies: Portrait of a Subculture.* Exeter: Exeter University Press, 1986.

Holland, S. and Scourfield, J. B. "Managing Marginalised Masculinities: Men and Probation." *Journal of Gender Studies* 9(2), 2000: 199–211.

Howarth, D. "Discourse Theory." In D. Marsh, D and G. Stoker, eds., *Theory and Methods in Political Science.* London: Macmillan Press, 1995.

Huntington, S. *The Soldier and the State: The Theory and Politics of Civil-Military Relations.* Cambridge: Harvard University Press, 1957.

Ingram, L. *The Study of Organizations: Positions, Persons and Patterns.* 1st ed. Westport, CT: Praeger, 1995.

Izraeli, Dafna N. "Gendering Military Service in the Israeli Defence Forces." *Israel Social Science Research* 12(1), 1997: 129–166.

Janowitz, M. *Essays in the Institutional Analysis of War and Peace.* London: Sage, 1975.

Janowitz, M. *The Professional Soldier: A Social and Political Portrait.* Free Press, New York, 1971.

Janowitz, M. and Van Doorn, J., eds. *On Military Intervention.* 1st ed. Rotterdam: Rotterdam University Press, 1971.

Jefferson, Tony. *The Case against Paramilitary Policing.* Milton Keynes: Open University Press, 1990.

Jenkins, R. *Social Identity.* London: Routledge, 1996.

Jennings, Christian and Weale, Adrian. *Green-Eyed Boys.* London: HarperCollins, 1996.

Jessup, C. *Breaking Ranks: Social Change in Military Communities: The Inter-relationship of Domestic and Working Lives in the Armed Forces.* London: Brassey's, 1996.

Jolly, R. *Changing Step: From Military to Civilian Life: People in Transition.* London: Brassey's, 1996.

Jolly, R. *Military Man, Family Man: Crown Property?* London: Brassey's, 1989.

Kaplan, Danny and Eyal, Ben-Ari. "Brothers and Others in Arms: Managing Gay Identity in Combat Units of the Israeli Army." *Journal of Contemporary Ethnography* 29 (2000): 396–432.

Keeley, Lawrence H. *War before Civilization: The Myth of the Peaceful Savage.* New York: Oxford University Press, 1996.

Kelly, L. "The Continuum of Sexual Violence." In J. Hanmer and M. Maynard, eds., *Women, Violence and Social Control.* London: Macmillan, 1987.

Keshen, Jeffrey A. *Propaganda and Censorship during Canada's Great War.* Edmonton: University of Alberta Press, 1996.

Kickbusch, Ilona. "New Perspectives for Research in Health Behaviour." In R. Anderson, ed., *Health Behaviour Research and Health Promotion,* pp. 237–243. Oxford: Oxford University Press, 1988.

Kimmel, Michael. *Manhood in America: A Cultural History.* The Free Press: New York, 1996.

Klein, Uta. "Das zionistische Projekt und die Geschlechterfrage." *Inamo. Berichte und Analysen zu Politik und Gesellschaft des Nahen und Mittleren Osten,* Heft 13, Frühjahr, 1998: 17–21.

Klein, Uta. "'Our Best Boys': the Gendered Nature of Civil-Military Relations in Israel." *Men and Masculinities* 2(1), July 1999.

Kovitz, Marcia. *Mining Masculinities in the Canadian Military.* Montreal: Concordia University Press, 1998.

Laclau, E. *The Making of Political Identities.* 1st ed. London: Verso, 1994.

Lieblich, Amia. *Transition to Adulthood during Military Service: The Israeli Case.* Albany: State University of New York Press, 1989.

Lister, Ruth. "Women, Economic Dependency and Citizenship." *Journal of Social Policy* 19(4), 1990: 445–467.

Lloyd, Genevieve. "Selfhood, War and Masculinity." In Carole Pateman and Elizabeth Gross, eds., *Feminist Challenges: Social and Political Theory.* Boston: Northeastern University Press, 1987.

Lukowiak, Ken. *Marijuana Time: Join the Army, See the World, Meet Interesting People and Smoke All Their Dope.* London: Orion, 2000.

Lukowiak, Ken. *A Soldier's Song: True Stories from the Falklands.* London: Phoenix, 1993.

Macinnes, J. *The End of Masculinity.* Buckingham: Open University Press, 1998.

McCallion, H. *Killing Zone.* London: Bloomsbury, 1995.

McFarlan, Donald M. *First for Boys: The Story of the Boys' Brigade, 1883–1983.* London: Boys' Brigade, 1983.

McGowan, R. and Hands, J. *Don't Cry for Me Sergeant Major*. London: Futura, 1983.

McKay, J. *Masculinities, Gender Relations and Sport*. London: Sage, 2000.

McNab, A. *Bravo Two Zero*. London: Corgi, 1993.

McNab, A. *Immediate Action*. London: Bantam, 1995.

Miedzian, Myriam. *Boys Will Be Boys*. London: Virago, 1992.

Mills, C. W. *The Sociological Imagination*. New York: Oxford University Press, 1959.

Morgan, D.H.J. *Discovering Men*. London: Routledge, 1992.

Morgan, D.H.J. "'It Will Make a Man of You': Notes on National Service, Masculinity and Autobiography." *Studies in Sexual Politics*, No. 17. University of Manchester Department of Sociology, 1987.

Morgan, D.H.J. "Men, Masculinity and the Process of Sociological Enquiry." In H. Roberts, ed., *Doing Feminist Research*. London: Routledge & Kegan Paul, 1981.

Morgan, David. "Masculinity and Violence." In Jalna Hanmer and Mary Maynard, eds., *Women, Violence and Social Control*. Atlantic Highlands, NJ: Humanities Press International, 1990.

Morgan, David. "Theater of War: Combat, the Military and Masculinities." In H. Brod and M. Kaufman, eds., *Theorizing Masculinities*, pp. 165–182. London: Sage, 1994.

Mort, Frank. *Dangerous Sexualities*. London: Routledge & Kegan Paul, 1987.

Moskos, C. *The Military: Just Another Job?* London: Brassey's, 1988.

Mosse, George. *Fallen Soldiers: Reshaping the Memory of the World Wars*. New York: Oxford University Press, 1990.

Mosse, George. *The Image of Man: The Creation of Modern Masculinity*. New York: Oxford University Press, 1996.

Newsinger, John. *Dangerous Men*. London: Pluto Press, 1997.

O'Brien, S. "Morale and the Inner Life in the Armed Forces." *Therapeutic Communities* 14(4), 1993: 285–295.

Oldfield, Sybil. *Women against the Iron Fist*. Oxford: Basil Blackwell, 1989.

Parker, T. *Soldier, Soldier*. London: Heinemann, 1985.

Rogers, Barbara. *Men Only*. London: Pandora, 1988.

Royle, T. *The Best Years of Their Lives: The National Service Experience, 1945–1963*. London: John Murray, 1992.

Ryan, Chris. *The One That Got Away*. London: Ted Smart, 1995.

Sacks, Karen. *Sisters and Wives*. Westport, CT: Greenwood Press, 1979.

Segal, David R., Wechsler-Segal, Mady and Booth, Bradford. "Gender and Sexual Orientation Diversity in Modern Military Forces: Cross-National Patterns." In Mary Fainsod Katzenstein and Judith Reppy, eds., *Beyond Zero Tolerance: Discrimination in Military Culture*. Lanham: u.a., 1999.

Segal, L. *Slow Motion: Changing Men, Changing Masculinities*. London: Virago, 1990.

Segal, M. "The Military and the Family as Greedy Institutions." *Armed Forces & Society* 13(1), 1986: 9–38.

Segal, Mady W.; Segal, David R.; Bachman, Jerald G.; Freedman-Doan, Peter; and O' Malley, Patrick M. "Gender and the Propensity to Enlist in the U.S. Military." *Gender Issues* 16(3), 1998: 65–87.

Seidler, V. *Embodying Masculinities*. London: Sage, 1997.

Shapiro, M. J. *Violent Cartographies: Mapping Cultures of War*. Minneapolis: University of Minnesota Press, 1997.

Shaw, Martin. *Post-military Society*. Cambridge: Polity, 1991.

Showalter, Elaine. *The Female Malady*. London: Virago, 1987.

Smith, Joan. *Misogynies*. London: Faber & Faber, 1989.

Stanko, Elizabeth. *Everyday Violence*. London: Pandora, 1990.

Stanley, L. and Wise, S. *Breaking out Again: Feminist Ontology and Epistemology*. 2nd ed. London: Routledge, 1993.

Stanley, L and Wise, S. *Georgie Porgie*. London: Pandora, 1988.

Stiehm, Judith Hicks. "The Protected, the Protector, the Defender." *Women's Studies International Forum* 5(3/4), 1982: 367–376.

Stoltenberg, John. *Refusing to Be a Man*. New York: Meridian, 1990.

Stone, Tessa. "Creating a (Gendered?) Military Identity: The Women's Auxiliary Air Force in Great Britain in the Second World War." *Women's History Review* 8(4), 1999: 605–624.

Summerfield, P. "'She Wants a Gun Not a Dishcloth!' Gender, Service and Citizenship in Britain in the Second World War." In Gerard DeGroot and Corinna Peniston-Bird, eds., *A Soldier and a Woman: Sexual Integration in the Military*. Harlow: Pearson Education, 2000.

Summerfield, Penny and Peniston-Bird, Corinna. "Women in the Firing Line: The Home Guard and the Defence of Gender Boundaries in Britain in the Second World War." *Women's History Review* 9(2), 2000: 231–255.

Sunindyo, Saraswati. "When the Earth Is Female and the Nation Is Mother: Gender, the Armed Forces and Nationalism in Indonesia." *Feminist Review* 58(1), 1998: 1–21.

Theweleit, Klaus. *Male Fantasies*. Cambridge: Polity, 1987.

Titunik, Regina F. "The First Wave: Gender Integration and Military Culture." *Armed Forces & Society* 26(2), 2000: 229–257.

Van Creveld, M. *On Future War*. London: Brassey's, 1991.

Van Gennep, Arnold. *The Rites of Passage*. Translated by M. B. Visedom and G. L. Caffe. Chicago: University of Chicago Press, 1960.

Warner, Philip. *Auchinleck: The Lonely Soldier*. London: Sphere, 1982.

Warner, Philip. *The SAS: The Official History*. London: Sphere, 1983.

Weeks, Jeffrey. *Sex, Politics and Society*. London: Longman, 1981.

Wheelwright, Julie. *Amazons and Military Maids*. London: Pandora, 1989.

Wheelwright, Julie. "'A Brother in Arms, a Sister in Peace': Contemporary Issues of Gender and Military Technology." In Gill Kirkup and Lauri Smith Keller, eds., *Inventing Women: Science, Technology and Gender*. Cambridge: Polity Press, 1992.

Willetts, T. *Canada's Militia: A Heritage at Risk*. Canada: Conference of Defense Associations Institute, 1990.

Woodward, Rachel. "'It's a Man's Life!': Soldiers, Masculinity and the Countryside." *Gender, Place and Culture* 5(3), 1998: 277–300.

Woodward, Rachel. "Warrior Heroes and Little Green Men: Soldiers, Military Training and the Construction of Rural Masculinities." *Rural Sociology*. 65 (2000): 640–657.

Index

About the Contributors

LOIS BIBBINGS is a Lecturer in law at the University of Bristol. Her work focuses on issues of gender and embraces an interdisciplinary approach which includes reference to history, sociology, cultural studies, literary studies, feminist linguistics, and medicine. She has published widely on feminism, the body, body alteration, human rights, criminal law, and masculinity and violence. In 2000 she co-edited *Feminist Perspectives on Criminal Law* and is currently completing a monograph on masculinity and conscientious objection to military service in World War I.

ANDREW BICKFORD spends his time between the Rutgers University Department of Anthropology and the Berlin Program for Advanced German and European Studies. He has served in the U.S. Army and his doctoral work focuses on male identity in the former German Democratic Republic.

GREGORY A. CAPLAN spends his time between Georgetown University and Berlin. His doctoral thesis explored the relationship between military service, citizenship, and nationalism in German-Jewish history.

SAMANTHA REGAN DE BERE has worked as a Lecturer and Research Fellow at the University of Plymouth since 1994. She has an interest in military sociology, the subject of her doctoral thesis. Her current interests include: career change and local labor markets; career/family interfaces; military identity; and resettlement of ex-service personnel. She is Convenor of the Plymouth Military Studies Group.

DEBORAH HARRISON is a Professor of Sociology and Past Director of the Muriel McQueen Fergusson Centre for Family Violence Research at the University of New Brunswick. She is author of *the Limits of Liberalism: the Making of Canadian Sociology* (1982), co-author of *No Life Like It: Military Wives in Canada* (1994), and national coordinator of the research project, the Canadian Forces' Response to Woman Abuse in Military Families, which was carried out jointly by the Muriel McQueen Fergusson Centre at UNB and the RESOLVE Violence and Abuse Research Centre at the University of Manitoba. She is a member of the Canadian Forces Advisory Council of Veterans Affairs Canada.

JEFF HEARN is a visiting Professor based in Helsinki. He is a leading contributor to the Men's Studies literature in terms of both its theoretical and empirical development.

PAUL R. HIGATE is a Lecturer at the University of Bristol. He served in the Royal Air Force for eight years before going on to examine the links between military service and homelessness, the focus of his doctoral thesis. He is in the final stages of a Ministry of Defence Fellowship, looking at the resettlement of armed forces personnel and their families into civilian life. His research interest has developed into the field of gender relations and peacekeeping.

JOHN HOCKEY works as a Research Fellow at the University of Gloucestershire. He is author of the groundbreaking work *Squaddies: Portrait of a Subculture* (1986), and has served in the British Army.

JOHN HOPTON is a Lecturer in the Department of Applied Social Studies at the University of Manchester. Among his many research interests is the influence of military-masculine discourse in the British public sector.

UTA KLEIN is Associate Professor of Sociology at the University of Muenster in Germany. She has been guest Lecturer at Hebrew University and Fellow of the Jerusalem Van Leer Institute. Among other subjects related to gender studies, she has written on Israeli society, the Palestinian conflict, and civil-military relations in Israel. Her book, *Military and Gender in Israeli Society*, was published in 2001.

MARCIA KOVITZ is a Research Associate of the McGill Centre for Research and Teaching on Women, and Professor of Sociology at John Abbott College in Québec, Canada, where she teaches courses in gender studies, social differentiation, and qualitative research methods. She is interested in understanding how the social organization of warfare interacts with the social construction of gender, both cross-culturally and historically. As well as advocating social change through her teaching, she has been involved in third world development/education and in local social justice issues. She has also authored a forthcoming book that examines the construction of gender in the Canadian Forces.

ROBERT MCGREGOR works as a Tutor in the Department of History at the University of Newcastle, Australia. His interests include eighteenth-century British and European history, with a particular focus on naval history.

CORINNA PENISTON-BIRD is a Lecturer in cultural history at the Department of History at Lancaster University. She is co-editor, with Gerard DeGroot, of *A Soldier and a Woman* (2000).

PENNY SUMMERFIELD is a Professor of Modern History at the University of Manchester. She has written widely on gender and the Second World War and has co-edited, with Tess Cosslett and Celia Lury, *Feminism and Autobiography: Texts, Theories, Methods* (2000).

RACHEL WOODWARD is a Research Fellow in the Centre for Rural Economy at the University of Newcastle upon Tyne. She has interests in the nexus that links space with identity, in particular, military masculinity and rurality.